EXCHANGE RATE FLEXIBILITY

*A Conference Sponsored by the
American Enterprise Institute for Public Policy Research
and the U.S. Department of the Treasury*

D1417141

EXCHANGE RATE FLEXIBILITY

*Edited by Jacob S. Dreyer, Gottfried Haberler, and
Thomas D. Willett*

American Enterprise Institute for Public Policy Research
Washington, D.C.

Library of Congress Cataloging in Publication Data

Main entry under title:
Exchange rate flexibility.

    (AEI symposia ; 78c)
    "Edited proceedings of a conference sponsored jointly by the
American Enterprise Institute and the U.S. Department of the Treasury."
    1. Foreign exchange problem—Congresses.
I. Dreyer, Jacob. II. American Enterprise
Institute for Public Policy Research. III. United States.
Treasury Dept. IV. Series: American Enterprise Institute
for Public Policy Research. AEI symposia ; 78c.
HG3821.E88   332.4'5   78-7379
ISBN 0-8447-2124-7
ISBN 0-8447-2123-9 pbk.

AEI Symposia 78-C

Printed in the United States of America

This volume is dedicated to the memory of Harry G. Johnson and Egon Sohmen in grateful recognition of their decisive contributions to our understanding of the foreign exchange market and the balance-of-payments adjustment mechanism.

PARTICIPANTS

Sven W. Arndt
University of California, Santa Cruz
(U.S. Treasury Department)*

Franz Aschinger
Swiss Bank Corporation

Geoffrey Bell
Schroder International Ltd.

C. Fred Bergsten
The Brookings Institution
(U.S. Treasury Department)*

Edward M. Bernstein
EMB (Ltd.)

Joseph M. Burns
U.S. Treasury Department
(Commodity Futures Trading Commission)*

James Burtle
W. R. Grace Company

Harold van B. Cleveland
Citibank

Sam Y. Cross
International Monetary Fund

Rimmer de Vries
Morgan Guaranty Trust Company

Thomas de Vries
International Monetary Fund

---

*Present affiliation

Jacob S. Dreyer
New York University
(U.S. Treasury Department) *

Horst Duseberg
European-American Banking Corporation

William Fellner
American Enterprise Institute

Margaret Greene
Federal Reserve Bank of New York

Armin Gutowski
Bank for Development, Frankfurt am Main

Gottfried Haberler
American Enterprise Institute

H. Robert Heller
International Monetary Fund
(Bank of America) *

Randall Hinshaw
Claremont Graduate School

Fred Hirsch
University of Warwick

Harry G. Johnson
University of Chicago

John Karlik
Joint Economic Committee, U.S. Congress
(U.S. Treasury Department) *

C. Dirck Keyser
U.S. Treasury Department

Donald J. Kirk
Financial Accounting Standards Board

Nicolas Krul
Lombard & Odier
(Gulf and Occidental Investment Company S.A., Geneva) *

Dennis E. Logue
Dartmouth College

Fritz Machlup
New York University

---

*Present affiliation

Josef Molsberger
University of Cologne
(University of Tübingen) *

Sean Mooney
W. R. Grace Company

Robert Mundell
Columbia University

Scott Pardee
Federal Reserve Bank of New York

J. J. Polak
International Monetary Fund

Robert V. Roosa
Brown Brothers Harriman

John Rutledge
U.S. Treasury Department
(Claremont Men's College) *

Walter S. Salant
The Brookings Institution

Wilson E. Schmidt
Virginia Polytechnic Institute and State University

Wolfgang Schmitz
Austrian Federal Economic Chamber

Franz Scholl
Deutsche Bundesbank

Robert L. Slighton
U.S. Treasury Department
(Chase Manhattan Bank) *

Egon Sohmen
University of Heidelberg

Robert Solomon
The Brookings Institution

Saul R. Srole
Department of Commerce

Richard James Sweeney
U.S. Treasury Department
(Claremont Men's College) *

---

*Present affiliation

---

*Present affiliation

CONTENTS

PART THREE
INTERNATIONAL TRADE AND INVESTMENT UNDER
FLEXIBLE EXCHANGE RATES

PART FOUR
INTERNATIONAL GUIDELINES AND PRINCIPLES FOR
NATIONAL FINANCIAL AND EXCHANGE RATE POLICIES

PART FIVE
INTERNATIONAL LIQUIDITY UNDER FLEXIBLE EXCHANGE RATES

POSTSCRIPT

FOREWORD

One of the most significant international economic developments of the past decade was the breakdown of the system of adjustably pegged exchange rates on which the post-war international monetary system had been based and the widespread adoption of more flexible exchange rates. By the fall of 1975 we had accumulated sufficient experience with the new system of flexible exchange rates to attempt a major effort at evaluation of the initial performance of floating rates. With this purpose in mind the Treasury Department and the American Enterprise Institute decided to jointly sponsor a conference on this subject to be held in the spring of 1976.[1] It was also decided to broaden the coverage of the conference to include two of the most important challenges facing the new international monetary system based on flexible exchange rates—multilateral surveillance of exchange rate and balance of payments policies and the management of international liquidity.

Primary responsibility for organizing the conference fell to Gottfried Haberler and myself. In the process we were fortunate to be able to draw heavily on the advice of large numbers of colleagues from the American Enterprise Institute and the Treasury, especially Sven Arndt, William

---

[1] This is the fourth and last of a series of conference volumes sponsored or cosponsored by the Research Office of the Assistant Secretary for International Affairs of the U.S. Treasury (OASIA Research) as a part of its program of policy-related external research. (This office has since been transferred to another portion of the Treasury.) The primary objectives of this conference series were to help clarify the analysis of major international economic questions, stimulate longer-run policy-related research, and contribute to the quality of debate on major international economic policy issues. It is hoped that the publication of these volumes will help the accomplishment of these objectives by making the conference papers and discussions available to a much broader group than could participate in the conferences themselves. The three previously published volumes in the series are Carl H. Stem, John H. Makin, and Dennis E. Logue (eds.), *Eurocurrencies and the International Monetary System* (Washington, D.C.: American Enterprise Institute, 1976); Ryan C. Amacher and Richard J. Sweeney (eds.), *The Law of the Sea: U.S. Interests and Alternatives* (Washington, D.C.: American Enterprise Institute, 1976); and Peter B. Clark, Dennis Logue, and Richard J. Sweeney (eds.), *The Effects of Exchange Rate Adjustments* (Washington, D.C.: U.S. Treasury Department, 1977).

Fellner, Thomas Johnson, Robert Slighton, and Richard J. Sweeney. Jacob Dreyer, then of New York University, agreed to serve as rapporteur for the conference, and he has kindly taken the major responsibility for preparing the summaries of the conference sessions and editing the conference papers.

A persisting difficulty in discussing the various aspects of exchange rate flexibility has been the considerably less than perfect communication between practitioners and researchers. Over the past decade noticeable progress has been made in increasing communication between these two groups,[2] and it was an important objective of the conference to attempt to contribute to this dialogue. However, a great deal of the current economic research on exchange rate behavior involves technical mathematical and statistical analysis which would make communication with nontechnical experts quite difficult. Furthermore, much of this research was at an early stage in which there was not yet general agreement on many issues of methodology even among technical experts. In an attempt to deal with this problem, it was decided to hold, prior to the conference, a two-day workshop in February 1976 on technical studies related to exchange rate flexibility to evaluate our current state of knowledge (and ignorance) in this area. Several of the participants in the technical workshop were invited to participate in the conference itself.

Papers presented at the conference by Richard Sweeney and myself attempted to summarize some of the empirical results and major points of agreement and dispute which emerged from the technical workshop. Both the workshop and conference proved to be extremely useful in analyzing the extent to which various types of technical studies were relevant to actual problems of exchange rate behavior and management, and in considering ways in which such studies could be improved.

While the discussions at the workshop and conference left many points of dispute over analysis and policy unresolved, the organizers' hopes for lively discussions and the achievement of greater clarification or reasons for dispute were fully met and numerous areas of widespread agreement among the participants did emerge. Most notably, despite a wide range of views regarding the final appraisal of the performance of floating exchange rates and the most appropriate strategies for official management of floating rates, the vast majority of the participants considered the system of flexible rates definitely superior to a system of

---

[2] An important earlier contribution to closing this communication gap was made by the series of "Bürgenstock" Conferences organized by C. Fred Bergsten, George Halm, Fritz Machlup, and Robert Roosa. See George Halm, ed., *Approaches to Greater Flexibility of Exchange Rates: The Bürgenstock Papers* (Princeton: Princeton University Press, 1970).

generally pegged exchange rates. Indeed, under present circumstances the latter was not viewed as a practical possibility.

THOMAS D. WILLETT
Horton Professor of Economics,
Claremont Graduate School and
Claremont Men's College.
Former Deputy Assistant Secretary
of the Treasury for International
Research and Planning

INTRODUCTION AND SUMMARY

Jacob S. Dreyer, Gottfried Haberler, and Thomas D. Willett

This volume contains the edited proceedings of the Conference on Exchange Rate Flexibility and the International Monetary System, cosponsored by the American Enterprise Institute and the U.S. Treasury and held at the American Enterprise Institute on April 20–22, 1976. The conference brought together leading researchers, officials, and members of the business and financial communities from the United States and abroad to analyze the performance of the new system of flexible exchange rates and to discuss the major policy issues concerning exchange rates and the international monetary system.

The conference was divided into five sessions. The first three focused primarily on the behavior and effects of floating exchange rates. The fourth and fifth sessions centered on two of the major issues facing the new international monetary system—the international surveillance of exchange rate and balance of payments policies and the management and control of international liquidity. The first session was designed to provide a broad overview of the experience with floating exchange rates, while the second and third sessions concentrated more narrowly on two major aspects of the experience with floating rates, the operation of the foreign exchange market, and the effects of flexible exchange rates on international trade and investment. Each session began with the presentation of one or more papers followed by the comments of a number of lead panelists and then general discussion among the participants. Summaries of the general discussion are presented at the end of each session.

The three papers delivered at the first session—Evaluation of the Performance of the Floating Exchange Rate Regime—differed considerably in their points of emphasis. Edward M. Bernstein, president of EMB (Ltd.) and a former high official with both the U.S. Treasury and the International Monetary Fund, indicated a number of areas in which floating rates had performed relatively successfully. He concentrated, however, on what he felt had been a major shortcoming of their performance, that is, the high volatility of certain exchange rates. This became a major topic of discussion continuing through the first three

1

sessions. While many participants were in agreement with Bernstein's focus on the exchange rates of a small number of currencies of the major industrial countries and his judgment that a substantial portion of their movement had not been related to underlying economic and financial conditions, a number of others felt that this view exaggerated the degree of the overall volatility of exchange rates. A number of participants expressed the opinion that changes in underlying conditions together with plausible expectations could explain the major part of variation in exchange rates, without need of explanations based on destabilizing or insufficiently stabilizing speculation. It was also emphasized by a number of participants in this and following sessions that as the instability of underlying conditions was reduced and market participants gained experience with operating under floating rates, the volatility of exchange rates had been reduced.

Josef Molsberger, now of the University of Tübingen, offered a much more favorable evaluation of the experience with floating than did Bernstein. He presented a critical analysis of much of the European literature on floating exchange rates, and emphasized as a major benefit of floating the greater control over monetary policy which had been restored to his country, West Germany. Thomas D. Willett reported on a large number of technical studies on exchange rate flexibility and discussed the experience with floating rates in terms of the expectations of both their advocates and their critics. His general conclusions were that while it was not difficult to find areas in which floating rates had performed less than ideally, on balance the experience with floating had come closer to the predictions of the strongest advocates of floating than it had to those of the staunchest critics.

The comments of the lead panelists began with Harold van B. Cleveland, who presented observations on the performance of floating rates from his perspective as an economist and commercial banker. C. Fred Bergsten concentrated on the relationship between the international transmission of inflation and the exchange rate regime. Gottfried Haberler's and Harry Johnson's comments were mainly devoted to policy implications of flexible exchange rates.

The papers in Part Two—The Foreign Exchange Market under Flexible Exchange Rates—dealt with the characteristics and behavior of the foreign exchange market. John Rutledge reported on his interviews with foreign exchange traders and summarized their perceptions of its working. Richard Sweeney presented a summary of results of statistical tests of speculative behavior and the efficiency of foreign exchange markets. Wilson Schmidt focused on the role of official participants in the market: He discussed the intervention methods of the Federal Reserve Bank of New York and reported on interviews with private participants in the market on how they perceive this intervention. The general thrust of all three papers was to discount the danger of badly behaved private speculation, which has frequently been alleged to be a major problem under freely floating rates.

A greater diversity of views was found among the lead discussants of this session. These discussants—Horst Duseberg, Nicolas Krul, Scott Pardee, and Dennis Weatherstone—discussed the operation of foreign exchange markets under floating from their perspectives as foreign exchange operators and private and central bankers. While views differed about the existence of speculative bandwagons and about the appropriate role of official intervention in the foreign exchange markets, most of the participants appeared to feel that the exchange markets had adjusted quite successfully to operating under flexible exchange rates. Of particular interest was the exchange of views on the appropriateness of various criteria for judging the operation of the exchange market and of the concepts held by various participants of the meaning of *efficiency* in this context. While general agreement on this issue was not reached, the discussion clearly indicated the importance of reaching greater understanding of the various criteria used by different analysts.

The subject of Part Three—International Trade and Investment under Flexible Exchange Rates—was also covered in three papers. Issues taken up in each of these papers focused upon different aspects of the influence of floating rates upon the attitudes and behavior of those engaged in foreign trade and investment activities. James Burtle and Sean Mooney of W.R. Grace Company, discussed the effects of uncertainty associated with floating from the point of view of managers of a multinational manufacturing concern and summarized the results of several surveys on this subject. Joseph Burns, of the U.S. Treasury, analyzed the accounting procedures of multinationals operating in an environment of floating currencies and the consequences of these procedures for the economic behavior of managers of large multinational companies. Burns's analysis, greatly expanded, was subsequently published by the American Enterprise Institute as a separate study, *Accounting Standards and International Finance: With Special Reference to Multinationals* (1976). The present volume therefore contains only a summary of his paper. The last paper in part three, by Alan Teck of the Chemical Bank, analyzed the practice of foreign exposure management by private firms having a substantial portion of their total assets and liabilities denominated in foreign currencies.

These papers were discussed by an expert in accounting, Donald Kirk, of the Financial Accounting Standards Board, by an international investment banker, Geoffrey Bell, and by a professor of finance, Dennis Logue. An extensive discussion among the conference participants fol-

3

lowed. It became clear from these discussions that we have much to learn about the effects of uncertainty on business firms and that fluctuations of exchange rates (or prices or interest rates) as an independent cause of uncertainty must be distinguished from those that merely reflect underlying economic and financial instabilities and uncertainties. Another question that attracted discussion was to what extent, under current accounting procedures, changes in exchange rates might influence managerial decisions even though these changes do not affect the "real" economic position of a firm.

Part Four—International Guidelines and Principles for National Financial and Exchange Rate Policies is preceded by a luncheon address given by Under Secretary of the U.S. Treasury for Monetary Affairs Edwin Yeo. He assessed the Rambouillet and Jamaica agreements on international monetary reform and discussed current major issues concerning the operation of the new international monetary system. The fourth session started with a presentation by Sam Y. Cross, U.S. executive director of the International Monetary Fund, on the general problem of international surveillance of the payments adjustment process and avoidance of beggar-thy-neighbor policies, and the issues facing the International Monetary Fund in developing a new set of guidelines for countries' exchange rate policies under the new international monetary system based on flexible exchange rates.

Extensive comments on the various topics raised by Cross were provided by two IMF officials, Thomas de Vries and J. J. Polak, by a government economist, Thomas Willett, and by three university economists from different countries, Marina Whitman, Armin Gutowski, and Fred Hirsch. These were followed by an extensive general discussion and Sam Cross's concluding rejoinder. There was general agreement that international surveillance could not be confined to exchange rates in isolation, but must consider the consistency between exchange rates and underlying economic and financial conditions. Some participants argued that international agreement should be sought on target zones for exchange rates to serve as benchmarks for international surveillance. A good deal of skepticism was expressed, however, over whether such an approach could be expected to work well. Considerable support was expressed for the view that the primary focus of surveillance should be on discouraging manipulation of the exchange markets by governments. It was recognized that a precise definition of manipulation was not easy. There was much sympathy for the view that the issue was too complex for immediate agreement on a highly detailed definition of manipulation. Instead, it was felt that reliance should be placed initially on some simple rules, and in time a set of precedents based on the treatment of actual cases should lead to the adoption of more detailed

4

principles of surveillance. In essence, this approach was subsequently adopted by the International Monetary Fund in its new set of "Principles of Fund Surveillance over Exchange Rate Policies," issued in 1977.

Part Five—International Liquidity under Flexible Exchange Rates— began with a presentation by Robert L. Slighton of the U.S. Treasury, followed by the comments of four academic economists: Fritz Machlup, Walter Salant, Egon Sohmen, and Robert Triffin, by a commercial banker and economist, Franz Aschinger, and by a former central bank president, Wolfgang Schmitz. In his presentation Slighton stressed the complexities of analyzing international liquidity, caused by major recent developments such as widespread abandonment of fixed exchange parities, the rapid expansion of official borrowing from the private international financial markets, and the huge increases in international reserve holdings of the oil-exporting countries. He warned against the use of some highly popular but oversimplified theories of international liquidity. The conference participants expressed a wide range of views on whether the new international monetary agreements provided sufficient control over international liquidity. In the course of the discussion, however, considerable progress was made in narrowing the range of disagreement over the scope of the analysis of international liquidity problems in the new international monetary environment. Of particular significance was the agreement that many important issues of management and control of international liquidity should be approached through international surveillance of the operation of the adjustment process. Thus the topics of parts four and five were seen to be much more intimately connected than had been realized.

As should be clear from this brief summary, the conference offered little support for the view that floating exchange rates have solved all major international monetary issues or have operated with textbook perfection. But the general sense of the conference appeared to be that the adoption of floating rates—when compared with realistic alternatives —had made an important positive contribution to the operation of the international monetary system and that floating should continue to play a major role in balance of payments adjustment.

It is hoped that this volume will prove useful in the continuing analysis and debate over national exchange rate policies and in the search for ways to improve our new international monetary system based on flexible exchange rates.

PART ONE

EVALUATION OF THE PERFORMANCE OF THE FLOATING EXCHANGE RATE REGIME

THE ECONOMICS OF FLUCTUATING EXCHANGE RATES

Edward M. Bernstein

Function of Exchange Rates

The exchange rate is a price, and like all prices one of its functions is to equate supply and demand. The exchange rate, however, is much more than an ordinary price; it is the link between the price structure of one country and those of all others, and thus between the national economy and the world economy. Occasionally, prices set in a market result from mistaken assumptions as to the future course of supply and demand. It is not usually of great consequence if this happens from time to time in the price of one or a few commodities. It is another matter, however, if the exchange rate is not suited to a country's relative position in the world economy. An inappropriate price for one or a few commodities has a minimal effect on the prices and production of other commodities. An inappropriate exchange rate affects the relation of domestic to foreign prices of a wide range of goods and services and to some extent the relation of one group of domestic prices to others. A substantially inappropriate exchange rate for a prolonged period would seriously disturb the economy.

A country's international transactions are an integral part of its economy. As they affect output and employment, prices and real income, and money and capital markets, the international transactions should be at a level and in a pattern that contribute to a country's economic well-being. Economists have long accepted the proposition that the benefits from international transactions are maximized when trade reflects comparative costs and the flow of capital reflects comparative interest rates and profits. From an economic point of view, the primary function of the exchange rate is to help bring about such a pattern of international trade and capital flows. That function, it should be emphasized, is the same whether a country has a fixed par value or a freely fluctuating exchange rate for its currency.

As this implies, the appropriate balance of payments does not depend on the exchange system. In fact, the strongest argument for floating rates over fixed rates, is that in an unstable world they are more

9

likely to bring about an appropriate balance of payments. In an appropriate balance of payments, each sector should reflect the country's international economic position. The trade in goods and services should reflect comparative costs of production, and capital flows should reflect comparative rates of interest and profits. As a corollary to this principle, the balance on capital flows should offset the balance on goods and services over a few years. An excessive or inadequate balance on goods and services that is matched by an inadequate or excessive balance on capital flows is not an appropriate balance of payments—the distortion in trade is offset by a distortion in capital flows.

A fixed rate system in order to work satisfactorily requires a certain degree of harmony in the domestic policies of the industrial countries. As the only common policy they could agree on would be one based on stability of relevant prices and costs, it follows that the exchange rate can perform its function in such a system only if countries succeed in achieving a high degree of stability. If for some reasons the countries cannot maintain stability of the relevant prices and costs, the system of par values will break down. Moreover, no country can by itself maintain an appropriate exchange rate under a fixed system, even if it avoids inflation, because the rise in prices and costs in other countries will generate an overvaluation of their currencies and an undervaluation of its currency. Because the industrial countries could not adjust their policies to the par values of their currencies, it became necessary to adjust their exchange rates to their policies. That is what floating rates are intended to do.

It is sometimes said that fluctuating exchange rates give a country greater freedom on fiscal and monetary policies. That is true only in a negative sense. If a country cannot maintain the policies required for a fixed par value, it can avoid the consequential disruption in its balance of payments and in its domestic economy by letting the exchange rate fluctuate. Having shifted to floating rates, however, a country is not completely free to pursue any fiscal and monetary policies and to ignore all fluctuations in exchange rates. It still must take account of the effect of those policies on output and employment and on prices and costs. For the same reason, a country with floating rates must have a positive exchange rate policy because an inappropriate rate will be destabilizing for the economy. An exchange rate that overvalues the currency will tend to restrain output and employment; a rate that undervalues the currency will tend to raise prices and costs. To avoid negating the objectives of its fiscal and monetary policies, a country's exchange rate policy will have to be directed to achieving an appropriate balance of payments.

Three Years of the Floating Dollar

After two formal and unsuccessful devaluations, the attempt to establish an appropriate par value for the dollar was abandoned in March 1973. Since then the dollar has been a floating currency. More than fifty countries have linked their currencies to the dollar and a number of others have linked it to special drawing rights (SDR) whose dollar value changes only moderately. Significant fluctuations in the dollar exchange rates are confined to the currencies of the industrial countries, and the degree of fluctuation varies considerably among these currencies. Changes in the dollar rates for the Japanese yen and the Canadian dollar have been relatively small and gradual. Changes in the dollar exchange rates for sterling and the lira have been large, but they have drifted downward rather than fluctuating around some trend. Changes in the dollar exchange rates have been very large for the currencies in the European common float and the Swiss franc. These were true fluctuations in the sense that the dollar rates for these currencies rose and fell considerably in short periods without large net changes over the past three years.

How well has the floating rate system for the dollar worked? If the test is whether fluctuations in exchange rates have succeeded in clearing the market, the conclusion must be that the system has worked quite well. Of course, the exchange market is cleared under *any* system of exchange rates. The difference with floating rates, however, is that the dollar exchange market has been cleared without requiring official intervention and usually with a minimum of net intervention, particularly by the United States. Moreover, this has been achieved without generating the monetary crises that used to occur when large-scale intervention became necessary to support the par value for the dollar. That is not an insignificant achievement in a period of marked instability of exchange rates and in an environment of persistent inflation, widespread imbalances in international payments, and recently severe recession.

The more important economic test is how floating rates have affected the U.S. economy and the world economy. The reason for allowing exchange rates to fluctuate is to enable them to respond to changes in underlying economic conditions and to facilitate the maintenance of an appropriate balance of payments. For example, if relevant prices and costs rise at a rate of 9 percent a year in the United States and 5 percent in Germany, the dollar-to-mark exchange rate should rise by 4 percent a year as long as the difference in inflation continues. Or if the United States eases monetary policy in a recession and short-term interest rates fall by 3 percent while they are unchanged in Switzerland, the dollar-to-Swiss franc rate should rise immediately and then decline at a rate that measures expectations on the length of the change in interest-rate differentials. The decline in the dollar-to-mark rate would maintain the competitive position of the United States vis-à-vis Germany despite the higher rate of inflation. The decline in the dollar-to-Swiss franc rate with the expectation of its recovery would maintain the relative attractiveness of holding short-term funds in the two currencies. This is how a floating rate system should work if it is to keep an appropriate balance of payments.

In fact, differences have developed between what actually happened and what, according to the floating rate model, was supposed to happen. Fluctuations in the dollar rates of exchange for the currencies in the common float have risen and fallen alternately by 10 to 20 percent over three- to four-month periods, returning approximately to where they were before the large gyrations. The chart below shows the end-of-month changes in the dollar-to-mark exchange rate since it began to float on March 19, 1973. As is evident from the magnitude of the fluctuations, the rate changes could not have been in response to relative changes in underlying economic conditions because the latter changes are small and gradual and their effects are not quickly reversed.

Large fluctuations in the dollar rates for currencies in the common float were mainly caused by speculative capital flows in anticipation of changes in exchange rates. Exchange speculators operate on a very short time span; they are concerned with what the exchange rate will be in the next few days or weeks, not what it should be or may be several months later. Once a decline begins, although initially justified by changes in underlying economic conditions, speculators enter the market as sellers expecting the decline to continue. When this happens, the exchange rate falls until the depreciation has become so large that either speculators recognize the great risks in holding a short position or the monetary authorities intervene. When the decline stops, speculative expectations are reversed, short positions are liquidated or covered, and the exchange rate rises until the appreciation is halted by developments similar to those at the end of the decline. Such fluctuations in exchange rates, mainly in response to changes in speculative expectations, perform no economic function.

It is frequently said that the large fluctuations in the dollar rates for the currencies in the common float give an exaggerated view of the degree of instability in exchange rates. An average of the changes in dollar rates for a large number of currencies, weighted by U.S. export and import trade with each country, shows much smaller fluctuations. Such an average, however, has no economic significance. It cannot measure the change in the U.S. competitive position with other countries because it takes no account of changes in their prices and costs in domestic currencies that occurred simultaneously with the changes in exchange

Figure 1

**Change in Dollar-to-Mark Exchange Rate
under Floating Rates**

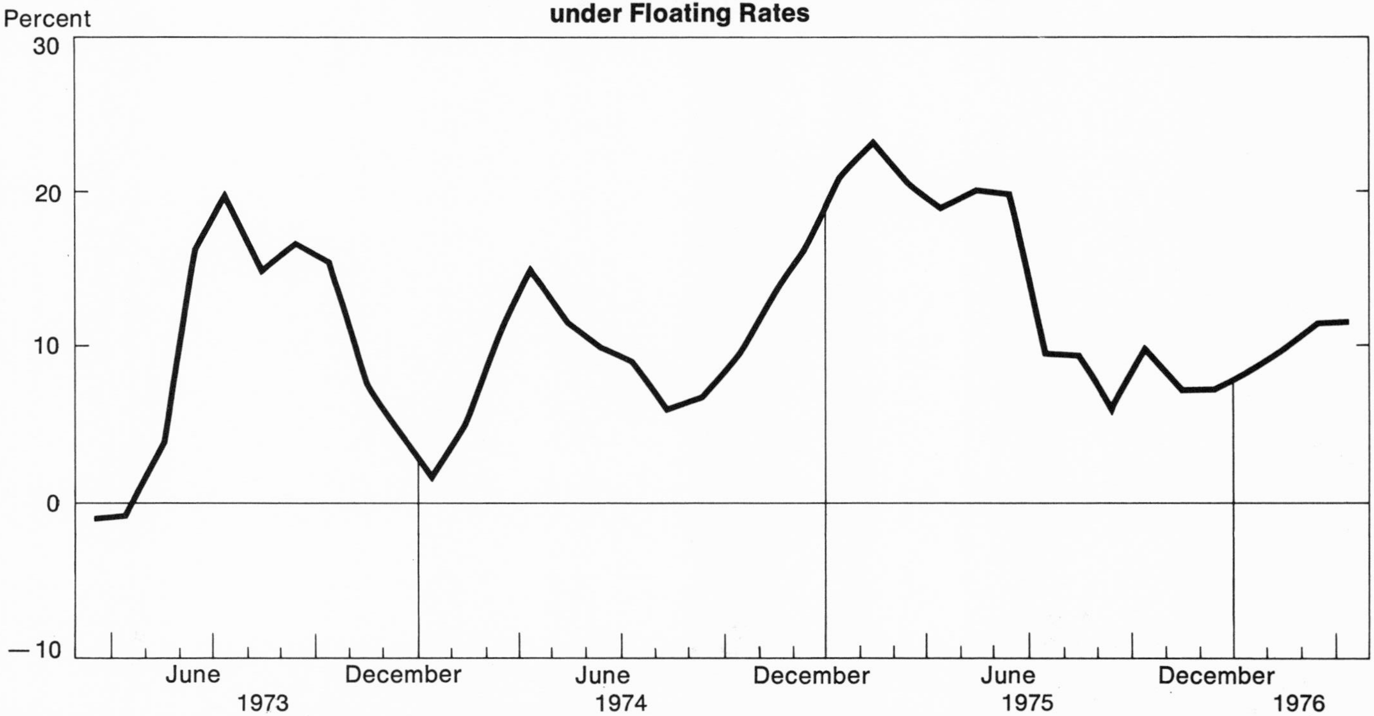

Note: The figure shows the percentage above or below the rate on March 19, 1973, on the last day of each month, from March 1973 to April 1976.

rates. Nor is there any reason for including in the average the rates for the currencies tied to the dollar, which have a great effect in holding down the average. The United States is not trying to reduce its imports of coffee, sugar, wool, metals, and other basic commodities from developing countries. It is not even trying to displace their domestic manufactures with U.S. exports. Actually the United States is trying to displace their imports of manufactured goods from other industrial countries with U.S. goods. That depends primarily on the dollar rates for the currencies of the industrial countries, not on the rates for the currencies of the developing countries.

The most useful measure of the effect of changes in exchange rates on the competitive position of the United States would be the average of changes in the dollar rates for the currencies of other industrial countries, weighted not only by their direct trade with the United States but also by their shares in world exports of manufactured goods. That average is very much higher than the one weighted by U.S. direct trade with forty-seven countries which is published in the U.S. *Treasury Bulletin*. Such an average, however, would still have a glaring shortcoming: It would not measure the change in the U.S. competitive position because it does not allow for the differences in the inflation of domestic prices and costs. Without elaborating the point, it is safe to say that no average of the changes in the dollar exchange rates for any number of currencies can by itself have any clear economic meaning.

A direct-trade-weighted average change in dollar rates hardly measures the exchange risk to which U.S. exporters and importers are exposed. Most U.S. trade is invoiced in dollars. Even for the trade invoiced in other currencies, exporters and importers can eliminate the exchange risk for the relatively small cost of forward cover. Incidentally, although the premiums and discounts on forward exchange are higher than previously, this is only partly because of fluctuations in exchange rates. Differences in interest rates determine the difference between spot and forward rates. Because interest rates are generally higher and differences larger than a few years ago, forward premiums and discounts are greater than previously. In my opinion, the fluctuations in the dollar exchange rates that have economic significance were large in the past three years and exceptionally large in the rates for the currencies in the common float and the Swiss franc.

Economic Effects of Excessive Fluctuations

The economic justification for a floating rate system is that in an inflated world it is a necessary means of maintaining an appropriate balance of payments. It will succeed in this, however, only if the fluctuations are in response to changes in underlying economic conditions. Yet large and rapid fluctuations in exchange rates are disturbing because they cause changes in the balance of payments that are not suited to a country's position in the world economy. To be specific, when the dollar exchange rates for the currencies in the common float rise and fall by 10 to 20 percent in three or four months and then reverse this movement in the next three or four months, the fluctuations must distort the pattern of trade. During these excessive fluctuations, the dollar becomes overvalued at some point and undervalued at another. When the dollar is overvalued, the exchange rate becomes an implicit tax on exports and a bounty on imports. When it is undervalued, the tax and bounty effects are reversed. That is the result not of fluctuations as such but of much greater fluctuations in exchange rates than can be attributed to changes in underlying economic conditions.

Assuming that excessive fluctuations in exchange rates are undesirable, how seriously have they distorted trade? The volume of world trade increased at a satisfactory rate in 1973 and 1974, and, although it fell in 1975, that was a typical response to a worldwide recession. Actually, the rise and fall in world trade were about the same as in 1956–1958, the previous coincident cycle in the industrial countries. In fact, there is no reason for thinking that the volume of world trade would be adversely affected by excessive fluctuations in exchange rates unless they led to restrictions on imports. What one country is prevented from exporting by the overvaluation of its currency, a competing country is induced to export by the undervaluation of its currency.

Excessive fluctuations in exchange rates have distorted the pattern rather than the volume of trade, and here too there is a major difference between trade in basic commodities and trade in manufactured goods. Exports of basic commodities could not have been much affected by large fluctuations in exchange rates that were reversed in a few months because of the short-term inelasticity of supply. The instability of exchange rates, however, intensified the fluctuations in the dollar prices of such commodities and in the dollar equivalent of the foreign exchange receipts of developing countries dependent on such exports. Similarly, imports of basic commodities could be only marginally affected by fluctuations in exchange rates because of the inelasticity of demand in response to changes in price. On the whole, excessive fluctuations in exchange rates probably had a greater effect on the terms of trade for basic commodities than on either the volume or the pattern of such trade.

The main distorting effect of excessive fluctuations in exchange rates was on trade in manufactured goods. Even on such trade, however, measures taken by exporters and importers moderated the effect. Traders do not lightly surrender their foreign connections because of an adverse

15

change in the exchange rate, particularly if they expect it to be reversed. If necessary, they keep prices at an unremunerative level for a time in order to retain an established position in a major market. They can also use the forward exchange market to hedge their domestic costs or prices against foreign prices. For example, when the dollar was very high relative to the mark, West German exporters sold dollars forward, confident that at that exchange rate the U.S. price would cover their future domestic costs. Similarly, when the dollar was very low relative to the mark, West German importers bought dollars forward, confident that at that exchange rate they could sell U.S. goods later at profitable domestic prices. Such defensive action helped to mitigate the distortions in trade, but it could not entirely prevent them.

Excessive fluctuations in the dollar exchange rates for the currencies in the common float also disturbed the trade of other countries and not merely through the substitution of U.S. and European goods for each other. As the dollar rates for the yen and the Canadian dollar fluctuated much less than the rates for the currencies in the common float, Japanese and Canadian exporters gained an advantage over their European competitors when the dollar was undervalued and suffered a disadvantage when it was overvalued. Even developing countries with dollar-linked currencies found that their manufacturers were helped in competing in the domestic market when the dollar was undervalued and were hurt when it was overvalued. As this indicates, excessive fluctuations in the dollar rates for the currencies in the common float greatly influenced the pattern of trade in manufactured goods.

Excessive fluctuations in exchange rates, however, do much more than distort trade. When the dollar is overvalued, the U.S. balance on goods and services is less than it would otherwise be, and this is accompanied by a reduction in the net outflow of capital. The shift is in the opposite direction when the dollar is undervalued. As the level of output is affected by the balance on goods and services, the shift in net exports is transmitted to the economy as a whole. This may not be very important in the large U.S. economy, but it could be decisive in a country where the external sector is a much larger part of its economy. Changes in the balance on goods and services also occur under a system of fixed but appropriate par values. The difference, however, is that with the appropriate par values the changes are generally stabilizing—that is, the balance on goods and services increases during a recession and decreases during an expansion. Large fluctuations in exchange rates under the present system followed no regular cyclical pattern. Consequently, changes in the balance on goods and services had a haphazard effect on the economy. If fluctuations in exchange rates were solely in response to changes in underlying economic conditions, they would not of themselves effect changes in the balance on goods and services. That would allow the contracyclical policies of the monetary authorities to have the intended effect on output and employment, without being negated or distorted because of excessive rate fluctuations.

There is another aspect of excessive fluctuations that is of particular concern at present. The exchange rate is the link between the price structure of one country and those of all others. In one way or another, changes in prices and exchange rates will be brought into harmony. That will occur more quickly and to a greater extent by the adjustment of the exchange rate to a change in prices. It will take place more gradually and to a lesser extent by the adjustment of prices to a change in the exchange rate. If a change in the rate results because of a relative rise in domestic prices and costs, it serves to bring the prices of imports, and perhaps some exports, into line with domestically produced goods sold in the home market. If the change in the rate is more than the relative rise in prices and costs, it becomes an independent contributor to inflation.

The tendency for prices to respond to excessive changes in the exchange rate is most marked for the prices of basic commodities, those that the United States imports and exports. Excessive depreciation of the dollar will also affect the prices of imported manufactured goods, ultimately perhaps more than the prices of basic commodities although not as promptly. Even U.S. prices of domestic manufactured goods may tend to rise in response to an excessive depreciation of the dollar if competition with foreign producers has been a dampening factor on prices. Of course, appreciation of the dollar not resulting from a relative decline in domestic prices will tend to slow the rise of prices.

Although higher world prices for oil and foodstuffs fed the inflationary fires in 1973 and 1974, the prolonged inflation in the United States has been primarily due to domestic causes. The excessive depreciation of the dollar during parts of these two years probably had only a minor effect on the rate of inflation, mainly because the depreciation was reversed within a few months. Yet, it compounded the difficulties of slowing the inflation. The incremental rise in prices that it caused must to some extent have led to larger wage increases. When this happened, U.S. prices and costs were raised permanently to a higher level than they would otherwise have reached. Of course, the later recovery in the exchange rate had a dampening effect on prices, but that was not so promptly or so fully reflected in more moderate wage increases. As this asymmetrical effect was also experienced by other countries, excessive fluctuations in exchange rates probably aggravated the worldwide tendency to inflation even if they minimally affected the trend of dollar rates.

Should Fluctuations in Exchange Rates Be Dampened?

Not everyone would agree that fluctuations in the dollar exchange rates for the currencies in the common float were excessive or that it was possible or desirable to prevent or moderate them. In part, this reflects a conviction that the market is always right and that every fluctuation in exchange rates is the consequence of economic developments that should be allowed to manifest themselves, even if the causes are not clearly visible. One can have considerable faith in the usually beneficent effects of the invisible hand while recognizing that this does not necessarily apply to sleight of hand. Nevertheless, some of those who would agree, at least in retrospect, that fluctuations in the dollar rates for some European currencies have been excessive would hesitate to concede the desirability of intervention because of the uncertainty regarding what was an appropriate exchange rate under the very unstable conditions that prevailed. That is a concern that must be considered.

The principle that the balance of payments should be appropriate to the relative international economic position of a country is of only limited help in determining whether fluctuations in exchange rates are excessive at the time they occur. The fact is that we do not know precisely what structure of the U.S. balance of payments is appropriate, particularly after an extended period of deficits with an overvalued dollar and at a time of vast surpluses and deficits throughout the world. In some respects, with a fixed rate system it is easier to recognize whether the balance of payments is appropriate. Essentially, it is a balance of payments that is neither in deficit nor in surplus on an official reserve basis over a few years. With a universal floating rate system, there will be no surplus or deficit on an official reserve basis if the monetary authorities do not intervene in the exchange market. Nevertheless, the structure of the balance of payments may be inappropriate in the sense that the balance on goods and services may be too large or too small, although it is offset by net capital flows.

For the United States, the nonuniversality of the floating rate system adds another problem in bringing about an appropriate balance of payments. Sizable enclaves of fixed exchange rates exist within the present system of floating rates. When countries with dollar-pegged currencies have a deficit in the aggregate, they meet it by drawing down their dollar reserves. Unless the United States has an equivalent surplus on an official reserve basis, these funds will be sold in the exchange market to make payments to countries with floating dollar rates for their currencies. That would depreciate the dollar. Similarly, when a country in the common float finds that its currency is at the bottom of the permissible range, it uses reserves to support the exchange rate. If the reserves are dollars, the dollar will depreciate unless the countries whose currencies are at the top of the range add an equivalent amount of dollars to their reserves.

This difficulty would not arise in a universal fixed rate system. If some countries have a deficit, others must have a surplus. Although the deficit countries draw down their reserves, the surplus countries add an equal amount to their reserves. Reserve transactions would not affect the U.S. balance of payments. A problem would arise, though, if the deficit countries use dollars while the surplus countries accumulate other reserve assets. In that case, the United States would face the need to convert the dollars acquired by the surplus countries into other reserve assets. As an equal decline in reserve assets and reserve liabilities would impair the liquidity of the United States, such conversions could create difficulties. With floating rates, the United States has no obligation to convert dollars into other reserve assets, although dollars are convertible in the exchange market. When dollars held in reserves are converted in this way, the dollar depreciates.

This raises the question whether the United States should offset fluctuations in exchange rates which result from the drawing down of dollars by the monetary authorities of other countries, including shifts from dollars to marks and Swiss francs. As a practical matter, the United States cannot offset fluctuations in exchange rates resulting from changes in official dollar holdings because that would amount to restoring the convertibility of the dollar into other reserve assets. If the United States does not intervene, however, depreciation of the dollar will create a balance of payments that is out of line with the country's position in the world economy. Moreover, as the United States cannot undertake to intervene to offset such dollar reserve transactions, the dollar exchange rates for the currencies in the common float must be expected to fluctuate considerably more than the dollar rates for other floating currencies, apart from the effect of private speculation on exchange rates.

Even if an appropriate balance of payments qualified for changes in dollar reserves were the objective, there would still be the question what exchange rate this would require. Since March 1973 the dollar-to-mark rate has fluctuated between 34.7 cents and 44.3 cents. One can understand the uncertainty at any given time about the proper rate within this vast range. Changes in relevant price and cost indexes in the United States and West Germany would help little in this regard because such indexes lack a satisfactory base period, apart from the fact that other economic factors affect the exchange rate. The average rate over this period would not be a reliable guide for estimating the appropriate dollar-to-mark rate, as there may have been a gradual trend toward a higher rate for the mark. The problem is further complicated by the fact that, during the past three years, West Germany has posted sizable trade surpluses, almost certainly too large for a balanced pattern of international payments after the deficits with the oil-exporting countries are sharply reduced.

Calculating an appropriate dollar rate for the mark under such conditions is hopeless. An appropriate rate could have been anywhere between the high and the low during this period, and intervention might at some stage have prevented the exchange market from reaching it. The case for dampening excessive fluctuations in exchange rates, therefore, is not that intervention would result in an appropriate rate, but would reduce very large divergences from it. Regardless of what the appropriate rate may be, intervention that reduces extreme fluctuations would be helpful from an economic point of view. If the appropriate rate were the high or the low of a wide range, intervention that reduced fluctuations might not reduce the average divergence from that rate, although that is unlikely. Even then, as the divergences would not be as extreme as they would otherwise be, they would have had a less disturbing effect. From an economic point of view, a divergence of 10 percent from the appropriate rate is not as disturbing as alternate divergences of 0 and 20 percent. And if the appropriate rate were lower than the high and higher than the low, intervention would reduce the average divergence as well as the extreme divergences from that rate.

Many countries preferring the fixed rate system and those with floating rates are recognizing that fluctuations in the dollar rates for the currencies in the common float have been too large. For example, in London in October 1975, Chancellor Schmidt of West Germany contended that the excessive fluctuations in the dollar rates for the European currencies have been disruptive. He may have overestimated the effect, but his statement merits serious consideration.

> I believe, that volatile floating rates have contributed to the current world recession. The transition to floating exchange rates was, on the other hand, an unavoidable step if international trade and payments were to be kept free of restrictions in the face of balance-of-payments deficits and sizable differences in the rate of inflation. . . . Although exchange rates cannot just be fixed by Governmental decision and—in addition to that—be expected to stay at the fixed pegs, we should all be trying to ensure that oscillations do not become as large again as they were during the first phase of floating. Our attention at this time should be concentrated on flattening out the wild movements.[1]

---

[1] *Financial Times* (London), October 25, 1975.

At a meeting in Rambouillet, France, in November 1975, government officials from the United States, Germany, Japan, France, the United Kingdom, and Italy agreed on the need to cooperate in achieving greater monetary stability. Their communiqué stated that this requires efforts to restore greater stability in underlying economic and financial conditions—the sine qua non for monetary stability however defined. It also said that the monetary authorities of these countries will act to counter disorderly market conditions or erratic fluctuations in exchange rates. At a meeting of the Group of Ten in December 1975, the countries' finance ministers and central bank governors agreed to intensify their consultations for these purposes. Carrying out these commitments will require a policy and guidelines for a floating rate system.

The IMF and Fluctuating Exchange Rates

Recently the International Monetary Fund has sent to its members for approval a comprehensive second amendment to the Fund Agreement. Of particular interest is the amended Article IV on exchange arrangements. The amendment recognizes that a country may have any exchange system that it regards as suitable to its economy, including fluctuating rates. Regardless of their exchange system, members are under a general obligation "to collaborate with the Fund and other members to assure orderly exchange arrangements and to promote a stable system of exchange rates."[2] The amendment's essential feature is its recognition of the international interest in a country's exchange rate policy, regardless of the rate system. That would seem to be the meaning of the provision which states: "[The] Fund shall exercise firm surveillance over the exchange-rate policies of members, and shall adopt specific principles for the guidance of members with respect to those policies." Since widespread use of floating rates will continue indefinitely, it is useful to consider what principles the Fund could adopt for the guidance of members that have floating rates.

At first appearance, the basic principle, applicable to countries having either exchange rate system, would seem to be that each country's exchange policy should be conducive to a well-balanced pattern of international payments. A country that is accumulating reserves when it already has large reserves, or avoids such accumulation by extraordinary capital outflow, does not have a balance of payments in accord with this principle. Similarly, a country that is drawing down reserves rapidly on a large scale, or depends extensively on reserve credit to finance a deficit, or undertakes heavy official borrowing in private markets to avoid a

---

[2] Sections 1 and 3(b) of Article IV as proposed in the amendment.

deficit, has a balance of payments that is not conducive to a well-balanced pattern of international payments. Even this basic principle, however, would be difficult to apply at a time when the oil-exporting countries are accumulating very large reserves. And it is doubtful whether such a principle should apply to the United States if it has a surplus, because of its large reserve liabilities, or to Germany if it has a deficit, because of its large dollar reserves.

This principle would have to be applied in broader terms to assure an appropriate exchange rate policy in a country with floating rates. If such a country did not intervene and other countries did not use its currency in reserve transactions, the country's overall payments on an official reserve basis would always be balanced. The balance, however, could be achieved with an excessive surplus on goods and services offset by an excessive capital outflow. Such an overall balance would militate against achieving a well-balanced pattern of international payments. This particular point does not seem to be covered by Section 1 (iii) of the amended Article IV under which each member is especially obligated to "avoid manipulating exchange rates . . . in order to prevent effective balance of payments adjustment or to gain an unfair competitive advantage over other members." The provision would clearly apply to a country that intervenes in the exchange market during a recession in order to depreciate its currency and thus spur an export-led recovery. The provision would be more difficult to apply, however, to a country that eases monetary policy and lowers interest rates to deal with a recession and thus encourages a depreciation of the exchange rate. Such a country could find that its balance on goods and services responds more quickly to the depreciation of the exchange rate than home investment responds to monetary expansion. Moreover, the provision could not apply to a country whose exchange rates fluctuate erratically and excessively for reasons unrelated to its own policies.

The devising of principles that relate exchange rate policy to the state and structure of balance of payments can be left to the ingenuity of the IMF. The more immediate problem is how to deal with disorderly exchange markets and erratic fluctuations in exchange rates. If a disorderly market means that exchange transactions cannot be executed except with a large change in rates during a very few days, then that has not happened to the dollar. However, erratic fluctuations have occurred in the dollar exchange rates for the currencies in the common float. An article on the business situation, in the March 1976 *Survey of Current Business*, uses the term *erratic* in the accepted economic sense: "judging from the housing starts, which are subject to erratic month-to-month movements," the article states, "residential construction might have lost some momentum." One may question this conclusion, but not the use

22

of *erratic* to describe large changes, without an apparent economic reason, which are reversed. That applies even more clearly to the dollar rates for the currencies in the common float.

In the outline of reform of the international monetary system, the deputies of the Committee of Twenty discussed the exchange rate policy that countries with floating rates should follow. They recommended that the monetary authorities of those countries intervene from time to time to avoid or dampen excessive fluctuations in exchange rates in order to prevent them from having a disturbing effect on the economy. Among the specific points emphasized in the guidelines were the following.

(1) Intervention in the foreign exchange market should be undertaken when necessary to prevent or moderate sharp and disruptive fluctuations in exchange rates from day to day and from week to week.

(2) Intervention may be desirable to moderate movements in the exchange rates from month to month and from quarter to quarter. It should be undertaken where the factors causing the movements are recognized as temporary.

(3) If the exchange rate moves outside a reasonable range of the medium-term norm and is likely to be harmful to other countries, the Fund may encourage a country to moderate movements outside this range. A country would not, however, be expected to hold any particular rate against strong market pressures.

These guidelines would seem to be unexceptionable, although they do require judgments as to whether the factors causing movements in exchange rates are temporary and as to what norm or range of exchange rates is reasonable. Unfortunately, such determinations are more easily made after the event than when the exchange rate is in the course of moving.

The policy that should guide U.S. intervention in the exchange market should be more pragmatic. U.S. monetary authorities can have no responsibility for moderating changes in exchange rates, even large changes, if they are the result of a general weakness in another currency—as, for example, the recent decline in the rates for sterling and the lira. The United States should be most concerned with the dollar exchange rates for the currencies in the common float—a responsibility it should share with these countries. When the monetary authorities decide to intervene, they should remember that floating rates are supposed to be determined by market forces, provided the fluctuations are neither rapid nor excessive. For this reason, if exchange rates rise or fall by, say, 6 or 8 percent in a period of about two months, the monetary authorities should intervene only to prevent a disorderly market. The market may be adjusting the rates to an appropriate level, even though the economic reasons are not yet apparent. If after such a rise or fall, the rates continue moving in the same direction, the monetary authorities should intervene, not to halt the movement abruptly, but to limit it to a further 1 or 2 percent a month. Even this rule of thumb should be flexible, particularly if there are evident economic reasons for the change in exchange rates. If and when the movement is reversed, the monetary authorities would follow a similar rule, so that there would be a minimum of net intervention over a moderate period of a few months.

Such a policy in 1973–1976 would have reduced by about half the larger fluctuations in the dollar rates for the currencies in the common float. At the same time, it would have given the exchange market a generous amount of freedom to adjust exchange rates to underlying economic conditions. The policy would, however, have prevented massive speculative movements of capital from causing the wide fluctuations in exchange rates that had a disturbing effect on the economy. This is not a policy for fine-tuning rates in order to establish an ideal balance of payments. It is a practical policy for limiting obviously excessive divergences from the exchange rates suited to comparative costs and comparative rates of interest and profits.

HOW FLOATING EXCHANGE
RATES ARE WORKING:
A EUROPEAN VIEW

Josef Molsberger

In March 1973, the international monetary system which had been in existence since the end of World War II was replaced by a new system of international currency relations.

In the earlier system, established at the conference at Bretton Woods in 1944, fixed exchange relationships determined by governments—fixed parities—were, as a general principle, maintained between each national currency and gold, and thus between individual national currencies. Currency revaluations and devaluations were, however, permitted from time to time. After March 1973 officially fixed parities ceased to be maintained for a number of currencies. Exchange ratios between many currencies—the rates of exchange—have been determined by supply and demand on the foreign exchange markets. In response to market forces they have undergone fairly large changes over time. Nevertheless, the rates of every currency have not been flexible against all other currencies. A number of countries have formed various "currency blocs." Among the currencies of a "bloc," the maintenance of fixed exchange rates, or of rates which move only within narrow margins, has been agreed upon.[1]

The new currency system, "floating," has not had a good press in Europe. An entire catalog of disadvantages and defects has been attributed to it. It has been said to have caused inflation, produced the raw materials boom, endangered the unity of the Western world, led to an escalation of trade barriers and exchange controls, caused insecurity in world trade, favored multinational enterprises, and hurt small business.

---

[1] On June 30, 1975, 81 of the 126 member countries of the International Monetary Fund (IMF) had pegged their currencies to another currency. Nineteen countries had pegged their currencies to the special drawing right or to another composite of currencies. The currencies of eleven countries were floating independently; these countries accounted, in 1974, for 46.4 percent of the total trade of IMF members. In addition, seven countries were participating in the European joint float; they accounted, in 1974, for another 23.2 percent of IMF members' total trade. See International Monetary Fund, *Annual Report 1975* (Washington, D.C., 1975), p. 24, Table 9. Further details are given on p. 23ff.

Even though these disadvantages may not yet have materialized, they have been predicted for the next downswing in the trade cycle.

Are these assertions correct—if not in every detail, then as inherent tendencies? Worse, has floating failed even to produce the benefits over the fixed rate system that were expected of it? In attempting to answer these questions, first I shall have to clear away a large amount of "debris" (as Schumpeter once said) and discuss a number of adverse concomitant phenomena that have been charged against the flexible rate system, but which in reality are a legacy of the earlier currency system, or operating defects of still subsisting parts of the system of fixed parities. Secondly, I shall examine the thesis that floating has had adverse effects on international trade. Thirdly, I shall discuss the assertion that floating has not fulfilled the expectations of autonomy for national monetary policy which had been placed in it.

Misdirected Criticism

Disintegration? Otto Veit, a noted monetary theorist with a philosophical orientation, views the loosening up of exchange rates as related "to the phenomena of political, cultural and intellectual disintegration which have afflicted the Western world in more and more new areas." He considers floating "ominous," because with it "something is developing which must be regarded as a disintegration of order." [2] With all due respect for a famous name, it must simply be said that Veit is wrong. He has taken a symptom for the causes behind it. There is, in fact, political disintegration, but the rate of exchange is only the seismograph that registers the earthquake. Whoever thinks that tying down the indicator will protect him from the earthquake deceives himself.

The earthquake did not by any means begin on March 19, 1973, with the beginning of floating, but since that time the seismograph has been working. And now everyone can see what had been hidden before: the discouraging fact that the countries of the Western world do not agree on fundamental questions of economic policy, above all on the question of the stabilization of the domestic value of money.

This agreement had in fact been missing before March 1973, under the system of allegedly fixed rates of exchange. And because it had been missing, the rates of exchange—the official parities [3]—were not in fact at all rigidly fixed, but were on "adjustable pegs." They have not moved of

---

[2] Otto Veit, "Währungspolitik ohne Währungssystem," *Zeitschrift für das gesamte Kreditwesen,* May 15, 1975, reprinted in *Deutsche Bundesbank Auszüge aus Presseartikeln,* no. 33 (May 22, 1975), p. 9ff.

[3] The problem of the permissible margin of fluctuation is neglected here.

their own, but they have been moved by governments, at irregular intervals and in large abrupt jumps. The French franc, the pound sterling, the Italian lira, and many other currencies have been devalued again and again since the end of the war. The West German mark, the Swiss franc, the Dutch guilder, and a few other currencies have been revalued several times. Whenever foreign exchange reserves threatened to run out or to pile up too fast, the parity was changed. This would have been necessary even more frequently had stability of exchange rates not in many cases been nominally maintained by exchange controls or supported by half-begged, half-extorted, foreign borrowing.

This was the reality of the supposedly healthy world of fixed exchange rates of the Bretton Woods system. Differences between the monetary policies of individual countries were just as pronounced then as they are today with flexible rates. Very few countries wanted to relinquish "the sovereign right to inflate" (as President Holtrop of the Netherlands central bank once expressed it).[4] And even the countries which had decided on a sound monetary policy had to import a part of the inflation produced abroad. The "inflation producing countries" unloaded a part of the adverse effects of inflation on foreign shoulders, and were thus able in turn to inflate even more strongly than would have been tolerable had inflation been confined to their own territory. The currency system of Bretton Woods had a strong inflationary bias.

What is more, in the conditions that obtain today, *all* fixed rate systems—even the gold standard—would have a tendency to spread inflation.[5] For today wages are no longer flexible downward. There is no longer any deflation; there is at most an abatement of inflation. All disturbances of the balance of payments can be eliminated only through inflating in the surplus countries. In a fixed rate system under modern conditions, then, the inflationary countries set the trend, and thus international monetary disorder is institutionalized.

It was not, therefore, the introduction of flexible exchange rates that has caused "a development which must be regarded as disintegration of order" (to quote Veit once again), but rather the tendency to inflation which has long prevailed in many countries, and its transmission through fixed rates to inflation-resisting countries.

---

[4] M. W. Holtrop, "Is a Common Central Bank Policy Necessary within a United Europe?" *De Economist,* vol. 105 (The Hague, 1957), p. 655.
[5] See Gottfried Haberler, "The Future of the International Monetary System," *Zeitschrift für Nationalökonomie,* vol. 34 (1974), p. 390 (American Enterprise Institute Reprint No. 30); Hans Willgerodt, "Wirtschaftsraum und Währungsraum," in *Welwirtschaftliche Probleme der Gegenwart,* Schriften des Vereins für Social-politik, vol. 35 (Berlin: Duncker & Humblot, 1965), p. 348.

An End to Coordination? The assertion that floating put an end to international coordination of monetary policy is similarly distorted.[6] There was no more international coordination before than there is today, but this fact has been hidden behind camouflage. As proof of better coordination in the fixed rate system, it has been adduced "that for twenty-five years after the Second World War, every change in exchange rates required the approval of an international body, the IMF."[7] This argument confuses the norm of the law with reality.[8] For "the Fund never attempted to oppose a change in parity."[9] In many cases it was not even consulted. In practice parity changes were decided autonomously by the governments according to their national interests. The IMF could only take note of these decisions.

It was the same with the introduction or elimination of exchange controls by member countries of the IMF. Exchange controls on trade and capital movements were decreed by the individual governments—with little international consultation and cooperation: what counted was only the national interest, or whatever was considered as such. Exchange control is one of the crassest ways of refusing international cooperation, and the *Annual Report on Exchange Restrictions* published every year by the IMF has been of considerable bulk during the time of the fixed rate system.[10]

Measures of Control. Now, it has been said that measures of exchange control have been "much more widespread since the introduction of fluctuating rates than before." [11] Interventionism is said to be "expressed primarily in a rapid expansion of foreign exchange *dirigisme* in the form of capital controls." [12] If this were so, one should conclude that floating did impair the movement of goods and capital and thus international cooperation. In fact, however, the opposite is true. In the important

---

6 See Günter Keiser, "Erste Erfahrungen mit 'Floating Rates,'" *Zeitschrift für das gesamte Kreditwesen*, 1975, no. 3, p. 104.

7 Ibid., p. 107.

8 According to the Articles of Agreement of the IMF, the Fund could raise no objection to a change in parity if the new parity varied less than 10 percent from the original parity. See "Articles of Agreement of the International Monetary Fund (July 22, 1944)," Article IV, Sec. 5(c), in Keith Horsefield, *The International Monetary Fund 1945–1965, vol. 3: Documents* (Washington, D.C.: The Fund, 1969), p. 190.

9 Veit, "Währungspolitik," p. 7.

10 International Monetary Fund, *Annual Report on Exchange Restrictions* (Washington, D.C.: The Fund, 1950 and succeeding years).

11 Keiser, "Erste Erfahrungen," p. 106.

12 Kurt Richebächer, *Überforderte Wechselkurspolitik* (Tübingen: Mohr, 1974), p. 79.

trading countries, exchange controls have been relaxed since the introduction of floating.[13] On January 29, 1974, the United States abolished the interest equalization tax, the control of foreign direct investment, and the control of foreign credits.[14] At the beginning of 1974 all countries of the Common Market had abolished those capital controls which they had introduced a year earlier to ward off capital imports when rates of exchange were still fixed.[15] The Netherlands (on February 2, 1974), France (on March 21, 1974) and Italy (on March 22, 1974) abandoned dual exchange markets.[16] "The separate channel for financial flows with its attendant administrative complexities had become redundant in view of the exchange rate flexibility," was the IMF comment on these measures.[17] As of February 1, 1974, the German Bundesbank dismantled the authorization requirement for borrowing abroad, for the sale of domestic securities to nonresidents, and for foreign direct investments in West Germany.[18] As of August 1, 1974, the compulsory interest-free "cash deposit" (*Bardepotpflicht*) for capital imports to West Germany was abolished after this requirement had already been decisively relaxed on January 1 and again on February 1, 1974.[19] Finally the ban on paying interest on nonresidents' deposits with West German banks was lifted effective September 4, 1976.[20]

---

[13] See Hans Willgerodt, "Stabilitätsförderung durch marktwirtschaftliche Ordnungspolitik—Notwendigkeit und Grenzen" in *Stabilisierungspolitik in der Marktwirtschaft*, Schriften des Vereins für Socialpolitik, vol. 85/II (Berlin: Duncker & Humblot, 1974), p. 1454.

[14] See Rolf Hasse, Horst Werner, Hans Willgerodt, *Aussenwirtschaftliche Absicherung zwischen Markt und Interventionismus: Erfahrungen mit Kapitalverkehrskontrollen* (Frankfurt/Main: Knapp, 1975), pp. 203ff., 267. The IET officially expired on June 30, 1974; on January 29, 1974, the tax rate was fixed at zero.

[15] See *Sachverständigenrat zur Begutachtung der gesamtwirtschaftlichen' Entwicklung, Vollbeschäftigung für morgen: Jahresgutachten 1974/75* (Stuttgart and Mainz: Kohlhammer, 1974), p. 37.

[16] See Hasse, Werner, and Willgerodt, *Aussenwirtschaftliche Absicherung*, pp. 116ff., 150ff., 265ff.

[17] IMF, *Annual Report 1975*, p. 46.

[18] See *Report of the Deutsche Bundesbank for the Year 1974*, p. 55. Further details are given in the German version, *Geschäftsbericht der Deutschen Bundesbank für des Jahr 1974*, p. 89.

[19] See *Geschäftsbericht der Deutschen Bundesbank für das Jahr 1974*, p. 89. For the Swiss measures, see John R. Lademann, "Währungspolitische Chronik," *Aussenwirtschaft*, vol. 29 (1974), p. 245ff.; Hasse, Werner, and Willgerodt, *Aussenwirtschaftliche Absicherung*, p. 182ff.

[20] The ban had the technical form of an authorization requirement. See *Report of the Deutsche Bundesbank for the Year 1975*, p. 18. For further details see the German version of this report: *Geschäftsbericht der Deutschen Bundesbank für das Jahr 1975*, p. 90.

Objections. Two objections may be raised here. The first relates to the West German example just mentioned. A review of events will indeed show that on June 29, 1973, after the introduction of floating, the Bundesbank tightened controls on capital inflows.[21] This is true enough. But freely flexible rates of exchange were not in force—and are not in force today—within the bloc of European currencies which participate in the so-called currency snake. The rates of exchange among these bloc currencies are officially fixed and can move in relation to one another only within relatively narrow bands. If one of the participating currencies reaches the limit of the band, its rate of exchange must be supported by the central banks.

In the second half of June 1973 the deutsche mark had stood permanently at the upper limit of the "snake." The support of the exchange rate had necessitated the acquisition of foreign exchange equivalent to DM 4.5 billion. To alleviate this situation, the deutsche mark was revalued (on June 20, 1973) by 5½ percent relative to the other snake currencies.[22] The simultaneous tightening of controls on capital inflow was intended to help defend the new deutsche mark rate. It was not floating, however, which led to this intensification of exchange controls; on the contrary, it was an exception from floating, to wit, the retention of fixed rates within the European currency bloc. (This fact, by the way, throws significant light on the assertion that the fixing of parities within the European currency bloc acted as a stabilizer, and thus encouraged European integration.[23] Capital controls are usually not regarded as measures that encourage integration.)

The second possible objection seems to carry more weight. Its proponents do not deny that it was possible for some countries to reduce or entirely remove controls of capital movements. They even concede that this was made possible by the transition to flexible rates of exchange. But, so the argument runs, this possibility presented itself only to those countries whose currencies were appreciating on the foreign exchange market. Countries with weak currencies, on the other hand, would have had to increase their intervention in capital movement.[24]

Let us examine the situation. The countries with permanent tendencies to depreciate are the countries with the strongest inflation, relatively

---

[21] See *Report of the Deutsche Bundesbank for the Year 1973*, p. 21.

[22] Ibid. The central rate of the deutsche mark was revalued by 5½ percent in terms of special drawing rights; this implied a commensurate revaluation relative to the central rates of the other "snake" currencies.

[23] See, for example, Keiser, "Erste Erfahrungen," pp. 104-105.

[24] Martin Thomann and Daniel Kaeser, "Übertriebene Erwartungen," in *Feuertaufe für das Floating: Praktische Erfahrungen mit flexiblen Wechselkursen*, Neue Zürcher Zeitung, Schriften zur Zeit, no. 32 (Zurich: Neue Zürcher Zeitung, 1975), p. 59.

speaking. The depreciation of their currencies is due, in part, to attempts by wealth-holders to protect the value of their assets from inflation by transferring those assets abroad. The stronger the capital flight, the greater the decline in the exchange rate of the domestic currency. From this the "naive" exchange rate theory has drawn the conclusion that the increase in the price of foreign exchange would automatically place a brake on and finally stop the capital outflow. On the other hand, Wolfgang Stützel, in particular, has repeatedly stated that this is a fallacy.[25] To be sure, a unit of foreign currency costs more in domestic currency with the increase. But the new exchange rate will, of course, also apply to the retransfer of interest and capital. Later on, more units of domestic currency will be received for each unit of the foreign currency repatriated.

The question of interest payments may be left to one side; withdrawals of funds from inflationary countries are primarily a matter of protecting capital. The argument then runs: a devaluation of the currency of an inflation-prone country does not stop capital flight, because one can expect that after the end of the inflation one will be able to retransfer the capital at the currently prevailing or even at a lower rate of exchange. From this it is concluded that inflation countries with depreciating currencies will have to introduce capital controls—despite depreciation, indeed even because of it. Thus, floating will have failed.

But this again is fallacious, for it is not conceived in terms of a system of truly flexible rates of exchange. In such a system, the rate of exchange is basically flexible, both downwards and upwards. If domestic inflation is brought under control—and that is, of course, the decisive point—then not only would the rate stop its decline, but also its movement would reverse direction. The decline which previously occurred in the expectation of further inflation would be reversed. The movement of the French franc during its period of isolated floating (from January 19, 1974, to July 10, 1975) provides a textbook example: as soon as the government became serious about fighting inflation, the franc floated upwards again. This upward movement began when the French government announced, on June 12, 1974, a program of anti-inflationary measures. The franc rate further improved during the last months of 1974, when French monetary policy became very tight. In May 1975, the franc had regained its former position within the narrow margin of the "snake."[26]

Those who had moved capital out of France at the time of the franc depreciation and later repatriated it at an increased rate of exchange

[25] See Wolfgang Stützel, *Währung in weltoffener Wirtschaft* (Frankfurt/Main: Knapp, 1973), p. 221.

[26] See IMF, *Annual Report 1975*, p. 30. "Der Europäische Wechselkursverbund," *Monatsberichte der Deutschen Bundesbank,* vol. 28, no. 1 (January 1976), p. 23ff.

suffered losses as a consequence. What is more, the capital repatriation itself contributes to a further rise in the exchange rate and exchange losses thus become even larger.[27] With freely flexible rates, therefore, speculation on rate changes through capital transfers and retransfers is not without risk—a risk that acts as a brake on capital outflows from countries tending toward depreciation of their currencies.

In a system of fixed parities with intermittent rate changes, this risk did not exist. Once a currency had been devalued by government decision, exported capital funds could be repatriated with a sure benefit at the new (lower) rate of exchange, inasmuch as the probability that the government would revalue the currency shortly after a devaluation was practically nil. The only "risk" speculators would run would be that of no devaluation at all.[28] If we still had fixed parities today, the pressure to move capital from inflationary countries would thus be far stronger than it is. Consider what exchange controls would be necessary to contain this pressure.

Let me give an illustration. Because capital speculation is risky under floating rates the oil-exporting countries have never dreamed of making the (often luridly pictured) abrupt shifts of funds from one currency to another that aroused fears that the world monetary system might be destroyed. In the oil countries, solid businessmen make the decisions: what interest would they have in destroying the world monetary system? Moreover, they knew very well that, with flexible rates, such behavior would have led, not to the ruin of the world currency system, but quite possibly to their own. People in the oil countries had understood the system of floating more quickly than our own excited commentators.

Of course, sympathy for an economic system which steers itself with the help of markets is not very widespread nowadays. This is apparent, for example, from the universal reproach that floating, "this ruleless game with rates no longer bound to anything," could not even be called a "system."[29] It is said, moreover, not even to have been planned, but introduced only by force of circumstances. Those who experienced the first years after the West German currency reform of 1948

---

[27] See IMF, *Annual Report 1975*, p. 27, for the general principle, and p. 30, for the special case of the French franc.

[28] Gottfried Haberler ("Vorwort zur deutschen Ausgabe," in *Wirtschaftswachstum und Stabilität* [German edition of *Economic Growth and Stability*] [München: Verlag Moderne Industrie, 1975], p. 20ff.), and Harry G. Johnson ("World Inflation and the International Monetary System," *The Three Banks Review*, no. 107 [September 1975] p. 9ff.) have pointed out that some of the banks operating in the foreign exchange market had to learn that "outguessing the collective wisdom of the competitive market" was much more risky than "outguessing central banks on the tenability of their pegged exchange rates" (Johnson, "World Inflation," p. 10).

[29] Keiser, "Erste Erfahrungen," p. 104. See also Veit, "Währungspolitik," pp. 6, 9.

may remember that similar indictments were delivered after Ludwig Erhard abolished controls and reintroduced free market pricing for goods and services. The same happens now in respect to market pricing of national currencies. What Friedrich von Hayek has called "spontaneous order" [30] meets little applause—and even less understanding—least of all among politicians, whose avocation it is to busy themselves with the "fixable." And the lack of technical understanding frequently induces political activism reflected in pronouncements to the effect that "the fate of a currency is much too important to be left to the markets." [31] The result of such thinking is that central banks intervene in the markets; they buy and sell their own currencies for foreign exchange, in principle the same way they had done it in the fixed rate system. Instead of freely flexible rates, many countries practice a system of manipulated or "managed" floating.

There are good reasons why the appearance of central banks in foreign exchange markets seems appropriate even with floating. An "ironing out" of short-term rate fluctuations on the foreign exchange market—comparable to surveillance of quotations in the stock exchanges—has long been considered acceptable or even advisable by most advocates of flexible exchange rates. [32] Attempts to use managed floating to oppose long-run market tendencies are, however, much more problematical. Be that as it may, there is defective logic in denouncing unmanipulated free rate formation as a "ruleless game" while complaining that the transition to managed floating made "exchange rate policy the object of contention of diverse opinion and interest groups." [33] For what is criticized here is precisely an element of the fixed rate system that has been grafted onto floating. It is characteristic of a fixed rate system that each rate change is undertaken through a conscious political decision and thus it automatically becomes the object of political contention. The West German revaluations are illuminating examples of this. Whoever is unwilling to leave the fate of a currency to the markets should not complain if political groups attempt to exert influence on that fate. This is, however, not a failing of floating, but rather a failing of the fixed rate system.

---

[30] F. A. von Hayek, "Arten der Ordnung," *Ordo,* vol. 14 (1963), p. 11ff. Reprinted in F. A. von Hayek, *Freiburger Studien: Gesammelte Aufsätze* (Tübingen: Mohr, 1969), p. 32ff.

[31] Hannes Androsch, "Währungs- und integrationspolitische Ziele des neutralen Österreich," *Aussenwirtschaft,* vol. 29 (1974), p. 138.

[32] See, for example, Haberler, "Future of the International Monetary System," p. 394.

[33] Keiser, "Erste Erfahrungen," p. 107.

Has Floating Impeded International Trade?

Let us now turn to an argument that actually concerns the "flexible part" of the present conglomerate which goes by the name of "floating."

For international trade, floating is seen by many as a setback compared with the former fixed rate system. Rate fluctuations, it is said, have caused great insecurity and have thus represented "a strong obstacle to the international exchange of goods."[34] In connection with international trade, one author even speaks of the "inherent destabilizing effect of fluctuating rates of exchange."[35] The argument that international trade would not be able to bear the risks of rate fluctuations had already been proffered many times as a warning before the transition to floating.

In reality, however, world trade in 1973 showed a real increase—adjusted for price rises—of no less than 15 percent. In 1974—with world prosperity ebbing—it still showed a real increase of about 5 percent.[36] Naturally, one cannot "prove" with these figures that floating had the same effect on trade as fixed parities or a more favorable effect. The possibility cannot be logically excluded that under another exchange rate system world trade would have expanded even more strongly. Nevertheless, with the real growth rate of 15 percent attained in 1973, this is hardly probable: during the last years of the fixed rate system, the real growth rate had been between 5 and 10 percent.[37] One thing is clear in any case. The often alleged restricting effect of flexible rates on trade has not in fact occurred—at least not up to now—and this has surprised many people who had the strong rate fluctuations before their eyes and the complaints of the export industry in their ears.

Injury to international trade through exchange rate fluctuation has been claimed on two counts.

The export industry in countries whose currencies tend to appreciate points to the absolute magnitude of the appreciation of the domestic currency. The Swiss franc and the deutsche mark exhibited the widest movements under floating. The dollar rate of the deutsche mark was 20 percent higher at the end of March and again at the end of May 1975 than it had been at the end of March 1973 at the beginning of floating.[38] Rate movements relative to a single currency are certainly important to a firm that exports only to the one country in question. But they give a

---

[34] A. Frauenfelder, "Erschwerung des internationalen Güteraustausches," in *Feuertaufe für das Floating*, p. 22.

[35] Keiser, "Erste Erfahrungen," p. 104.

[36] *Report of the Deutsche Bundesbank for the Year 1974*, p. 45.

[37] *Börsen- und Wirtschaftshandbuch 1974* (Frankfurt/Main: Societäts-Verlag, 1974), p. 174. See also, IMF, *Annual Report 1975*, p. 11.

[38] See *Report of the Deutsche Bundesbank for the Year 1974*, p. 58.

false picture of the situation of the export business as a whole. Relative to the world as a whole the deutsche mark has appreciated by a weighted average of only 13 to 14 percent in the first two years of floating. And against the sixteen currencies most important to West Germany[39]—in which almost all trade transactions take place—the appreciation has been only about 11 percent.[40] For the export situation, the development of the exchange rates is only one among several decisive factors. Moreover, developments of costs and prices in the country of destination must be considered. In the first two years after the beginning of floating, prices rose strongly in West Germany, but substantially less than in its most important trade partners.

If the consumer price index is taken as a rough measure of comparison, we find that in the fourth quarter of 1974 in West Germany, this price index was 14.3 percent higher than it was in the fourth quarter of 1972. In the same period of time, the index in twelve of the sixteen important trading partner countries[41] rose on average by 26 percent. The average "price lead" of these countries was thus 11.7 percent after two years.[42] And this is to say that the rise of the deutsche mark exchange rate has on average approximately offset the stronger price rise in the trade partners. Of course this is admittedly not the case for each individual country. Great Britain, for example, has developed a "price lead" of 16 percent in two years. But the rate of exchange of the deutsche mark against sterling has risen approximately 25 percent. In Italy prices have risen by 25 percent more than in West Germany in two years. However, the deutsche mark–lira rate in March 1975 was 31 percent higher than it was two years earlier. For the United States the price lead was 7.2 percent, but the appreciation rate was 20 percent.[43]

For the West German export trade on average, what the Bundesbank states in its last annual report is true: the appreciation of the deutsche mark since the beginning of floating "was very largely, though not fully, offset for West German foreign trade by lower cost and price

---

[39] The currencies officially quoted in Frankfurt and referred to here are those of Austria, Belgium, Canada, Denmark, Finland, France, Great Britain, Italy, Japan, the Netherlands, Norway, Portugal, Spain, Sweden, Switzerland, and the United States.

[40] See *Report of the Deutsche Bundesbank for the Year 1974*, p. 58. As for the rationale of calculating a trade-weighted index of exchange rates see H. G. Johnson, "World Inflation," p. 12.

[41] Excluding Denmark, Finland, Portugal, and Spain.

[42] My calculation is based on *Report of the Deutsche Bundesbank for the Year 1974*, p. 55.

[43] My calculation is based on a press release from the Deutsche Bundesbank, May 23, 1975, in Deutsche Bundesbank, *Auszüge aus Presseartikeln*, no. 34 (May 27, 1975), and on *Report of the Deutsche Bundesbank for the Year 1974*, p. 55.

rises in the Federal Republic of Germany."[44] The Bundesbank adds, "It would, however, be more correct to say that the higher rate for the deutsche mark was primarily a consequence of the lower price rise in the Federal Republic."[45] Floating did not "kill" export trade with the relatively strong appreciation of the deutsche mark. On the average it caused differing rates of price rises to be readjusted, and it has, moreover, in part done away with disequilibria piled up during the time of fixed parities.

Unquestionably, this process can be very painful for individual export firms, just as it was painful for individual construction companies to adjust to the normalization of the construction boom: in both cases abnormal data were erroneously considered to be normal for the long run. But should the adjustment be prevented because of this? Who is to finance the overproduction of homes or the overproduction of export goods? There is reason to expect that, in the future, the continual adjustment of the rates will prevent the generation of such disequilibria as have occurred in the past and must now be painfully eliminated.

It has been said—very reproachfully—that: "Floating exchange rates do protect the state and national banks from exchange rate losses. However, they transfer the risk to the private sector."[46] The observation is correct. But who is "the state," this "great fiction," as Frederic Bastiat put it, through which everyone tries to live at everyone else's expense? To burden the state with a risk means to burden the general public. It is a principle of the market economy to make chances of gain and threat of losses private sector concerns, and this is what occurs through flexible rates.

The conditions in other countries are similar to those described here for the Federal Republic of Germany. In other countries, too, a false picture of the total effect of floating emerges if rate developments between only *two* currencies are considered. During the first two years of floating, for example, the dollar depreciated by almost 20 percent relative to the deutsche mark, but this strong depreciation is not representative of the foreign value of the dollar in general. Measured as a weighted average value relative to the sixteen currencies officially quoted in Frankfurt, the external value of the American currency was only about 1 percent lower at the end of March 1975 than at the beginning of floating two years earlier.[47] (It should be noted that none of these sixteen cur-

---

[44] *Report of the Deutsche Bundesbank for the Year 1974*, p. 58. A similar statement has been made by the IMF. See IMF, *Annual Report 1975*, p. 31.

[45] *Report of the Deutsche Bundesbank for the Year 1974*, p. 58.

[46] Rainer Hellmann in *Eurépargne*, quoted in *Blick durch die Wirtschaft*, no. 73, March 27, 1975.

[47] *Report of the Deutsche Bundesbank for the Year 1974*, p. 58ff. See also IMF, *Annual Report 1975*, p. 28ff.

rencies is tied to the dollar. Even the manipulation of floating should not be taken to have had a substantial influence over such a long time span. Merely "to offer a measure of resistance to market tendencies" during as much as two years,[48] a very considerable volume of *masse de manoeuvre* would have been necessary. That was certainly shown during the period of fixed rates of exchange.)

In addition, the fluctuations of the dollar value, measured as a weighted average of the rates against the sixteen aforementioned currencies, remained in the first year of floating within a margin of ±5 percent, and in the second year within a margin of ±2½ percent.[49] Since a considerable portion of international trade is still transacted on a dollar basis, businesses thus found generally much more stability than is commonly supposed. In this, as well, there lies a reason for the expansion of world trade during the period of floating.

Now it will perhaps be objected that what matters for international trade is not so much the long-term trend and still less is it the weighted averages. What is said to be decisive as an obstacle to the international exchange of goods is the strong fluctuation of individual currencies, the abrupt moves back and forth between appreciation and depreciation, the zigzagging of exchange rates. This objection has also been raised by businesses that emphasize the frequency of these fluctuations.[50] Two examples may be cited: Between March 1973 and August 1974 the dollar–Swiss franc rate showed, within some months, swings of 8 percent between highest and lowest rates. The rate of the deutsche mark to the Swiss franc showed, at times, changes of 6 percent within a month.[51] Such uncertainties deprived international trade of a basis for calculation—so it is said.

Economists have dealt with such objections by pointing to the possibility of concluding rate guarantee contracts. But practitioners have claimed that this is possible only in exceptional cases and that it is very expensive besides. As late as February 1975 an author close to foreign trade practice wrote, "The continually propagated expectation that commercial practice could protect itself with the help of futures transactions has been confirmed only to a limited extent. A broad and efficient

---

[48] "Guidelines for the Management of Floating Exchange Rates," in IMF, *Annual Report 1974*, p. 112.

[49] See *Report of the Deutsche Bundesbank for the Year 1974*, p. 5.

[50] See, for example, Frauenfelder, "Erschwerung," p. 21ff.; J. P. Christen, "Verrechnungsprobleme mit Auslandstöchtern," in *Feuertaufe für das Floating*, p. 27; Thomann and Kaeser, "Übertriebene Erwartungen," p. 58; J. P. Blancpain, "Wechselkursfloating—ein hoffnungsvolles Experiment," in *Feuertaufe für das Floating*, p. 69; Keiser, "Erste Erfahrungen," p. 105.

[51] Frauenfelder, "Erschwerung," p. 22. For examples of day-to-day and week-to-week movements of exchange rates see IMF, *Annual Report 1975*, p. 26.

futures market exists for only very few market relationships (dollar/ deutsche mark, dollar/Swiss franc, and dollar/sterling). Also, the costs of cover are often quite high."[52]

A glance at the facts shows that parts of this opinion are incorrect. First, in addition to the exchange futures market proper, there exist a number of further ways of covering the currency risk of foreign trade deals. These include foreign currency loans (in which an exporter raises a loan in foreign currency which is immediately exchanged into domestic currency at the current rate; the loan is repaid when the foreign currency receivables come in), discounting foreign exchange drafts (where an exporter makes a draft in foreign currency on a foreign importer; after acceptance the bill is discounted and passed to the credit of the exporter in domestic currency at the current rate of exchange), and factoring of foreign currency receivables (where an exporter assigns foreign currency receivables to a bank or a factoring firm; the amount is passed to the credit of the exporter in domestic currency at the current rate of exchange).[53] Besides, firms that engage in both export and import activities may be able to offset the currency risk within the firm itself.

In addition, it should be recognized that the larger part of foreign trade dealings is transacted in those currencies for which "a broad and efficient futures market" does exist. Indeed these forward markets developed because there were large foreign trade dealings in the currencies in question. For, as Harry Johnson has pointed out, "the development of a market of any kind is conditional on there being enough interested transactors to make the cost of establishing and operating the market worthwhile."[54] Forward deals are, however, also possible in other currencies; but in these, of course, they are relatively expensive.

Even exchange guarantee contracts over three to five years can be placed without difficulty.[55] Moreover, there is the possibility in most European countries of demanding a national export risk guarantee for long-term deals.[56] In West Germany, for example, the federal government has (since 1972) made possible the insurance of exchange rate risks through Hermes Kreditversicherungs-AG as the agent of the federal government.[57] Difficulties—mostly high costs—arise today only in the case of long-term rate guarantees for notoriously unstable currencies.[58]

---

[52] Keiser, "Erste Erfahrungen," p. 105.

[53] See "Katalog der Möglichkeiten zur Abdeckung des Währungsrisikos bei Aussenhandelsgeschäften," *Aussenwirtschaft*, vol. 29 (1974), p. 222ff.

[54] H. G. Johnson, "World Inflation," p. 11.

[55] See Hans Mayrzedt and Otto von Platen, "Dokumentation über Dreimonatsterminkurse (Geld) seit Anfang 1973," *Aussenwirtschaft*, vol. 29 (1974), p. 196ff.

[56] See "Katalog der Möglichkeiten," p. 223.

[57] See *Report of the Deutsche Bundesbank for the Year 1971*, p. 95.

[58] See Mayrzedt and von Platen, "Dokumentation über Dreimonatsterminkurse," p. 197.

But that was the case already at the time of fixed parities. Who, after all, can tell what will happen in Portugal or Italy in three years?

The *costs* of forward coverage, measured by the difference between spot and forward rates, were highest in the first half of 1973. A rate of 8.7 percent per annum effective at the end of March 1973 has been reported as the highest dollar discount against the deutsche mark on the three-month futures market in Frankfurt. In Zurich, the highest dollar discount against the Swiss franc, quoted at the end of July 1973, was 6.8 percent per annum. In Frankfurt, the highest discount for Swiss francs against the deutsche mark was 5.3 percent per annum (quoted at the end of February 1973, when the Swiss franc was already floating independently).[59] Forward coverage costs have receded sharply, though with fluctuations, since the middle of 1973. The fluctuations of the exchange rates have no (or at least no direct) influence on the cost of forward coverage, inasmuch as the costs are governed primarily by differences in interest rates between the currencies concerned in the Euromarket.[60] These differences in interest rates have narrowed during the time of floating—in part, it should be noted, because of floating.

Of course, the difference between the spot rate and the forward rate of a currency does not represent a cost to every participant in international trade who sells or buys this currency at the futures market. A discount for a seller of forward exchange means a premium for the buyer, and a discount for the buyer means a premium for the seller. An exporter who sells a foreign currency forward pays a cost only if this currency sells at a discount; if it sells at a premium the exporter makes an additional gain. Contrariwise, an importer who buys forward a foreign currency pays a cost only if this currency is quoted at a premium; if it is quoted at a discount the importer makes an additional gain. Thus, the difference between spot and forward rates is not a net cost to international trade as a whole: the exporter's cost is matched by the importer's gain, and vice versa. The net cost to society is only the spread between "bid" and "asked" prices of forward exchange.[61] It has been argued that "from the point of view of any one businessman, the asser-

[59] Ibid., pp. 205, 209, 211, 216ff. See also Hans Mayrzedt and Otto von Platen, "Dokumentation der Termindevisenkurse (3 Monate) in Zürich, April 1974 bis Mitte Mai 1975," *Aussenwirtschaft*, vol. 30 (1975), p. 145ff.

[60] H. Baschnagel, "Veränderte Bedingungen für das Devisentermingeschäft," in *Feuertaufe für das Floating*, p. 14ff. Hans Mayrzedt and Otto von Platen, "Die Bedeutung der Termindevisenkurse für das Aussenhandelsgeschäft," in *Aussenwirtschaft*, vol. 30 (1975), p. 140ff.

[61] See Fritz Machlup, "The Forward-Exchange Market: Misunderstandings between Practitioners and Economists," in George N. Halm, ed., *Approaches to Greater Flexibility of Exchange Rates: The Bürgenstock Papers* (Princeton, N.J.: Princeton University Press, 1970), p. 299ff.

tion . . . that his loss is some other's gain, can be hollow comfort."[62] But, over a longer period of time, even for one single exporter (or importer) the cost at one time can be offset or at least reduced by gains at another time if only the forward quotation of the currency in question changes over time from a discount to a premium (or from a premium to a discount)—which in fact has happened to several currency relationships since 1973.

Summarizing, we may say that in contrast to the statement quoted earlier, in practice exporters and importers had plenty of opportunities in the past three years to protect themselves very well against exchange rate fluctuations through forward transactions. And they have in fact done so extensively—as has been confirmed, for example, by a survey of business enterprises conducted by the Swiss Institute for International Economics, Regional Science and Market Research at Sankt Gallen. The institute reports that "many businesses have, somewhat belatedly, recognized the rate fluctuations as a daily risk against which they should protect themselves. Since then, this reorientation process has advanced considerably."[63] That was in spring 1974.

Meanwhile, Swiss banking circles have indicated that there was the impression "that commercially based coverage deals have decreased in importance." This is explained by the "assumption that the large adjustments in the currency structure are behind us." Strong rate fluctuations which exceed futures coverage costs are said to be no longer in prospect. Thus, despite floating, forward covering is becoming less necessary than it was earlier under fixed parities, when one frequently "did not know, whether and when an overdue devaluation (or revaluation) would occur."[64] This is in line with a statement that Secretary of the Treasury Simon made in July 1975: "The message I get from U.S. businessmen, bankers and investors who deal in the international area is a clear one— they are growing accustomed to a flexible rate system, and they find it much easier to cope with market-induced movements than the sudden impact of a closed market, a major par value shift, or the imposition of government controls."[65]

It turns out, then, that floating has not had destabilizing effects on foreign trade. Businesses have learned to live with flexible rates of ex-

---

62 John H. Watts, "Forward Currency 'Costs': A Zero Sum Game?" in ibid., p. 307.
63 Mayrzedt and von Platen, "Dokumentation über Dreimonatsterminkurse," p. 197.
64 Baschnagel, "Veränderte Bedingungen," p. 18.
65 "Statement of The Honorable William E. Simon, Secretary of the Treasury, before the Joint Economic Subcommittee on International Economics, and the House Banking, Currency and Housing Subcommittee on International Trade, Investment and Monetary Policy," *Department of the Treasury News*, July 21, 1975, p. 7.

change very quickly. Even Kurt Richebächer, certainly no protagonist of floating, finds, as he says, "consolation" in the "fact that international trade has flourished brilliantly despite extreme exchange rate fluctuations."[66]

It goes without saying that the need to obtain forward cover or exchange guarantees raises the costs of international trade, and thus is equivalent to an increase of transportation costs. In comparison with a system of rigidly fixed parities with coordinated monetary and business cycle policies, floating is a second best solution. But that ideal system is unreal under present political conditions. The only realistic alternative is a system of fixed parities with noncoordinated economic policies. That means, however, either sporadic rate changes, and thus again the necessity of forward cover or exchange guarantees for foreign trade, or the preservation of fixed parities through trade restrictions and exchange control, and thus also obstacles to foreign trade. By comparison, floating is the superior system.

A similar conclusion has been drawn by the IMF in its 1975 *Annual Report:* "On the whole, exchange rate flexibility appears to have enabled the world economy to surmount a succession of disturbing events, and to accommodate divergent trends in costs and prices in national economies with less disruption of trade and payments than a system of par values would have been able to do."[67]

Floating, Inflation, and the Autonomy of National Monetary Policy

The last argument against floating to be discussed here is that floating has failed to provide increased independence of national monetary policy, a fundamentally important matter.

This argument proceeds from the adjustment of exports and imports to shifts in the rate of exchange. In several countries, it has been observed since the beginning of floating that exports and imports have not reacted to changes of the exchange rate "according to the model," but rather "perversely." In West Germany, Switzerland, and Austria, exports increased despite a strong appreciation of the domestic currency. Conversely, in Great Britain and Italy exports decreased, despite a sharp

---

[66] Richebächer, *Überforderte Wechselkurspolitik,* p. 81.

[67] IMF, *Annual Report 1975,* p. 33. The IMF thus endorses Milton Friedman's statement of June 21, 1973 (before the Subcommittee on International Exchange and Payments of the Joint Economic Committee of the Congress) that "the introduction of a floating exchange mechanism has facilitated rather than impeded international trade and investment." Friedman, *How Well Are Fluctuating Exchange Rates Working?* American Enterprise Institute Reprint No. 18 (Washington, D.C.: American Enterprise Institute, 1973), p. 3.

depreciation, while imports rose. "According to the model," imports should have decreased in the depreciating countries and exports should have increased. In appreciating countries the reverse should have happened. A transitory "perverse" reaction of exports and imports—more correctly, a delay in the effect—had also been observed earlier for discrete exchange rate changes. But now it is claimed, a persistent perverse reaction of the current balance was evident.

For this alleged failure an explanation has been offered.[68] The decisive cause is said to be the highly advanced integration of markets in Europe. Imports consist mainly of finished goods and "in many markets, purchases from neighboring countries have become practically indispensable." In a depreciating country the importation from neighboring countries (with rising exchange rates) of "finished goods firmly anchored in the market" is said to raise prices.[69] These firm links between markets are believed to make it impossible to restrict imports, despite large price increases. On the other hand, a further price increase of the country's own exports is said to result from the rise in prices of imports through the worsening exchange rates: the import price rise raises the cost of living, causing pressure on wages, which in turn affects production costs and the prices of export goods. Thus, an export-promoting effect of the depreciation either evaporates quickly or does not occur at all. Rather, exports decline even more than they have declined because of the increase in costs caused by the depreciation. This, in turn, leads to a further worsening of the exchange rate and to another round of price increases.

The attentive reader will have noted that this is yet another version of the "motivated balance of payments theory" of exchange rates and inflation. This theory had already been supposed to explain the galloping inflation in Germany after World War I or rather to vindicate the creators of this inflation. The theory was that the war had caused a structural deficit in the balance of payments which—through the export of banknotes, a following depreciation of the deutsche mark exchange rate, and consequently rising prices for imports—continuously led to inflation.[70] This theory has often been refuted and believed dead, but again and again it celebrates a merry resurrection.

---

68 See Keiser, "Erste Erfahrungen," p. 105ff.

69 Ibid., p. 106.

70 A summary of this theory, given by one of its proponents, Karl Helfferich, is quoted in Gottfried Haberler, *The Theory of International Trade with its Applications to Commercial Policy* (Ninth impression, London: Macmillan, 1965), p. 58ff. For a critique of this theory, see Walter Eucken, *Kritische Betrachtungen zum deutschen Geldproblem* (Jena: Gustav Fischer, 1923), and Haberler, *Theory of International Trade*, pp. 30ff. and 59ff.

For appreciating countries a corresponding theory has been presented. In these countries "the cheapening effect of rising exchange rates affects imports in a correspondingly broad and rapid manner." Therefore it is, so the theory runs, "relatively easy for these countries . . . to check their price and wage increases and thus to maintain their competitive status or even to improve it."[71] Two conclusions have been drawn from these propositions which claim that floating has failed: floating encourages inflation, and it favors "the economically strong surplus countries obviously more than the weak deficit countries."[72]

These theories amount to the explanation that poverty comes from poverty. In reality, the reason imports in Great Britain and Italy have not decreased is not that they were "firmly anchored in the market." For them to have done so would mean that within a country a price increase, no matter how large, could never lead to a decline in demand, since "the anchoring in the market" is firmest within a country. Rather, imports in England and Italy have remained the same or even risen, despite depreciation, because demand has been expanded again and again by inflation. And the inflation was not caused by the depreciation of the currency; it was homemade. The costs of export production in these countries rose because of the tendency to give in to the escalating demands of the labor unions and simultaneously pursue inflationist financing. Finally, strikes in both countries paralyzed production for a long time: In Italy, the number of working days lost by strikes was 20,409,000 in 1973 and 16,742,000 in 1974; in Great Britain, the figures were 7,184,000 in 1973 and 14,730,000 in 1974. Working days lost by strikes in Italy and Great Britain made up 73 percent (in 1973) or 85 percent (in 1974) of total losses by strikes in the nine countries of the Common Market.[73] The result was that even export firms still

---

[71] Keiser, "Erste Erfahrungen," p. 106.

[72] Ibid. On "surplus countries," the opposite argument has also been proposed: It has been said that even countries with appreciating currencies could not avoid inflation by floating their exchange rate. See the discussion of this argument by Haberler, "Vorwort zur deutschen Ausgabe," p. 19.

[73] The comparative figures for France and the Federal Republic of Germany were 3,914,000 (1973) and 3,377,000 (1974), and 551,000 (1973) and 1,059,000 (1974), respectively. The picture is not altered if days lost by strikes are seen in relation to total working force: The number of working days lost by strikes per 1,000 gainfully employed in 1973 and 1974, respectively, was: Italy 1,564 and 1,246; Great Britain 317 and 647; France 233 and 198; Federal Republic of Germany 28 and 53. See Institut der Deutschen Wirtschaft, *Zahlen zur wirtschaftlichen Entwicklung der Bundesrepublik Deutschland, Ausgabe 1975* (Köln: Deutscher Instituts-Verlag, 1975), Table 81. Presse- und Informationsamt der Bundesregierung, *Aktuelle Beiträge zur Wirtschafts- und Finanzpolitik,* no. 10/1976 (Bonn, 21 January, 1976); Commerzbank AG, *EWG in Zahlen, Ausgabe 1975* (Frankfurt/Main: Commerzbank AG, 1975).

capable of competing abroad were physically unable to deliver and that, on the other hand, expensive foreign goods were imported because domestic goods were not being produced at all. Moreover, there was also the fact that in West Germany and Switzerland the domestic boom was curbed earlier than in other countries and therefore the export push became stronger.[74]

The "perverse" reaction of the current balance is thus a consequence of continuing inflation in some countries, and "the inflation differential between the various countries is the cause and not the consequence of exchange rate changes."[75] Of course, there is a grain of truth in the contrary theses: changes in the exchange rate do produce certain feedback effects; currency appreciation dampens domestic inflation while depreciation causes the reverse.[76]

Can one conclude from this that floating encouraged inflation in the world? To do so, one would have to show that the reinforcement of price increases in inflationary countries which depreciate have a stronger impact on the world economy than the moderation of price increases in countries which appreciate, as Lutz has already pointed out.[77] However, nothing speaks for this presumption.

On the contrary, one might even suspect that in the long run floating will dampen world inflation. Flexible rates on the one hand effectively shield countries with a solid monetary policy from inflationary impacts from abroad. In its last annual report the German Bundesbank stated plainly that the stabilizing course of monetary policy "could by and large be pursued without monetary disturbances from outside."[78]

On the other hand, flexible rates do prevent the moderation of inflation in the inflationary countries, which was possible under fixed rates by partially exporting inflation abroad. The countries that produce inflation must now "swallow" it themselves and cannot "export" it.[79] When things get worse in this way they may get better earlier. For the point is reached more rapidly where it becomes clear to everyone that "inflation cannot be countered by still more inflation."[80] The time that has to pass until this point is reached depends on the inflation sensitivity of the public, which may be different in different countries. But in the end an

---

[74] See *Report of the Deutsche Bundesbank for the Year 1974*, p. 12.

[75] Ibid., p. 32.

[76] Ibid.

[77] F. A. Lutz, "Vom Notbehelf zum Dauerzustand," in *Feuertaufe für das Floating*, p. 66.

[78] *Report of the Deutsche Bundesbank for the Year 1974*, p. 30.

[79] See Haberler, "Future of the International Monetary System," p. 391. See also Haberler, "Vorwort zur deutschen Ausgabe," p. 18.

[80] *Report of the Deutsche Bundesbank for the Year 1973*, p. 43

accelerating inflation can be cured only by domestic stabilization measures. In this sense it can be contended that "floating rates yield more direct signals to the public and the policymakers than reserve changes under fixed rates" and that floating thus is "more likely to alert the national public to monetary mismanagement by its governmental system."[81]

It has indeed been claimed by some, and with great indignation, that with the adoption of floating one has fallen victim to a professors' trick. There is autonomy of monetary policy, but it turns out to be for countries which strive for monetary stability. And floating did not yield the autonomy to continue inflating ever more strongly. Thus, perhaps floating might in the long run turn out even to have an anti-inflationary bias? That would not be the worst thing. Let us wait and see.

Conclusion

What then is the upshot of all this? Floating is not of the best of all conceivable worlds. But among the realistically possible solutions it is not a bad one. To quote the U.S. secretary of the Treasury, floating is "appropriate for the world as it is today, not as it once was or as we might like it to be."[82] We shall still have to wait for a currency system which—as Austrian Treasury Minister Androsch said ironically—"simultaneously reacts firmly but flexibly and therefore is crisis-proof to rate fluctuations, accommodates equally protectionists and export lobbyists in large countries, offers developing countries cheap and noninflationary increases in buying power through sufficiently interest-bearing special drawing rights, makes it possible, with the help of objective indicators, for individual countries to persist in their subjective desires to devalue or revalue, and, just on the side, guarantees flourishing world trade, business prosperity, full employment and price stability."[83]

Let us remain realists. Let us try to live with floating. Up to now it has not failed.

---

[81] H. G. Johnson, "World Inflation," pp. 15, 13. See also Arthur Burns, "Statement before the Subcommittee on International Finance of the Committee on Banking and Currency, House of Representatives, U.S. Congress, April 4, 1974," as cited in Haberler, "Vorwort zur deutschen Ausgabe," p. 18.

[82] "Address by The Honorable William E. Simon, secretary of the Treasury of the United States, before the 1975 Annual Meetings of the Boards of Governors of the World Bank Group and the International Monetary Fund at the Sheraton Park Hotel, Washington, D.C., September 2, 1975," *Department of the Treasury News,* September 2, 1975, p. 9.

[83] Androsch, "Währungs- und integrationspolitische Ziele," p. 137.

THE BEHAVIOR AND EFFECTS OF FLEXIBLE EXCHANGE RATES: A BRIEF REVIEW OF RECENT RESEARCH

Thomas D. Willett

I am going to try to summarize—briefly—some of the main results of the technical studies on exchange rate flexibility being carried out both by the Office of International Monetary Research at the U.S. Treasury and by various scholars at universities and other institutions. In doing so, I shall draw heavily on the summary paper presented by Charles Pigott, Richard Sweeney, and myself at the 1975 Konstanz Conference [1] and on the papers and discussions at the Treasury Workshop on Technical Studies on Exchange Rate Flexibility held in February 1976.[2] I shall be more or less dogmatic in trying to summarize quite a considerable amount of material and shall attempt only to highlight some of the major conclusions without spending a great deal of time on the methodology of the studies.

The studies of which I am aware tend to suggest that floating rates, while not having behaved in an ideal manner, have, on balance, worked much better than we had any right to expect. In terms of any set of reasonable expectations about how floating would work, I believe that floating rates must be given high marks on actual performance. Of course, it is easy to find instances where floating rates have fallen short of what some had hoped. Certainly they have not given national governments complete policy independence. But then no serious advocate of floating rates ever said they would result in complete policy independence. One gets into a grey area concerning how much greater policy independence has been obtained through floating.

If some are perhaps disappointed on this score, this disappointment must be balanced against the fact that we have not had a repeat of the 1930s, of the generation of chaos and beggar-thy-neighbor policies which

---

[1] "Some Aspects of the Behavior and Effects of Floating Exchange Rates" (presented at the Conference on Monetary Theory and Policy, held at Konstanz, Germany, in June 1975). Available as U.S. Treasury, OASIA-Research: Discussion Paper No. 75/31.

[2] A more detailed review of the experience with floating and extensive references to the studies on this subject are given in Thomas D. Willett, *Floating Exchange Rates and International Monetary Reform* (Washington, D.C.: American Enterprise Institute, 1977).

many critics of floating had prophesied if we did accept floating rates. In any general consideration of influences on policy, I believe that floating rates must be given high marks.

A second concern frequently expressed about the way floating rates have worked is that they have not eliminated many trade imbalances.[3] Of course, again, serious advocates of floating rates never asserted that floating would necessarily remove trade imbalances. As long as one grants that international capital flows are legitimate, one must recognize that trade imbalances are a part of equilibrium balance of payments structures for many countries.

Now, a more sophisticated brand of argument, associated with Robert Mundell and others, essentially posits that, under modern circumstances, exchange rate adjustments are not likely to be effective. We have spent a good deal of time at the Treasury analyzing such arguments and have concluded that while a number of interesting theoretical issues have been raised, when we combine an appropriate theoretical framework and empirical findings about the way the world is operating, we find that there is still a considerable balance of payments adjustment to be gained from exchange rate changes. This seemed to be the conclusion of most of the participants in a conference on this subject sponsored by the Treasury in 1974.[4]

A third area for criticism of how floating rates have worked concerns world inflation. Certainly floating rates have not been a panacea for world inflation. But again, it was not reasonable to expect that they would be.

Much more fascinating are debates on whether floating rates have, on balance, marginally contributed to greater inflation—say through a loss of discipline and through ratchet effects—or whether they have contributed more to a dampening of inflationary pressure by strengthening discipline and reducing the monetary imbalances and international transmission of inflation that may come through fixed exchange rates.

We have concluded there is no clear-cut answer whether a system of floating rates would be more inflationary than a system of genuinely fixed rates. Studies that purport to find a definite answer to this question have usually looked at only one or two of the mechanisms by which inflation is generated and transmitted internationally—for example, through the so-called ratchet effects. But the issue is much more complicated than this simple approach implies, and the answer depends on

---

[3] A convenient compendium of criticism of floating is given in "The Drift Back to Fixed Exchange Rates," *Business Week*, June 7, 1965.

[4] See Peter B. Clark, Dennis Logue, and Richard Sweeney, eds., *The Effects of Exchange Rate Adjustments* (Washington, D.C.: U.S. Government Printing Office, 1976).

many things: the type of disturbances one faces, the mechanisms and magnitudes of reserve creation, empirical assumptions about the nature of wage-price dynamics and government reaction functions, the relative importance of the different international transmission mechanisms, and so on.

On the inflationary impact of fixed and floating rates, we found it very difficult to draw any general conclusions, but I believe there to be a reasonable presumption that floating rates have tended to dampen inflationary pressures more than the adjustable peg system.

It has been said that floating rates have been excessively volatile and have contributed unnecessarily to the generation of instability and uncertainty and hence have distorted international trade patterns. This is an area in which it is extremely difficult to make hard and fast scientific judgments because the essential issue in the debate is the question of cause and effect. Our work in this area led me to the judgment that the considerable volatility of some exchange rates, the widening bid-ask spreads or increase of transactions costs, and the fact that forward rates have not been as good predictors of future spot rates under the current float as they were on average in the preceding decade are all primarily results of the increase in uncertainty about—and instability in—underlying economic and financial policies and conditions rather than of the poor performance of speculators in the foreign exchange market. There is much evidence consistent with this view, but it is extremely hard—indeed, I think, probably impossible—to provide a definitive scientific proof.

What we have done in our studies has been to consider statements to the contrary and we have found these statements very difficult to support. One such view would be that large rapid movements in the exchange rate could not be efficient (in the normal use of the term) because the underlying factors that ought to determine exchange rates are themselves not susceptible to rapid change. Hence, in this view large rapid changes in exchange rates would be per se an evidence of inefficiencies in the operation of the exchange market.

As a logical proposition, this view is hard to accept in the face of the modern theory of balance of payments and exchange rates which emphasize very heavily the role of expectations, the role of capital flows, and the role of exchange rates in clearing asset markets. Once one takes into account the expectations of changes in policies and other developments which are and should be reflected in movements of exchange rates, then it becomes not at all surprising that there has been a good deal of volatility of exchange rates. Consider the variability of the underlying circumstances—the large and variable differential rates of inflation, concern about the oil prices, where OPEC money is going, and the like.

All of these factors could give rise to a very large range of uncertainty as to what the appropriate exchange rate should be. And expectations could change quite rapidly. Thus one cannot argue that volatility per se is evidence of market inefficiency. Obviously, however, we cannot infer from this argument the obverse either, that the exchange markets have behaved with perfect efficiency.

This proposition will have to be treated as somewhat of an open question. I am not at all surprised to hear many judgments that exchange rates occasionally perform quite poorly in terms of reflecting underlying conditions, that there may have been episodes of significant destabilizing speculation, particularly in the earlier part of the floating period. But even if true, our research suggests that considerable caution should be applied in extrapolating those results to the future. For example, charts of the dollar–deutsche mark rate give the appearance of several clear-cut cycles consistent with the hypotheses of destabilizing bandwagon speculation or insufficiently stabilizing speculation. However, from the vast amount of work on testing for efficiency of other financial markets and work on the foreign exchange markets themselves, we also find that in a market that has been tested for years, like the stock market, there are many apparent cycles in market prices, although in fact this market has been found to be quite efficient.

The current research on statistical testing of the foreign exchange markets—such as random walk tests of the behavior of exchange rates and filter rules, which Richard Sweeney discusses later in this volume— suggests that it is not difficult to find ex post buy-sell rules that would have resulted in profits over short periods. Some viewers might take such results as evidence of destabilizing or insufficient stabilizing speculation. On the other hand, there are many plausible buy-sell rules which produce losses. Perhaps most significantly, quite a number of the plausible buy-sell rules which would give profits over the first part of the float, give losses over the last part.

By and large, results of this sort would be quite consistent either with having an efficient market the whole time or with initial transitional inefficiencies, while the market adjusted to new circumstances, followed by its settling down to more efficient behavior. The general conclusion from these studies is that a number of charges of the market's clearly suffering from poorly behaved speculation turn out, on close investigation, to be not clear-cut at all, particularly after the earlier part of the float.

The last category of studies I would like to discuss here is that dealing with the question of optimum currency areas. The findings that floating rates seem to have worked fairly well do not mean that there is no case for genuine fixed exchange rates under appropriate circumstances. A considerable amount of very interesting work on the appropriate economic conditions for genuinely fixed exchange rates and for floating exchange rates is being carried on. The general direction of these studies is to take into account more and more factors which tend to make us less and less certain as to what optimum economic boundaries for currencies would be.[5] But I think the strongest conclusion from recent experience is that the high degree of capital mobility we now face makes it much more difficult to run compromise systems between genuinely fixed exchange rates and relatively freely floating exchange rates. Compromise systems such as the adjustable peg have become much less viable in a world of high capital mobility. High capital mobility forces one away from compromises toward either floating rates or genuinely fixed rates.

A second major conclusion we can draw is that whatever is the first best economic optimum, as long as countries insist on following their own independent monetary policies rightly or wrongly, the most workable system is going to be one of relatively freely floating rates. The experiences over the last few years have made it clear that if one wants to make a system of fixed rates work among a group of countries, one must have extremely closely coordinated monetary and financial policies among those countries. Pegging exchange rates is just not a viable substitute for achieving stability in underlying policies and conditions. It is clearly desirable to achieve reduced volatility of exchange rates, but over the long run the only way in which this can be achieved is by securing greater stability in underlying conditions. Genuine exchange rate stability must be earned: it cannot be artificially imposed by official intervention except for brief periods of time. While it is hardly realistic to expect private speculation to be always correct ex post, we have found little evidence to support the view that it has tended to be systematically wrong, such that heavy official intervention in the foreign exchange markets would be called for to make up for insufficiencies of stabilizing speculation or offset destabilizing speculation.

---

[5] See, for instance, Edward Tower and Thomas D. Willett, *The Theory of Optimum Currency Areas and Exchange Rate Flexibility*, Special Papers on International Finance, no. 11 (Princeton: N.J., May 1976).

COMMENTARIES

C. Fred Bergsten

My comments will take the form of expressing, first, two hypotheses about the way floating rates have worked so far, and, then, one very deep concern about some problems arising from the manner in which they seem to be working.

The first hypothesis is that the effects of flexible rates on the world economy are anti-inflationary. The second is that flexible rates seem to have some significant impact on patterns of foreign direct investment by multinational corporations. The concern I shall express is a concern that the continuing system of nationally managed flexible exchange rates will give rise to some of the old problems of competitive intervention in exchange markets, with deleterious effects on international economic relations and world economic outcomes.

First, the hypothesis about the anti-inflationary impact of flexible exchange rates. Here, I side with Josef Molsberger and Thomas Willett, in his last conclusion on the subject, and I oppose Edward Bernstein. The first point here, as Molsberger indicated, is that flexible rates enable—or force—individual countries to bottle up home-grown inflation internally and thus they reduce the scope for exporting that inflation to the rest of the world. I think we have some empirical evidence that this has been happening. The deviations of national inflation rates from the world average have gone up quite sharply in the last couple of years. My colleague Walter Salant has put together data showing that those deviations from the world mean rate declined rather sharply in the 1960s as the world economy became more integrated under the continued efforts to maintain fixed exchange rates. Those deviations stayed pretty constant from 1970 through 1972 while we were in limbo and had not yet moved on to flexible rates. But then, as we moved to flexible rates in 1973, the deviations rose. They rose very sharply in 1974 and are continuing to rise now. The increase in those deviations would seem to suggest that the bottling up hypothesis has derived some support from events in the first three years of flexibility.

Thomas Willett made the second, and closely related point, that under flexible rates, with the ongoing adjustment of payments imbalances, there is less need for an expansion of world liquidity. This decreased need for liquidity reduces monetary impulses to world inflation that occurred during the 1960s and in the beginning of the 1970s.

Beyond that, it seems to me that the reaction functions of governments also suggest that flexible rates are less inflationary in their tendencies, as compared with the so-called disciplinary effect of fixed rates. Gottfried Haberler has argued for many years that a depreciating exchange rate would exercise a stronger disciplinary influence than would losses of reserves or the need for borrowing, which were the alternatives under fixed rates. The evidence so far suggests that he was probably right.

The matter is clearest, of course, for the United States. It seems that the depreciation of the dollar under the system of flexible rates has been taken more seriously into account by U.S. economic policy makers than the deficits under fixed rates ever were, at least after the very early 1960s when those deficits were a new phenomenon encountered with some surprise and disbelief in the Treasury and elsewhere. Certainly, compared with the almost total absence of impact of the growing balance of payments deficits in the late 1960s and early 1970s on internal U.S. policy (which was obviously related to the key currency role of the dollar and the absence of much larger reserve losses to the United States), it seems that the depreciating dollar has had a greater impact on U.S. internal policy in a stabilizing direction. The inflationary implications of the depreciating dollar come home immediately to the populace and, therefore, generate political pressure for anti-inflationary policies. That never happened under fixed rates, at least under fixed rates of the dollar standard variety in the Bretton Woods system.

In that context, I concur with Bernstein about the U.S. depreciation in 1973 and 1974 being inflationary. To a large extent it was a belated payment for our internal policies during the Vietnam War. During that period, because the dollar was the center of the system, it became overvalued. During that period we clearly exported some of our internally generated inflation to the rest of the world. But there was no free lunch, and, when the moment came, we had to pay our bill. Probably, because we delayed paying it, we may have paid a little more than we would have had to earlier under the system of fixed exchange rates.

Since the United States is still the largest country in the world economy, the fact that flexible rates contribute toward more anti-inflationary internal policies in the United States goes a long way toward improving the anti-inflationary performance of the entire world economy. The second major country, in terms of its impact on global inflation, is West Germany as the center of the deutsche mark zone and the dominant economy in Western Europe. West Germany has been helped in its anti-inflationary internal efforts by the steady appreciation of the mark. Prices may not fall in West Germany, but they rise less there than elsewhere. The virtuous circle in West Germany has spilled out to members of the deutsche mark zone and others in Western Europe, and so provided a mechanism through which the system of rate flexibility dampens world inflationary tendencies.

There is at least some evidence, although it is a little more conjectural, that the impact of rate depreciation has also been disciplinary on some of the other key countries. It is noteworthy that the British never adopted any kind of tough internal incomes policy until the sterling rate broke very sharply from $2.30. The French, after they left the deutsche mark zone in January 1974 (for the first time) not only intervened heavily, to keep the exchange rate from dropping more, but took some reasonably tough internal anti-inflationary measures. The Japanese, when the yen weakened sharply in the fall of 1973 and early 1974, responded with a tight money policy in part because of the weakening of the yen. There is a fair amount of evidence, both at the global level and at the national level, that flexible rates do have an anti-inflationary impact on the world economy.

My second hypothesis—and I submit it with an even greater degree of uncertainty—deals with the possible impact of greater rate flexibility on foreign direct investment by multinational corporations. There is a fascinating correlation—and I put it only as a correlation—between the ratio of foreign production by the affiliates of multinationals based in particular countries to the exports of those countries on the one hand, and the putative over- or undervaluation of the currencies of those countries on the other hand.

There are three home countries of multinational firms where the ratio of offshore production by the country's multinationals to their exports is very high, ranging from about 400 percent for the United States to over 200 percent for the United Kingdom, with Switzerland in between. All three countries, in part because of their major international financial roles, historically have had what I would regard as overvalued currencies—at least up until 1971, the most recent year for which data on trade and investment were available. This may have been an important factor, as Harry Johnson wrote many years ago, in promoting foreign investment rather than exports.

If we look at the ratios for Italy, Japan, and West Germany, we find that instead of ranging from 200 percent to 400 percent, they run around 40 percent—that is, their exports are much higher than offshore production by firms based in those countries. The other European countries and Canada range somewhere between 50 and 100 percent. Japan and West

Germany, and perhaps recently Italy, have been countries with basically undervalued exchange rates.[1]

How much of this correlation represents causality? It is too early to say anything definite, but it looks as though there may be some changes taking place in the U.S. pattern of foreign direct investment. If the estimates that now exist for 1976 hold true, it will be the first year in a long time in which domestic investment by U.S. firms grew more rapidly than foreign investment by U.S. firms. There are other factors involved, of course, and I do not mean to say this shows clearly that exchange rate relationships under flexible rates, being a better approximation of equilibrium, have changed the whole picture dramatically. But, at least suggestively, it appears that some changes may be taking place in investment patterns as a result of a more equilibrated exchange rate structure.

The other side of the equation, of course, is the big increase in direct investment in the United States by foreign firms, particularly from Western Europe and Japan. Of course, the question can be raised: Is this a one-shot change due to the parity realignments of 1971 and 1973, or is it a permanent consequence of new exchange rate relationships that have emerged under the flexible rate system? There seems to be a reasonably suggestive relationship between the pattern of foreign direct investment and the new rate structure that, I think, will certainly deserve additional attention and study as we get more experience with the new system.

The third point I want to make is a concern about the way that the flexible rate system is being managed. Despite agreements in principle at Rambouillet and Kingston, it clearly remains a unilaterally managed floating system. It seems to me that such management entails some risks. In 1973 and 1974, we saw a number of countries promulgating policies of competitive appreciation of exchange rates in order to try to export some of their internal inflationary pressures or, at a minimum, to avoid importing inflation. In some cases, countries which were actually intervening or pushing their exchange rates up through internal policy were not even running balance of payments surpluses.

Much more serious, it seems to me, is the current situation. I was surprised that none of our three authors mentioned the sharp exchange rate depreciations in the British and Italian cases and (even more notably) the nonappreciation of the Japanese yen. The unilateral management of exchange rates by the United Kingdom, Italy, and Japan raises a serious question of competitive depreciation or nonappreciation leading to a situation similar to what we had in the late 1960s and early 1970s. This situation not only brought on considerable international monetary

---

[1] This issue is elaborated in C. Fred Bergsten, Thomas O. Horst, and Theodore H. Moran, *American Multinationals and American Interests* (Washington, D.C.: Brookings Institution, forthcoming), esp. chapter 2.

difficulty but also was, in retrospect, the root cause of the onset of major protectionist pressures in the United States.

What is happening now is wholly understandable. The United States is the only country whose recovery from the world recession is clearly under way and booming. Both the Western Europeans and the Japanese are uncertain whether internal demand factors will be sufficient to reduce their rates of unemployment in what is for most of them an election year. So the exchange rate movements might indeed be predicted as countries try to export unemployment in a particularly sensitive political situation.

All this affects the United States in significant ways under the flexible rate system, as under the Bretton Woods system, and perhaps even more so. Other countries determine the exchange rate of the dollar through their more active intervention policies in the exchange market. Therefore the United States has, to some extent, some of the same kinds of worries it had in the later stage of the Bretton Woods system.[2] The policy implication is not that we should get rid of flexible exchange rates, but rather that we should implement the agreements that have been reached in principle to move from unilateral management of the floating rate system to multilateral management with a kind of joint surveillance, preferably through the IMF.

Harold van B. Cleveland

I would like to approach this question of flexible rates and our experience with them from the standpoint of someone who is fairly close to the markets, and whose primary concern is with interpreting what is happening, and even predicting what is going to happen, rather than with policy issues or normative questions. I would like to concentrate on four issues that seem to me important in revealing the nature of our system.

The first issue is the steady, though jerky, downward movement of two major exchange rates, the pound and the lira and, more recently, of a third, the French franc. The second is the famous instability of the dollar–deutsche mark rate around a relatively flat trend. If one drew a line through Mr. Bernstein's chart, one would find a pretty flat trend, beginning at the beginning of relatively free floating in February 1973.

The third issue I would like to discuss is one that has not yet been referred to in these papers but that strikes me as the most interesting and, certainly, the most difficult to understand. It is the large over-

---

[2] For a detailed analysis of this issue see C. Fred Bergsten, *The Dilemmas of the Dollar: The Economics and Politics of United States International Monetary Policy* (New York: New York University Press, 1976), esp. chapter 7.

valuation of the deutsche mark against the dollar, and by consequence, of some of the other snake currencies against the dollar. The evidence for this is what has happened to the relative purchasing power of the dollar and deutsche mark, and relative costs in the United States and West Germany, as indicated by consumer prices and by unit labor costs, compared at the present general level of the exchange rate.

Finally, there is the existence of two groups of currencies—a large dollar bloc and the European snake—with exchange rates within each group pretty well tied together or stabilized against each other—in a sea of considerably greater general instability of exchange rates.

Now, so far as theory is concerned, my stand is in agreement with the monetary approach, holding that the exchange rate is, in the long run at least, caused by the relative supply of and demand for the two kinds of money. In the long run, this implies purchasing-power parity. In the shorter run, we must have recourse to some notion of *expected* purchasing-power parity, or of expectations about the movement of the rate itself, assuming it tends to be strongly influenced by purchasing-power parity. In the short run, what seems to move exchange rates is market judgments about *future* relative price levels.

As in other economic expectations, there is here an element of adaptive expectation—that is to say, of expectations formed on the assumption that the past will continue into the future; and an element of rational expectations—that is to say, expectations that take into consideration other relevant information, most particularly including information with respect to policy. By other relevant information, I mean such things as policy decisions, policy trends, the background of policy, all those things from which exchange traders are accustomed to judge what is likely to happen to monetary and fiscal policy and to the price level itself.

Now, it is obvious, I suppose, from these points, that in a period where monetary policies have displayed rapid and diverse changes among countries, one cannot expect anything but instability in exchange rates. That is a point that Mr. Willett made well. One must factor into the rational expectations part of the expectation-formation process the behavior of the central bank in the exchange and money markets—that is, both its monetary and its exchange rate policies. If the central bank is seen to be intervening in the exchange market, and its intervention appears to be consistent with, and supportive of, a general trend in monetary policy (which, in turn, is consistent with the stability of the exchange rate in question), then I would suppose that the intervention policy of the central bank is of very great importance in determining where the rate will be in the near future. In other words, if the intervention policy is a *credible* policy, given the whole background of monetary and fiscal policy, and the political background, then it will have great power to influence the exchange rate in the short run. If, on the other hand, this is not the case, and the intervention policy seems to be running counter to the underlying trends of inflation and to short-run monetary-fiscal policies, then, of course, one would not expect the authorities to be able to control the rate. What we then have in the making is an exchange crisis. This is a shorthand description of what happened to the French franc in March–April 1976.

Of course, it does not require central bank intervention in the exchange market to produce stability of an exchange rate—in the monetary theory of exchange rates or in the real world. We have the case of the Canadian dollar and the U.S. dollar, in which the intervention policy of the Canadian government is mainly in the money market—that is, the Bank of Canada is mainly concerned with trying, over time, to align Canadian monetary policy with U.S. monetary policy, in order to stabilize the Canadian dollar close to parity with the U.S. dollar. And for that reason, the market, taking seriously the government's apparent intention to stabilize the Canadian dollar rate, will, indeed, act as though it expected the rate to remain stable, even when we have, as at present, a fairly large short-term divergence between Canadian and U.S. monetary conditions (as reflected in the difference in short-term interest rates).

Using a monetary approach to exchange rates is helpful in another way: it avoids confusion between stock-equilibrium and flow-equilibrium or disequilibrium effects. One should think of the exchange rate as being fundamentally a reflection of stock equilibrium—the balance between supply of and demand for the two kinds of money in the world economy—and not of the flow equilibrium in the exchange market.

An example of the way this distinction can be used to clarify exchange-rate movements is provided by the mistaken initial response of the exchange markets to the rise in the oil price in 1973–1974. The markets thought the dollar would rise steeply and stay high against the European currencies, because Europe was more dependent on imported oil than the United States, and also because most of OPEC's surplus revenues would be invested in dollars. On these expectations, the dollar did strengthen sharply against the deutsche mark and other European currencies. But the strength did not persist. The initial forecast was based on a flow analysis, which saw funds being pulled net out of Europe to pay for oil imports and then moving across the exchanges into dollars. But, in fact, the dollar–deutsche mark rate depends over time on the global supply and demand for dollars and deutsche marks—a stock equilibrium that the oil-price rise had not altered. Only the Bundesbank and the Federal Reserve had the power to change the relative supply of dollars and deutsche marks. The oil-producing countries could not alter that balance by acquiring ownership of more dollars. This distinction between stock equilibrium and flow equilibrium permits us to separate out a great many shorter-term or random influences (influences which affect net flows of funds across the exchanges) from the underlying determinants of exchange rates, which are monetary in character.

Now, there is no great mystery as to the behavior of the pound and the lira. Until quite recently, these currencies did seem to be declining more or less in line with their relative purchasing power. This year (1976), however, the depreciation seems to have run considerably faster than the decline in the purchasing-power parity of the pound and the lira. If an exchange rate runs ahead of purchasing-power parity, we must make the assumption that the markets are looking ahead; they are judging from what they see going on in government policy (and in the case of Italy in the political constellation) and concluding that policies will be more expansionary in Great Britain and Italy than they have been and, therefore, that the future relative purchasing power of their currencies vis-à-vis the dollar will be substantially lower than the current relative purchasing power.

It is also clear, I think, that there can be a ratchet effect on inflation in the two countries, provided the domestic authorities are willing—and they probably are—to validate the increase in the price level resulting from the sharp drop in the exchange rate below purchasing-power parity. And if the monetary authorities do, in fact, validate it, then there will be more inflation than there would have been if the whole phenomenon had not occurred.

As to the fluctuations of the dollar–deutsche mark rate, it seems to me that the fundamental explanation lies in the uncertainty about which country—the United States or West Germany—is going to have the lower rate of inflation in the longer run, or even in the relatively shorter run. I think we could carry this uncertainty back to the beginning of floating, but I shall only provide more recent evidence, beginning in mid-1975 when the Federal Reserve Board decided to tighten up against a background of a perceived slowing down of U.S. inflation in the first and in the second quarters of 1975—and also, against a perceived background of rather expansive West German monetary policy. Put together all of these perceptions and we have the makings of a shift in expectations about future relative rates of inflation in the two countries, which the markets then proceeded to discount in the exchange rate by moving the dollar up and the mark down.

Since the beginning of 1976, however, we seem to have had a shift again. U.S. monetary policy, at least as judged by M_2, appears to be quite expansive. West German monetary aggregates have slowed down considerably. Also the West German rate of inflation fell sharply in the fourth quarter of 1975—sharply even in comparison with the U.S. rate of inflation—providing what is apparently the makings of some shift back in favor of the deutsche mark. Analysis of data such as these is helpful, and sometimes even seems to yield a correct forecast.

Finally, on the mark's overvaluation, there is first of all a question whether that overvaluation exists, a question we could no doubt debate endlessly, but let us assume for a moment that it does exist. There are two possible explanations. One is simply that the history of the last ten years has convinced the markets, in some fundamental way, that in the longer run, the United States is likely to be a more inflationary country than West Germany. A thought we often hear in the exchange markets is that the mark is perennially a strong currency—meaning strong against all currencies. This observation must reflect some underlying expectation about relative inflation in Germany and other countries.

The second explanation, which is consistent with the first, is that there occurred in the early 1970s a marked change in the portfolio preferences of holders of international funds and short-term financial assets, against the dollar and in favor of the deutsche mark. This applies both to official holders and to private holders. Once exchange rates were free to move, this preference shift could only make itself felt by a shift in the relative purchasing power of the two currencies, effected in the short run through exchange rate changes.

In this second explanation, the shift could have occurred not because the holders of international funds think they know which way inflation in the United States will go relative to inflation in West Germany, but because they want to be diversified—hedged—between these two generally attractive currencies. They started in (say) 1969–1970 from a position of extreme nondiversification—heavily concentrated in dollars—and they now wish to reduce their exposure to a possible decline in the dollar. Given the manifest uncertainties, they want to be more evenly balanced than they were.

Looking at the magnitudes, I think we can explain the large departure of the dollar–deutsche mark rate from purchasing-power parity simply by assuming that the departure is necessary to equilibrate international portfolios in the currency proportions that their holders now wish to have. This is almost a tautology. The present equilibrium may be temporary. The currency preferences may shift back again or, in the long run, if they do not, one would expect price-level adjustments to occur in the United States and Germany which would bring the two currencies back to purchasing-power parity.

Perhaps I do not need to say much of anything about my fourth point—the formation of currency blocs. They are not hard to explain. They involve monetary leadership by a large country whose monetary policy is, as it were, imported by small-country followers. The followers choose to import the leader's policy because they believe they have a great deal to gain and relatively little to lose from the stability of their exchange rates vis-à-vis the leader's currency and the currencies of the other countries in the bloc.

Gottfried Haberler

This session is supposed to give an overview, and I thought it might be useful to try to formulate points of agreement and disagreement as they appear from these three excellent papers which cover a wide range, if not the full range, of professional opinion on floating.

Let me first briefly mention a few things on which all three panelists seem to be in substantial agreement. I refer to Bernstein's paper, because he is the one who is perhaps a little less enthusiastic about floating than the others. He said that the abandonment of the universal system of fixed par values was essential in order to allow the world economy to cope with the instability and uncertainty of recent years. In other words, floating was unavoidable and will be unavoidable for the near future—even for the distant future, I would say. This is one thing on which we agree, and we need not spend much time on it.

A second point on which there seems to be full agreement is that widespread floating does not mean that all currencies of the world or even most of them float against each other. According to the statistics of the International Monetary Fund in 1975, fifty-four currencies were pegged to the dollar. But we should remember that these fifty-four countries account only for 12.4 percent of the member countries' trade, while eleven currencies which floated independently accounted for 46.4 percent of that trade.[1] In any case, floating does not mean that 126 currencies float against each other. There will always be many pegged currencies.

A third point on which there seems to be agreement—and there I was a little surprised—is that forward cover for exporters and importers was, on the whole, available at a reasonable cost. Again I quote Mr. Bernstein who said that exporters and importers can eliminate the exchange risk for the nominal cost of forward cover; the premiums and discounts on forward exchange rates are higher than they were, but this is largely due to the higher nominal interest rates which in turn are due to inflation, and only to a minor extent to fluctuating exchange rates. That is, I think, a very interesting case of agreement.

---

[1] IMF, *Annual Report 1975*, p. 24. Since 1975 the precise figures have changed but the general picture has remained the same.

Then, fourth, there is agreement that speculation under floating is a much more risky business than under fixed rates or semi-fixed rates. The reason is that under the Bretton Woods adjustable peg system the speculator speculated against the central banks, whose hands were tied behind their backs, while under floating the speculators speculate against each other. While we now agree on that, it is natural that it took the operators in the market quite some time and a good deal of money in the form of losses from speculation to learn the lesson.

Still another point of agreement is that inflation in the United States was largely homemade. Again I quote from Mr. Bernstein's paper: "The prolonged inflation in the United States"—and, I think, we can say in most, though not all, other countries—"has been primarily due to domestic causes. The excessive depreciation of the dollar during parts of these two years probably had only a minor effect on the rate of inflation."

One more point that I think is highly important. Harry Johnson in a number of papers has called attention to the fact that the exchange market is like the stock market. Mr. Cleveland has also touched on that point, that the equilibrium in the exchange market is a *stock* equilibrium, rather than a flow equilibrium, and that expectations with respect to stocks and the future development of stocks are the decisive factor.

Now, may I come back to Bernstein's paper. He speaks of the appropriate balance of payments, and the appropriate exchange rate— and he says that the function of the exchange market is to bring about the appropriate balance of payments and an appropriate exchange rate. But he makes it quite clear that this formulation is only of very limited help in determining whether the fluctuations are excessive. He says that we do not know what the appropriate structure of the balance of payments is and that it is hopeless to calculate an appropriate dollar rate for the deutsche mark.

I think it is important to keep this in mind, insofar as that ties in with the vision of the exchange market as a stock market, rather than as a market where short-run flows are equated.

This brings me to the first major disagreement between Mr. Bernstein and the two other papers.

There are those who would draw the conclusion from the fact that we do not know what the appropriate exchange rate and the appropriate balance of payments structure are, that the authorities should refrain from official interventions or, at least, that official interventions should be modest and cautious. But Mr. Bernstein does not draw that conclusion. He is definitely of the opinion that interventions in certain cases are necessary. Let me make a few remarks on the dollar–deutsche mark exchange rate. If we look at the chart from the Bundesbank, which is in

Mr. Bernstein's paper, it is even ex post extremely difficult to determine the causes of these fluctuations. In 1973–1975 the world economy went through a turbulent period: high inflation and the oil shock were followed by a severe recession. Neither the inflationary explosion in 1973 nor the sudden deepening of the recession in the last quarter of 1974 were foreseen by anybody and nobody knew where the flood of petrodollars would flow and where it would settle down. Differential inflation, the differential impact of the oil shock and of the recession, smashed the par value system and made floating unavoidable.

It is not surprising that under these circumstances the market produced some fluctuations in exchange rates which ex post look excessive. Would the intervening authorities have done any better? Bernstein is very careful in his proposals for interventions. He does not want to suppress the fluctuations but only to make them milder. But is it wise to lay down rules for interventions beforehand—numerical rules on how to judge whether a movement is excessive and is likely to reverse itself? I have my doubts. Some recent experiences with intervention in Britain, France, and Italy are anything but promising. Britain has intervened on a massive scale using reserves and public or semipublic borrowing abroad (by nationalized industries)—a case not of dirty floating but of dirty fixing. The same is true of Italy and to a lesser extent of France. The exchange rates have been fixed for a while and then dropped sharply. The interventions have accentuated the fluctuations and have saddled the countries with a heavy foreign debt.

This is, of course, not the type of intervention that Bernstein recommends. He does not speak of the British pound or of the lira but of the dollar–deutsche mark rate. I personally would not rule out interventions, and this not merely because it would be hopeless to persuade governments to refrain from intervening. But I do believe that the danger is that most governments have a strong propensity to intervene too much rather than too little and that we should not encourage that propensity.

Let me mention one more important point on which there seems to be less than full agreement. How much independence does floating provide for internal stabilization policies? Bernstein has this to say:

> It is sometimes said that fluctuating exchange rates give a country greater freedom on fiscal and monetary policies. That is true only in a negative sense. If a country cannot maintain the fiscal and monetary policies required for a fixed par value, it can avoid the consequential disruption in its balance of payments and in its domestic economy by letting the rate fluctuate. Having shifted to floating rates, however, a country is not completely free to follow any fiscal and monetary policies and to ignore all fluctuations in exchange rates. It still must take ac-

count of the effect of those policies on output and employment and on prices and costs.

I fully agree that even under floating a country "must take account of the effect of [its fiscal and monetary] policies on output and employment and on prices and costs." No advocate of floating would deny that inflation or deflation remains a problem under floating. I also agree that under floating a country cannot safely ignore "all fluctuations in exchange rates." For example a depreciating currency tends to intensify inflationary pressures. Advocates of floating have been fully aware of this and have argued that for precisely this reason a falling exchange rate under floating will be a stronger inducement for the monetary authorities to step on the monetary brake than would a loss of reserves under fixed rates. This conjecture of theorists has been confirmed many times. For example Arthur Burns, not an ardent floater, pointed out that under floating "faster inflation in the United States than abroad would tend to induce a depreciation of the dollar, which in turn would exacerbate our inflation problem." He drew the conclusion that "under the present regime of floating it is more necessary than ever to proceed cautiously in executing an expansionary policy."[2]

The question how much protection from outside disturbances and how much freedom for fiscal and monetary policy floating provides, I would answer as follows: We must sharply distinguish between monetary and real influences from abroad. Floating protects only from monetary influences. No country need submit to deflation (contraction of money or of money GNP), because the rest of the world suffers from deflation. Nor need a country follow an inflation which is raging outside its borders, provided it lets its currency appreciate. But floating provides no protection from *real* disturbances from abroad and it must be kept in mind that inflation and deflation, inflationary booms and cyclical deflation and depressions (or inflationary recessions for the matter), are almost always accompanied by real changes. Floating does not protect particular industries that may have lost their foreign market nor does it protect a country from adverse changes in the terms of trade or protectionist reactions abroad in a recession or from export restrictions which foreign countries may impose to keep prices down at home. Furthermore, floating does not protect from domestic inflation that may have been induced by real disturbances from abroad. If, for example, a country supports its exporters who have lost their foreign market by buying up their products and finances these purchases in an inflationary way (a policy that Italy has pursued on a large scale in recent years), we have a case of domestic

---

[2] Statement before the Subcommittee on International Finance of the Committee on Banking and Currency, House of Representatives, April 4, 1974.

inflation which was induced by a real disturbance that had its origin abroad; against this inflation floating is of no help.

On the other hand, under fixed exchanges a heavy loss of exports may spell a general depression ("secondary deflation") which the central bank could not, or could not fully, contain because of the balance of payments constraint. Floating gives the country the freedom to counteract and to offset any secondary deflation, including the freedom to do *more* than to offset the deflation—that is, to inflate. Such a policy of overcompensation may be characterized as an abuse of the new freedom. Apart from providing freedom for offsetting policies, floating provides some automatic offsetting by stimulating exports and checking imports when the currency depreciates as a consequence of the loss of exports.

Conceptually the distinction between real and monetary disturbances from abroad is quite clear-cut. But, as it is usual in economics, there may exist borderline cases where the quantitative separation of the effects of the two types of disturbances is difficult.

Harry G. Johnson

I am in a bit of difficulty here, because I agree, generally, with most of what has been said except that I cannot avoid singling Bernstein's paper out for criticism.

One thing that puzzled me, having spent time with him in the Review Committee on the Balance of Payments Statistics, was that I find him using the term "balance of payments" in a quite different way from the way he once did. The balance of payments, now, is the *balanced* balance of payments—balanced by adjustments in the exchange rate. What we are worried about now is the composition of the balance of payments.

But we know that there is nothing we can do about the composition without changing other policies. We cannot run a surplus on current account unless we are saving enough—and not consuming enough—to make the real resources available. So that seemed to me a bit difficult to fit in with general theory.

Secondly, I was a bit puzzled by the information that the United States is not trying to reduce its imports of primary materials, that it is not even trying to sell manufactures as such to other countries. What it really wants to do is to knock the Germans out of the markets for industrial goods. But it seems to me that if that is our purpose, exchange rates are exactly the wrong way of going about it, because what we need is a discriminatory subsidy policy to promote American exports in those markets. No one who argues about exchange rates ought to be caught trying to say that exchange rate changes are designed to hit a particular kind of trade in a particular market and to leave everything else alone.

Finally, I was rather impressed by the tenaciousness of ideas that have been around now for about fifteen years. There is not all that much difference, theoretically, between Bernstein's idea that we should set limits to movements of exchange rates over short periods—say, an initial maximum of 6 percent or 8 percent, and then after that only 1 percent a month—and the old proposal for the crawling peg. Both ideas are subject to the same criticism—that they would allow some adjustment to take place, but short of what the market says is the necessary degree of adjustment.

A couple of other points have come up more generally. Among these is the question of wage and price stickiness, in which one could, I think, argue first that the idea that wages are always sticky downwards and never move downwards is very much an overgeneralization of British 1920s and 1930s experience, which John Hicks's recent writings have made the basis of a new economics of sorts. If instead we look around our own economy and see what is happening, we find that there are occasionally reports of workers accepting reductions of money wages. In other words the assumption that we must always have an inflationary adjustment seems to me to be a rule of thumb which may not be entirely valid, and we ought to be cautious about assuming it before we make it a basic principle. Particularly this should be the case now that we have a sharp squeeze on public employees of various kinds connected, in the case of New York City, obviously, but also in other places, with pressures to cut down on the costs of various kinds of public or semi-public employment. We do find teachers, for example, occasionally willing to take a wage cut. And since this is one of the major areas where the problem of inflexibility of wages is an important issue, we ought, perhaps, to look a little more carefully at it.

Turning to Fred Bergsten's comments, we must recognize that when we talk about competitive devaluations, we are talking about a concept that comes from the 1930s. It is closely connected with pegged rates that can be changed when a currency is devalued. It is also connected with the problem of world liquidity, specifically its shortage in the 1930s, and with the idea that there was no other way of maintaining full employment besides stimulating exports. In other words, it is a very mercantilist view.

Now, in a floating rate system, admittedly, if some country sets out to create employment for itself by running a current account surplus, this does pose problems for other countries, but these other countries can— as some people remarked at the time when the oil crisis was at its height —satisfy the would-be surplus countries by issuing assets to them. If they want to accumulate assets, there is nothing to stop countries from printing more assets. The only problem is to be able to adjust one's own domestic policies so that one does print assets rather than accept unemployment. That means, I think, that the dangers and risks of competitive devaluation in the present system are much less than would be implied by conjuring up the 1930s. It is not clear, actually, that there was much competitive devaluation even in the 1930s. There was a lot of writing about it, and it became an article of faith among opponents of the gold standard—and of floating rates, too, for that matter—but it is not clear that such cases were very prevalent. Economists went over this question in the professional literature just after World War II, when the question of fixing exchange rates was an issue between the agreement in Bretton Woods and the establishment of the IMF. The question could be gone over again. But it is clear enough that if some countries are insisting on creating employment this way—let them. Let them give their goods away, providing they do not reduce employment in other countries.

Finally, we come to something which seems to come out of the discussion and on which everybody seems to be agreed. This is that the one thing we are having trouble with is understanding the German case. Cleveland made that a major point in his discussion. We seem to be able to explain most other cases fairly satisfactorily. It is the Japanese case that Bergsten worries about, but the German seems to be the one that is most difficult to understand. Actually, if we go to a smaller scale, the Canadian case is pretty difficult to understand at the present time, but nobody worries about that, especially not the Canadians. And as far as the research side on foreign exchange markets is concerned, the German case is the one that really requires more work.

Another point I wanted to comment on was Willett's remark about his speculation rules—that they made money in the first half of the period and lost money in the second. One would assume that a clever speculator would have followed the reverse of the rule and made money both times, once he became aware that it was possible to do so. It is not really an argument against rules to say that they made money consistently for part of the time and lost consistently the rest of the time. If the distinction between two periods is that clear-cut, it should be possible to reverse the rule. Maybe that would make a stronger case for Bernstein's stand.

Just to complete the discussion, it seems to me that the indication coming out of this is that while the floating rate system has not worked particularly well, one cannot easily see how to make it work better. That would suggest that following Bernstein's advice and intervening in the market is a bit dangerous, since we do not know what we are trying to do when we do intervene.

SUMMARY OF DISCUSSION

The general discussion that followed the presentation of papers and the commentaries revolved around the appraisal of the performance of floating rates during the first thirty months of the new regime. The discussion centered on the search for relevant criteria for such an appraisal and on the evaluation of some consequences of floating for the world economy in general and for international economic relations in particular.

In connection with such an appraisal, the issue which attracted the attention of many discussants was the reason for relatively large fluctuations in some exchange rates, especially in the dollar-mark rate. Among causes considered, in addition to changes in underlying economic conditions, were speculative movements of liquid funds, shifts in asset preferences resulting in long-term capital movements, changing expectations about the future and changing assessment of the past, lack of experience of central banks in managing floating rates, and political instability. The question of how large the fluctuations in exchange rates must be to deserve the label "excessive" was aired, and the problem of proper assumptions about the behavior of the participants in the foreign exchange market was touched upon.

Appraisal of the performance of floating rates entails an evaluation of their effects, especially in contemplating the adoption of certain policy measures. In analyzing those effects the discussants encountered the problem of separating positive from normative questions. They agreed that such separation is vital for a rational discussion of exchange rate policies, along with the relationship between those guidelines and other economic policies, designed to enhance the beneficial effects of flexible exchange rates and alleviate those that are harmful.

Assessment of the Performance of the Regime of Floating Rates

Robert Mundell objected to judging the performance of floating rates on the basis of such criteria as greater ease in reducing payments imbalances. He juxtaposed the pre-1971 period of exchange rate stability, coinciding with a period of smooth and stable growth of the world

69

economy, and the post-1971 period of variable exchange rates, coinciding with perceptible deterioration of the global economic environment. His conclusion was that the burden of evidence weighs heavily against the superiority of floating rates to an arrangement of the Bretton Woods type.

Mundell doubted that the relative ease with which oil deficits were financed was a consequence of floating rates. He argued that these deficits were financed through expansion of international reserves, mainly dollars held both by monetary authorities and by private parties. More generally, he expressed his belief that an evaluation of an exchange rate system should not be based on its ability to facilitate short-run adjustments in the market. Instead, it should be viewed in a long-run perspective. Mundell pointed out that the framers of the Bretton Woods agreement had given the exchange rate experience of the 1930s an interpretation quite different from our view of this episode. In order to assess the exchange rate experience of the 1970s we ought to project ourselves ahead into the future.

Mundell vigorously attacked the proposition that floating rates necessarily preclude the resurgence of protectionist tendencies. He pointed out that in Britain and Italy more than just a fleeting thought was given to the possibility of introducing exchange controls in order to offset the depreciation of the pound and the lira. He believed, however, that the depreciation was inevitable in view of the British and Italian reserve positions and balance of payments situations. Under such circumstances, labeling the depreciations of these two currencies "competitive" amounts to looking for a pretext for imposing exchange controls or other restrictions.

Neither did Mundell subscribe to the opinion, voiced by some, that floating rates ensure elimination of trade imbalances. The appreciation of the deutsche mark did not prevent West Germany from enjoying huge trade surpluses, a phenomenon not as paradoxical as it appears to be. The exchange rate under floating is determined to a large extent by the capital account. When West German factories are shipped abroad instead of being built at home, exports go up and imports down. Thus, a highly valued mark may be coupled with a huge deficit on the capital account and a correspondingly large surplus on the trade account.

Mundell stressed that, in his view, the present system is not a system at all. It is not even a world of genuinely floating exchange rates. The only difference, he claimed, between the present situation and the pre-1971 world is that the dollar bloc had shrunk slightly and countries with a persistent balance of payments surplus, mainly Germany and Japan, had had to appreciate substantially their currencies.

Mundell's remarks were followed by a string of interventions by other discussants expressing their strong disagreement with Mundell's evaluation of the system of floating exchange rates.

Edward Bernstein expressed his desire to dispel the notion (implicit in Harry Johnson's remarks) that he was opposed to a regime of floating exchange rates as such, and especially to the floating of the dollar against the West German mark and the snake currencies. Mundell's objections notwithstanding, Bernstein did not challenge the opinion that floating rates have performed better than fixed rates would have. The relevant question is whether they have performed as well as possible. He claimed that they have not, and therefore it is worthwhile to look for ways of improving the performance of the system of floating exchange rates.

Bernstein noted that plausible explanations of wide swings in certain key exchange rates did not mean that these swings had been beneficial to the U.S. or any other economy. Large fluctuations of exchange rates are justifiable only if they reflect large changes in underlying economic conditions—differentials in the rates of inflation and interest rates among countries, as well as other factors affecting relative balance of payments positions and, hence, the exchange rates. Bernstein's concentration on the dollar–deutsche mark exchange rate stemmed from his conviction that a 20 to 25 percent change in this rate within a short period of time cannot be explained by invoking changes in underlying economic conditions in the United States and West Germany.

Nicolas Krul disassociated himself from what he had perceived as the panelists' conclusion on the performance of floating rates. Even if floating rates were advantageous to the U.S. economy, from the European point of view, he believed, they have definitely entailed disadvantages, especially political disadvantages not readily measurable in economic terms.

Josef Molsberger took exception to Mundell's assertion that the present exchange rate system is not a system at all. He followed up with a rhetorical question: For a monetary arrangement to be recognized as a system, do we need formal agreements on all kinds of exchange controls and trade impediments? Molsberger objected to the criteria suggested by Bernstein for evaluating the performance of floating rates. To say that floating rates could have worked even better than they had is to state the obvious. An alternative to floating was the continuation of the Bretton Woods system, and Molsberger argued that the only sound evaluation of a system is its comparison with other relevant alternatives. On this criterion, at least during the period from 1973 to 1975, the performance of floating rates should be given high marks.

Robert Solomon's remark referred to Mundell's view on the explosive growth of world liquidity since the advent of floating. According to

71

the IMF statistics, from March 1973 through the end of 1975, 87 percent of world reserves has accrued to the thirteen OPEC countries. The reserves of the rest of the world have risen only by one percent over the entire period of thirty months. The skewness of the distribution of newly created reserves among countries indicates that oil-importing countries, unwilling to see their foreign exchange reserves dissipated, resorted to borrowing in order to finance their balance of payments deficits. This mode of financing payments imbalances was bound to result in an accumulation of assets—claims on the rest of the world—in the hands of OPEC countries.

In Solomon's view, Mundell has an opportunity to deplore an explosive growth of world reserves only because the International Monetary Fund defines the claims of OPEC as reserves. Solomon noted that if, instead, the IMF chose to define these claims as long-term capital outflows, which in his opinion they are, then they would appear "above the line." Under that definition of assets being accumulated by OPEC the explosion of world reserves would not have occurred.

Causes of Large Fluctuations in the Exchange Rates

Sven Arndt noted that Bernstein and Molsberger had arrived at diametrically opposite conclusions regarding the magnitude of fluctuations in some exchange rates, the former claiming that they were excessive, the latter that they were just right. In this connection Arndt inquired what kind of choice-theoretic models underlie the behavior of economic agents causing the exchange rates to fluctuate. He inquired, in particular, what choice-theoretic model would describe speculative behavior of a "bandwagon" variety which, according to Bernstein, was responsible for exchange rate volatility. What kind of a model would describe such a behavior not only during a particular episode but over a lengthy period encompassing a number of reversible movements in exchange rates?

By analogy, Arndt's question addressed to Molsberger would be: What are the specific behavioral assumptions moving speculators, exporters, and importers to appraise changes in exchange rates as temporary or permanent? What is the mechanism translating these appraisals into investing and trading decisions resulting in exchange rate movements being "just right"?

Walter Salant submitted that Bernstein's opinion that movements in some exchange rates were too large was a consequence of his neglect of possible changes in asset preferences. In Bernstein's treatment equilibrium flows of capital among countries are a reflection of relative interest rates and profits. However, if the possibility of changes in asset preferences is admitted, one must recognize the existence of temporary capital flows induced by attempts to readjust internationally diversified portfolios in accordance with a new set of asset preferences. Thus, during a transitory period of stock adjustment, departures from equilibrium are unavoidable. Under a system of fixed exchange rates the balance of payments will depart from its long-run equilibrium level; under a system of floating rates the departure from the long-run level of equilibrium will be exhibited by the exchange rate.

Moreover, not only must the initial change in the exchange rate take place for the shift in preferences to be translated into actual change in the mix of assets held, but also a subsequent reversal in the direction of the exchange rate change must be allowed for as well. The reversal will occur when the portfolio adjustment is completed and the temporary capital flow comes to an end.

Thus, to disregard shifts in asset preferences may lead to erroneous conclusions regarding fluctuations of exchange rates about their equilibrium levels. Furthermore, Salant emphasized that, if changed asset preferences are to be accommodated, the mere fact of sizable movements in exchange rates and their subsequent reversals is not sufficient for establishing that these movements are per se undesirable. Whether such sizable movements in the dollar–deutsche mark rate, deplored by Bernstein, were due to shifts in assets preferences or (as Bernstein assumed) to destabilizing speculation is an empirical question.

Egon Sohmen expressed his entire lack of surprise regarding either the average dollar–deutsche mark exchange rate or its fluctuations. Data published by the West German Statistical Office imply that 2.55 to 2.60 marks to the dollar is the exchange rate corresponding to the purchasing power parity. Roughly the same result is obtained by using the bundle of goods typical for West German consumers and the bundle typical for U.S. consumers. Furthermore, consumer prices are not the main determinant of the exchange rate, which is primarily influenced by the prices of exports and imports. And although West German consumer prices may be relatively high, prices of producer goods—West Germany's main export category—continue to be moderate in comparison with the prices of West Germany's competitors.

As far as the fluctuations in the mark–dollar rate are concerned, Sohmen submitted that even the largest departures from the average rate could be explained without recourse to Bernstein's argument of destabilizing speculation. Sohmen suggested that the all-time low for the dollar against the deutsche mark in early 1975 was a result of the fact that the U.S. and German monetary policies were out of phase at this time. The resulting interest rate differential, especially in the long-term bond market, tended to attract funds to West Germany. With a 1 to 2 percent interest is less likely to be at one of the extremes of the range of fluctuations than between them. If the rate were stabilized in the middle of the range, at worst, we would always be 10 percent off the proper rate. According to Bernstein, the resulting tariff or subsidy of 10 percent is more desirable, or less detrimental, than being 0 percent off the proper rate and then, soon thereafter, 20 percent off the proper rate.

Bernstein agreed that if, as Solomon contended, the system were settling down—that is, fluctuations in key exchange rates were becoming less pronounced—the need for official stabilization of the rates within a narrower range would disappear. Modest fluctuations in exchange rates, Bernstein claimed, were in themselves an indication that the movements were in response to changes in underlying economic conditions, and not a result of volatile flows of speculative funds.

Salant, although he found it difficult to find support for the view that excessive changes in exchange rates were due exclusively to destabilizing speculation, concurred with Bernstein's position that violent and later reversed movements in exchange rates may be harmful per se. He acknowledged that even if these movements had been a consequence of large and abrupt shifts in asset preferences, one could argue that adjustment to these shifts should have been made gradual through a policy of official intervention that would have limited the degree of exchange rate changes taking place in any given period of time. Judicious use of intervention would still allow shifts in asset preferences to be translated into new composition of portfolios. It would, however, permit partial accommodation of new asset preferences through changes in net official reserves, thus stretching out over time a portion of capital flows which otherwise would have to be financed by counterflows of private funds induced by changes in the exchange rate. The justification for such intervention policy would depend on the cost comparison of temporary official financing of autonomous shifts in asset holdings and of changes in exchange rates that would have to be much larger in absence of that financing.

Salant also noticed that while the main point of Bernstein's paper was that the behavior of certain exchange rates had been too erratic during the first three years of floating, Willett argued in his paper that large and reversible movements in exchange rates could be easily explained when the role of expectations is taken into account. Salant perceived Willett's unwillingness to accept that movements in exchange rates had clearly been excessive as resting on the implicit assumption that any behavior of the market explicable in rational terms is socially desirable.

This is precisely the notion Bernstein challenged. He did not claim that the observed exchange rate movements could not be explained.

Bernstein professed, however, that such movements were socially undesirable and, hence, should have been dampened by means of appropriate policies. Willett's denial of this proposition, Salant contended, stemmed from confusion between points of positive and normative analysis.

Willett rejected Salant's charge, although he agreed that explicability of a phenomenon does not necessarily make it socially desirable. He pointed out that a comprehensive normative theory is still in the making. For instance, Willett said, he was not convinced by Bernstein's assertion that a disequilibrium exchange rate permanently 10 percent off the equilibrium rate is preferable to a fluctuating exchange rate, at times coinciding with the equilibrium rate and at times being 20 percent off it.

Nonetheless, Willett recalled, some of the propositions embodied in welfare economics are widely accepted. One of them is that large and erratic exchange rate movements from destabilizing speculation are socially undesirable. But this proposition entails neither a conclusion that all large and rapid exchange rate movements are caused by destabilizing speculation nor a conclusion that an occurrence of such movements, whatever their cause, justifies official intervention. Willett concluded that the very type of analysis involved in testing efficiency of foreign exchange markets deals simultaneously with positive and normative aspects of economic theory.

Molsberger remarked that, if by social undesirability of large exchange rate changes one understands an increased risk facing exporters and importers, the harm from these changes had been greatly reduced by the availability of forward cover. His understanding was that the cover had been relatively cheap and available even during the periods of most hectic activity on the foreign exchange market. In his opinion, as long as the markets are able to cope with the problem of increased risk, extreme caution ought to be exercised in recommending official intervention.

Krul disagreed that forward cover had been always available at a reasonable cost, at least for all currencies. The discount on the lira in terms of the Swiss franc went up from February to April 1976 from 4 percent to 26 percent (annualized). Similarly large changes took place in the forward rate for the French franc and the pound. Since Italy, France, and England are important trading partners of Switzerland, sharp variations in the cost of forward cover for their currencies affected the structure of Swiss foreign trade.

John Karlik joined Bernstein in his concern over the possibility of floating rates facilitating competitive depreciation. He remarked that similar concern is likely to be shared by the IMF. Its reflection can be discerned in the text of the amended Article IV, which calls upon member countries to abjure using movements in the exchange rate in order

PART TWO

THE FOREIGN EXCHANGE MARKET UNDER FLEXIBLE EXCHANGE RATES

AN ECONOMIST'S VIEW OF THE FOREIGN EXCHANGE MARKET

Report on Interviews with West Coast
Foreign Exchange Dealers

John Rutledge

Introduction

The large variations in bilateral exchange rates observed since the adoption of floating exchange rates in 1973 have caused concern over the operation of foreign exchange markets under flexible rates. Recent international agreements to counter "erratic fluctuations and disorderly market conditions" have amplified this concern and generated considerable discussion of the appropriate official intervention policy for ensuring orderly markets.

There is now substantial agreement that "disorderly markets" are not to be identified by reference to some target rate or by simply looking at the magnitude of exchange rate variations. Instead, they should be identified by certain characteristics of technical market performance. Moreover, it would appear desirable to use the accumulated experience of market traders in selecting and evaluating these characteristics. This paper reports information on exchange market performance based on several recent interviews with West Coast foreign exchange dealers.

The Role of Private Speculators in a
Regime of Flexible Exchange Rates

If asset prices are to serve their function as signals for efficient resource allocation, they must successfully transmit all relevant information about present and future market developments to the ultimate suppliers and demanders of the asset. In the foreign exchange markets (when they are not dominated by official intervention), the information-transmitting function of exchange rates depends largely on the actions of private speculators.

By private speculators we mean those market participants who gather and process information about the likely behavior of the many factors which determine exchange market equilibrium, and then use that information to buy and sell currencies in anticipation of price movements. Speculators can act on their own behalf, or as agents for ultimate wealth holders engaging in no other business activity, or they can use their anticipations about likely exchange market developments to make decisions about the size, timing, and placement of ordinary business transactions. By definition, then, there are a great many who play the role of private speculator in the foreign exchange markets.

Asset markets in which prices accurately reflect all available information are called efficient markets. There exists massive evidence that equity markets in the United States are efficient markets. New information about firms' underlying return distributions is quickly reflected in price changes; there is no evidence of cyclical, or otherwise easily predictable, variations of stock prices about their equilibrium values; and stock prices do not systematically overreact or underreact to new releases of information.

We are now in a period of furious research activity in international finance, asking the same questions about exchange rates that we once asked about stock prices. Do the markets always overreact? Are there "bandwagon effects"? Do exchange rates move cyclically? Do exchange rates reflect the underlying determinants of exchange market equilibrium? Is speculative activity stabilizing or destabilizing? One must reflect for a moment on why we are having such a difficult time nailing down answers to these questions for the exchange markets when they have been so convincingly demonstrated for equity markets.

The answer, of course, is that stock prices are determined entirely by private traders—there are literally thousands of observations of stock price behavior from which to draw conclusions. There is no direct official intervention in the equity markets. In contrast, *there has never been a significant length of time during which exchange rates have been determined entirely by private market forces, free of all official intervention.* As a consequence, the researcher's job becomes much more difficult. Weak-form tests for efficient markets—which simply examine observed price behavior for evidence of inefficient cyclical and nonrandom price movements—cannot discriminate between price movements caused by private speculators and those caused by the intervention authorities. Strong-form tests, which account for official intervention by building detailed structural models of exchange market equilibrium, are the appropriate alternatives. Effective application of strong-form tests, however, is still beyond our reach since there are nearly as many competing hypotheses about the formation of speculators' expectations as there are independent market observations, since official intervention data are both confidential and unreliable.

Having pointed out some of the major difficulties with traditional approaches to examining the performance of private speculators, I shall report the preliminary results of a second—or perhaps third—best approach: interviewing participants in the foreign exchange markets. The objective is to obtain some information about the technical efficiency of the foreign exchange markets in facilitating transactions between ultimate buyers and sellers, and about private traders' views of the role of official intervention in international exchange markets.

Do Private Speculators Create Bandwagon Effects?

The hypothesis that private speculators exert a stabilizing influence on the foreign exchange market is based on the presumption that private speculators evaluate the fundamental determinants of exchange market equilibrium, then take open positions based on the difference between the market rate and their forecast of the equilibrium rate, or their forecast of some range of rates compatible with exchange market equilibrium. Speculative purchases of currencies which traders feel are temporarily undervalued and speculative sales of currencies which traders feel are temporarily overvalued tend to eliminate foreseeable (that is, ex ante) deviations of the market exchange rate from the rate implied by the fundamentals. If speculators fail to perform this stabilizing role then, in principle, exchange rates could diverge from "equilibrium" rates for substantial periods of time, causing transactions to be based on a set of inefficient prices.

The econometric problems outlined above make it difficult to make empirical judgments on the behavior of speculators since the float. My view, however, is that, in principle, there is little difference between the equity markets and the foreign exchange markets. The presumption is thus that foreign exchange markets, like equity markets, are "efficient markets," and that speculators play a largely stabilizing role. We shall, therefore, take stabilizing speculation and efficient markets as the null hypothesis: it remains for critics of floating rates to present evidence that private speculators have exhibited unstable behavior. One such allegation that has received much recent attention is that speculators generate "bandwagon effects."

In all the discussions of bandwagon effects and destabilizing speculation, I have yet to see a careful description of the precise roles played by various market traders. The basic story, however, goes something like this. A group of speculators in a smoke-filled room decides to take a currency (the Bolumbian Mambo, for example) for a ride. They begin massive purchases of mambos. Other speculators, seeing the mambo rate rise, will not want to miss out on a good thing, and they will also place buy orders for mambos. Thus for a time the increases in rates will—in bootstraps fashion—beget further rises in rates, until the mambo rate is far out of line with the underlying equilibrium rate.

Then—and this is where the art comes in—the smart speculators dump their mambos at the premium price and reap handsome profits. Other speculators, of course, catch the scent and place their mambos on offer. As a result there is a prolonged decline in the mambo rate.

Viewed as a time series, then, bandwagon effects imply a speculative bubble in the exchange rate. Clearly, from a welfare point of view, such exchange rate movements serve little useful economic purpose.[1] Worse still, the false signals given off during the transitory exchange rate movement may distort real resource flows and result in a decrease in net welfare.

Markets which are dominated by bandwagon effects provide the strongest case for official intervention. Central bank intervention that succeeds in smoothing out bandwagon cycles—or, in the spirit of Kondratieff and Jevons, what we may call "Bernstein Cycles"—will not only avoid costly resource misallocations associated with disequilibrium exchange rates; it will also make a profit for the public treasury (a wealth transfer that would have been applauded neither by Marshall nor by Fisher, although certainly by Galbraith).

Not surprisingly, this rationale for official intervention has not been overlooked by the authorities. The foreign exchange reports of the Federal Reserve Bank of New York tell of speculative attacks on the dollar and other currencies, and of central banks defending their currencies from speculative onslaughts. Furthermore, speculative activity is often characterized as unreliable, as capricious, and as overreacting to each snatch of news as it hits the foreign exchange market. Thus, the existence of bandwagon cycles is an important issue for policy as well as for theory.

As my earlier arguments imply, however, it is not very easy to test for the existence of bandwagon effects over relatively short time periods.

To augment the statistical studies, I have asked several foreign exchange traders for their views on the existence of bandwagon effects. Invariably traders responded yes, that private speculators can and do have powerful effects on exchange rate movements, and that speculators gang up on an exchange rate to force adjustments.

Before we pick up our intervention shovels and head for the trenches, however, note that exchange market intimates overwhelmingly felt that such speculative swings in exchange rates were mainly an intraday phenomenon, lasting for a few hours. I did not see any agreement with the story that bandwagons can persist for several months at a time, or that they can be used to explain the mysterious behavior of the dollar-mark rate over the past three years.

---

[1] Except the transfer of wealth from dumb speculators to smart ones, which after all, both Marshall and Fisher agree is only right.

Nor did traders feel that there was any reliable way of distinguishing short-run speculative pressure on a currency from fundamental adjustments due to changing evaluations of market forces. Speculative cycles in exchange rates, it seems, can only be identified through the rear-view mirror. One trader, when asked about speculative "cycles" remarked, "I have been in this business for more than twenty years, and have yet to see one."

Official intervention, on the other hand, presumes that the authorities are endowed with the ability to discriminate between exchange rate adjustments which are bandwagon-induced and those which are more fundamental. U.S. intervention, moreover, has been based on the existence of recognizable bandwagon cycles lasting for several months—witness the practice of repaying swaps within several months, and the sizable U.S. one-way intervention pursued during early 1975. It would seem that the burden of proof on both counts ought to be with the intervention authorities. They have supplied no evidence, to my knowledge, either that speculators cause bandwagon effects, or that they—the intervention authorities—are especially good at picking out these effects from all the other factors which impinge on exchange markets.

Is There Enough Speculation?

Paradoxically, many of the same people who urge that speculators are responsible for large and prolonged bandwagon cycles argue at other times that there is not enough private speculation to give depth and stability to the foreign exchange markets. The problem, they say, is that the inter-bank market is too thin—traders are either unable or unwilling to take "large enough" open positions in foreign exchange. This is the legacy of the Herstatt and Franklin National failures.

Traders with whom I talked agree that they are more cautious in foreign exchange operations today than they were in the quasi-fixed-rate era; open positions are smaller, and bid-asked spreads are wider for both spot and forward exchange. This is not because speculators are faint-hearted, however, but rather because the variability of the underlying determinants of exchange market equilibrium has increased. It is also because "the drinks are no longer on the house," that is, traders cannot always count on a benevolent central bank to guarantee that they can complete a transaction for a customer with little exchange risk. As with any other industry, when a subsidy is reduced or removed, the volume of business done by the industry shrinks.

It has also been suggested by some analysts that today's foreign exchange markets are so thin that a fairly large purchase order—say DM 30 million—would disrupt the market, and would unduly interfere with a trader's sleep while he tried to sneak his order into Australia, Hong Kong, and London at various points during the night. Traders indicate that this is not so! To be sure, a West Coast trader would send for an aspirin if he received such an order late Friday afternoon, when both New York and the European markets are closed. But there are two reasons why this is not likely to be a major problem. First, customers are usually able to foresee such large purchases, and would likely time their order to coincide with the most favorable market conditions. Second, the risk to the trader can be partly shifted to the customer if the trader contracts on a "best I can do" basis, rather than at a quoted rate. Naturally, traders say, if a customer demands a quotation one will be given, and it will include a premium for the estimated impact of the contract on the exchange rate, plus an allowance for risk.

The final point we shall consider is that institutional constraints on traders' speculative positions inhibit the stabilizing speculation that would otherwise be forthcoming. Such constraints could conceivably interfere with market efficiency. Traders claim that this is incorrect. First, huge intra-day open positions can be carried while meeting *any* constraint on overnight open positions. Second, constraints on forward open positions typically do not differentiate according to maturity. A trader can carry a forward open position in a currency by simultaneously buying a contract for one maturity and selling a contract for a different maturity, while showing zero open position in total forward contracts for that currency.

A corollary of this argument is that auditing schedules of banks and other firms prevent them from holding positions long enough to speculate on medium-term movements in the fundamentals. I propose, to the contrary, that the horizon of the speculators is irrelevant to questions about market efficiency. Even if speculators only act on two-week horizons, every future date at which we observe the exchange markets will have been preceded by days during which that date was within the speculators' horizon.

In summary, traders with whom I spoke agreed that the system of market-determined exchange rates, while not perfect, has performed admirably in spite of the generally high level of uncertainty about the underlying economic and financial conditions over the past three years. Exchange market participants react quickly to new market information, but do not generate the variety of cyclical or "bandwagon" exchange rate behavior which have been used to justify prolonged periods of market intervention.

REPORT ON TECHNICAL STUDIES ON SPECULATION AND MARKET EFFICIENCY

Richard James Sweeney

I am pleased to have the opportunity to report here on technical studies on speculation and efficiency in the foreign exchange markets.[1] Let me begin by summarizing those studies' results, as I see them.[2] The results seem to me consistent with the viewpoint that the markets have behaved efficiently; at worst, they are merely inconclusive. In any case, they provide absolutely no guidance to would-be speculators on ways to make profits, or guidelines for central bank interveners who believe they can improve on the markets' workings.

While much of the testing, in its detail, is (or appears) highly technical, it is in fact concerned with very down-to-earth and practical problems, for example, with the bandwagon effects invoked by Edward Bernstein or, more generally, with short-run self-reversing movements in the exchange rates.[3] That such self-reversing fluctuations have been recognized as a possible problem in the literature, I would like to illustrate with two quotations that present divergent views about the seriousness of one problem in a world with speculators.

---

[1] "Efficiency" is used here in the technical sense that there exists an efficient market if each time the exchange rate changes it embodies all economically relevant information. On this concept, see E. F. Fama, "Efficient Capital Markets: A Review of Theory and Empirical Work," *Journal of Finance*, May 1970.

[2] The studies discussed here are primarily those carried out in the Research Office, U.S. Treasury—mostly by P. A. Cummins, D. E. Logue, R. J. Sweeney, and T. D. Willett. These include Cummins, Logue, Sweeney, and Willett, "Aspects of Efficiency in U.S./Canadian Foreign Exchange Markets," U.S. Treasury/Research Discussion Paper, 1975; Logue and Sweeney, " 'White Noise' in Imperfect Markets," *Journal of Finance*, 1977; Logue, Sweeney, and Willett, "The Speculative Behavior of Foreign Exchange Rates, during the Current Float," *Journal of Business Research,* 1978; and Logue and Sweeney, "Efficient Information Processing in Foreign Exchange Markets: Tests and Results," U.S. Treasury/Research Discussion Paper, 1976. Several unpublished papers on similar topics were presented at the February 1976 Treasury Workshop on Technical Studies on Economic Interdependence and Exchange Rate Flexibility. The results presented are noted below though the authors' requests not to cite or quote their papers are honored.

[3] See Bernstein's paper in this volume.

Speculation or Official Intervention

One view is from R. M. Goodwin[4] who says,

> There is a fundamental ambiguity in the meaning of stability
> which we encounter in the question of stabilizing the market.
> Technically, by degree of stability, we mean the rapidity of
> approach to equilibrium, defined here as the equality of supply
> and demand.
> However, for a market with shifting supply and demand
> curves, the equilibrium price will hop about so that the more
> stable, in this sense a market is, the more agitated its price will
> be.
> This contradicts our common sense notion of stability and,
> what is more important, is normally undesirable. In fact, we
> want the market, as dominated by the authorities, to be mark-
> edly sluggish. To be stable in the popular sense and not very
> stable in the technical sense.
> More specifically, I assume that ideal behavior for the
> exchange rate is to be insensitive to short-run fluctuations in
> demand and supply. Thus, the authorities are to try to equate
> supply and demand, but only in the long run, not in the short
> run.

This, I think, is partly what Walter Salant was getting at, in speaking about shifts in asset preferences and the resulting short-run self-
reversing changes in the exchange rates that might well be stabilized by
the authorities.

A different view of the process, though, is given by Milton Friedman
in his classic "Case for Flexible Exchange Rates."[5] Friedman writes,

> If a country has an incipient surplus of receipts over pay-
> ments—an excess demand for its currency—the exchange rate
> will tend to rise. If it has an incipient deficit, the exchange rate
> will tend to fall. If the conditions responsible for the rise or
> fall in the exchange rate are generally regarded as temporary,
> actual or potential holders of the country's currency will tend
> to change their holdings in such a way as to moderate the
> movement in the exchange rate. If a rise in the exchange rate,
> for example, is expected to be *temporary*, there is an incentive
> for holders of the country's currency to sell some of their hold-
> ings for foreign currency in order to buy the currency back
> later on at a lower price. . . . On the other hand, if the change

---

[4] R. M. Goodwin, "Stabilizing the Exchange Rate," *Review of Economics and Statistics*, May 1964, pp. 160-162.
[5] See Milton Friedman, "The Case for Flexible Exchange Rates," *Essays in Positive Economics*, 1953, pp. 161-162.

in the exchange rate is generally regarded as produced by fundamental factors that are likely to be *permanent*, the incentives are the reverse of those listed above, and speculative transactions will speed up the rise or decline in the exchange rate and thus hasten its approach to its final position [italics added].

Thus, we have Friedman putting forward the view that speculators, in effect, will do what other economists think that central bank intervention is required to do.

Tests of the Efficiency of Speculation

Let me recount some of the tests for the possibility that there are cycles in the exchange rates (or that there are other sorts of inefficiency). The most naive test, and the most dangerous, is simply to look at a plot of the time path of the exchange rate. As we well know from work on the stock market, the eye has a tendency to pick out cycles in prices that simply do not exist in the data, so that "eyeballing" the data is a very dangerous sort of "test." But there are two somewhat less dangerous tests that might be applied, two so-called "weak-form" tests. These have been applied, at length, in studies of stock markets.[6] They are not at all as easy to apply to studies of foreign exchange markets as we shall see.

These two possible "weak-form" tests are correlation tests and so-called filter rules. Correlation tests are based on the following sort of notion. Suppose that we assume that a bandwagon is started—for example, the dollar price of the deutsch mark begins to rise, and this rise is then followed by successive rises until the bandwagon is reversed and a fall is followed by successive falls.[7] We might expect, then, to be able to look at correlation coefficients between changes in the exchange rate at various lags and find significant relationships, if there are bandwagon effects. It might be objected, though, that correlations depend on linear relationships and are too stringent a test. For example, the shocks, themselves, may come at random intervals,[8] and the reactions to the shocks—the bandwagon effects—may be highly nonlinear.

One way of getting at these nonlinearities is to make use of filter rules, which my colleague Willett and Professor Harry Johnson briefly

---

[6] See Fama, "Efficient Capital Markets," for a survey of earlier work on stock and bond markets. Cummins et al. ("Aspects of Efficiency") apply a rather informal semi-strong form test to the Canadian-U.S. dollar exchange rate.

[7] For a more detailed discussion of this line of reasoning, see R. J. Sweeney and T. D. Willett, "Concepts of Efficiency and Speculation in the Foreign Exchange Markets," U.S. Treasury/Research Discussion Paper, 1976.

[8] On this problem, see Logue and Sweeney, " 'White Noise.' "

discussed in Part One. These filters are buy-and-sell rules of the form, "If the dollar price of the DM rises X percent above its previous low, buy DMs on the assumption that the price is going to continue to rise; however, if the dollar price of the DM falls Y percent from its past high, sell DMs on the assumption that the dollar price will continue to fall."[9]

It is highly important, however, when we use these filter rule techniques for looking at how much profit we could have made speculating against the market (trying to "beat the market") that we compare this profit with what we would have made simply putting our money in the market and holding it there. If the dollar price of the deutsche mark is generally rising, we would naturally expect to make some profits going in and out of deutsche marks. The question is, will we make *more* profits by following these speculative rules than we would have made by simply buying deutsche marks at the start and holding them.[10]

Let us look here at some representative results of these weak-form tests. Two cases of considerable interest are the Canadian-U.S. dollar spot exchange rate and the deutsche mark–U.S. dollar spot exchange rate. Canadian-U.S. dollar exchange markets are among the most intensively studied—in part, because of the Canadian float of the 1950s, and in part because of the importance of mutual trade for the two countries. The deutsche mark–U.S. dollar rate is extremely important for world markets, and, in addition, tests of the deutsche mark–dollar rate involve anomalies and difficulties in interpretation that are also met in some other markets.

Philip Cummins, Dennis Logue, Thomas Willett, and I carried out tests on about 800 successive daily observations on the Canadian/U.S. exchange rates,[11] and found none of the significant correlations between changes in the rate that one would expect if there were cycles or bandwagon effects. Moreover, the buy-and-sell rules that we tested showed no greater profits from speculating against the Canadian dollar than could be obtained by buying and holding Canadian dollars. The Canadian spot market thus seemed, by and large, to behave quite efficiently, according to these tests that we ran.

---

[9] For further discussion of such rules, see the references in notes 6, 7, and 8, above.

[10] For this buy-and-hold rationale as applied to stock markets, see Fama, "Efficient Capital Markets," and E. F. Fama and M. E. Blume, "Filter Rules and Stock-Market Trading," *Journal of Business,* January 1966, part 2, pp. 226-241.

[11] Cummins et al., "Aspects of Efficiency." Data were supplied by the Board of Governors of the Federal Reserve System for the period December 1970 to March 1974. Canada returned to a floating rate in September 1970 after ten years of *de facto* and then *de jure* pegging.

Technical Difficulties in Interpreting Test Results for the
Deutsche Mark–U.S. Dollar Exchange Rate

The case with the deutsche mark–U.S. dollar rate is somewhat different from the Canadian case and presents difficulties in the interpretation of the results.[12] The correlations we found between changes in the deutsche mark–U.S. dollar exchage rate, at various lags, were significantly larger than these should have been if the market were efficient. There are, however, a number of technical difficulties in interpreting these results, two of which I would like to go into here. One is that our tests of what correlations are significant are based on the hypothesis that these changes in the exchange rate are drawn from a normal distribution. (Many of our statistical tests, in economics, are of course based on this assumption.) However, the distribution of changes in the deutsche mark–U.S. dollar exchange rate is highly non-normal, and it is non-normal in a way that may bias an observer toward saying the market is inefficient, in cases where, in fact, it is efficient.[13]

A second problem is the following. The bandwagon effects we have considered occur when there is a constant trend to the changes in the exchange rate, but cycles around this trend: these cycles would be inefficient. An alternative hypothesis, consistent with the efficiency, is that the trend itself changes randomly and unpredictably from time to time, but that—whatever the trend is—there are no cycles around it.[14]

---

[12] We used approximately 700 daily observations, from the series compiled by the Board of Governors of the Federal Reserve System, for the period April 1973 through January 1976. By April 1973, Germany and most Western nations had moved to generalized floating.

[13] There is a substantial literature on the possibility that stochastic processes generating changes in stock and bond prices cannot be characterized as normal. See Fama, "Efficient Markets"; B. Mandelbroit, "The Variation of Certain Speculative Prices," *Journal of Business,* October 1973; and A. Barnea and D. Downes, "A Reexamination of the Empirical Distribution of Stock Price Changes," *Journal of American Statistical Association,* June 1973, pp. 348-350.

In essence, the "tails" of the distribution of changes in exchange rates are "fatter" than with the normal distribution. Under the null hypothesis of no autocorrelation, coefficients of a given magnitude are more likely to be observed in a sample from such fat-tailed distributions than from normal distributions. Hence, usual tests of significance will too often reject the null hypothesis of no autocorrelation.

[14] The matter is worth further examination here. In the examination, let us distinguish three separate characterizations of the exchange rate and outline the way these relate to market efficiency.

First, the exchange rate x might be characterized as having a constant mean a with random fluctuations around the mean, or

$$x_t = a + u_t \qquad (1)$$

where u_t is a random variable that may be serially correlated. Note that we expect x to return to a, so that deviations from a are temporary and self-reversing. In this case, x is said to be *mean-stationary*, in the sense that the mean of x is constant. Fluctuations in x around a should allow for large speculative profits, inasmuch as when x differs from a, we know that x will tend to revert to a. Statistical tests show that exchange rates, including the deutsche mark–U.S. dollar rate, are indisputably *not* mean-stationary. In particular, the autocorrelation functions decay in the slow way typical of nonstationary series.

Secondly, we might suppose that *changes* in x are equal to a constant b plus a random component, or

$$\triangle x_t \equiv x_t - x_{t-1} = b + \epsilon_t. \tag{2}$$

Now, if ϵ_t is a purely random, serially uncorrelated variable (or "white noise"), the only predictable aspect of changes in x is that they will on average equal b, or their expected value is b. If ϵ_t displays no serial correlation, $\triangle x$ will display none. In particular, one cannot expect to make any speculative profits (beyond b per period) from finding patterns in $\triangle x$, for by this hypothesis there are no patterns.

In fact, examining the autocorrelation function of $\triangle x$ is the most common test of the *random walk hypothesis*. Under the hypothesis that b is constant, efficiency requires that ϵ be serially uncorrelated (or at least display no greater correlation than the small amount that could be straightforwardly explained on the basis of transactions costs, risk, and so forth). Lack of serial correlation is a necessary (but not sufficient) condition for efficiency under the maintained hypothesis that b is constant. Sample autocorrelation coefficients are larger than expected if b is constant and ϵ_t is both normally distributed and serially uncorrelated. Such autocorrelation might then be taken as raising the possibility of inefficient behavior in this market.

Third, the change in the exchange rate might be alternatively modeled as equal to a given value c plus a random term v_t, or

$$\triangle x_t \equiv x_t - x_{t-1} = c + v_t \tag{3}$$

where c shifts from time to time in a totally unpredictable way. Speculators, then, could make no profits by betting on changes in c. Efficiency further requires that v_t be "white noise"—given c, there are no profits to be made by cycles around c.

Such a process is not mean-stationary. Over long enough periods, when c has changed sufficiently, sample autocorrelations will begin to appear to be statistically significant. That is, if we have an efficient market described by the process in equation [3], we will tend to judge the market as inefficient if we view it as modeled by equation [2]—the nonstationarity of changes in c will be judged to be serial correlation in ϵ_t.

As explained by R. J. Sweeney, "Efficient Information Processing in Output Markets: Tests and Implications," U.S. Treasury/Research Discussion Paper, 1976, the first difference of the change in the exchange rate, $\triangle(\triangle x)$, will have a theoretical autocorrelation function with a coefficient somewhere between zero and —.5 at lag 1, and zero at all other lags, *if* v_t is white noise and c varies completely unpredictably. As reported by Logue and Sweeney, "Efficient Information Processing," $\triangle(\triangle x)$ does seem to behave in this manner for many exchange rates where $\triangle x$ seems not to be "white noise." They argue that for such markets, one should adopt the model of equation [3] and decide not to reject the hypothesis of efficiency, rather than adopting the model of equation [2] and rejecting efficiency. They note, however, that their evidence that $\triangle x$ is nonstationary is hardly overwhelming. It consists primarily in dividing the entire period into three subperiods and noting that $\triangle x$ appears to be "white noise" in many of the subperiods while appearing nonwhite in other subperiods and the whole period. This is exactly what is expected if some subperiods contain few or unimportant changes in c, but other subperiods and the overall period contain many or important shifts in c.

Unfortunately, the correlation tests cannot by themselves enable us to distinguish which of the two hypotheses is correct. They do not provide sufficiently clear-cut results to allow us to discriminate between a constant trend with cycles around it, and no cycles with unpredictable shifts in the trend. It is consequently difficult to interpret the results (though I myself strongly lean toward the latter hypothesis).

We had hoped that our filter rule results might resolve some of the difficulties, inasmuch as filter rules can be a very powerful technique. They present a way of approaching the data that might give us some insights on how to "beat the market." However, one must use a little sophistication in interpreting filter rule results. For the overall period, from April 1, 1973, through January 6, 1976, Logue, Willett, and I ran filter rules, and found that *all* the filter rules we used made a lot more money than simply buying deutsche marks and holding them.[15] But we must not jump to the conclusion that these results conclusively indicate inefficiency in this market. First, I might note that other students, using the same data but starting March 12, 1973, and ending in September 1975, found *some* filter rules that made substantial amounts of money. But, when results were averaged across all the filter rules they tried, they showed losses. These filter rule profits are evidently sensitive to beginning and ending dates. Nor do the problems end there.

When we pick a filter rule to use, we cannot, of course, go back to 1973, and make our decisions *then* on the basis of what we know now. Instead, we must look at the data and, on the basis of what it tells us, try to pick a rule to use in the *future*. To get at this forecasting aspect of the problem, we split the period into three subperiods of virtually equal length. In the first of these subperiods we looked at, all of the filter rules made substantially more money than would have been made by buying and holding deutsche marks. It looked like the problem of selecting a rule was solved: all one would have to do is pick all of these rules—use all of them—or, perhaps, just use the best rule, the one that made the most money in the first period. But, alas! Using the rule that made the most money in the first period would have lost money in the second period. In fact, on average, the rules from the first period would have lost money in the second period (see Table 1). Nor is this the worst. Suppose that we believed we had learned our lesson and did not use any of the rules in the third period. It turns out that we could have made a lot of money in the third period by using several of the rules that were profitable in the first period.

---

[15] Note that we selected rules that *a priori* seemed likely candidates for making excess profits. In particular, our results do not mean that every possible rule would make profits. Rather, in judging efficiency, the most profitable rules must be sought in order to build the best case against efficiency in the market.

The implication of what Harry Johnson said in Part One was that if things continue in their present fashion, speculators will catch on. Note, however, that the speculator I have been considering here who used these rules had little success in beating the market, and may well not beat the market in the future.

Let me conclude by going back to the propositions that I started with. I find the results of these tests at least consistent with the hypothesis that markets behave efficiently. At worst, these tests are inconclusive and certainly—best or worst—they present substantial difficulties in interpretation. Nevertheless, the results of the filter rule tests indicate that at least for movements of several months, the rules provide no guidance for a central banker who would act to assist the market.

Table 1
Net Filter Rule Profits: Germany
(Based on daily data, April 1, 1973–January 7, 1976)

Buy/Sell Rule (percent)	Whole Period	First Subperiod	Second Subperiod	Third Subperiod
.5	13.70	8.04	−3.55	−6.81
1.0	24.32	18.38	−2.32	4.83
1.15	14.03	6.94	−4.88	10.20
2.0	22.80	7.71	2.63	9.47
3.0	14.73	11.48	−2.85	4.62
4.0	14.39	9.41	0	3.61
5.0	6.01	12.90	0	2.48
6.0	−1.08	1.51	0	0
7.0	−10.93	−8.34	0	0
10.0	0	0	0	0
15.0	0	0	0	0
Average filter rule profit	18.78	12.33	11.93	−5.49
Buy and hold	9.87	7.28	12.93	−9.31

Note: Profits are net of the gains from buy and hold. For example, in the whole period, the .5 percent filter rule began with $100 and immediately bought deutsche marks; it ended with $123.57, for a profit of $23.57. Buy-and-hold profits are seen to be $9.87 (=$109.87 −$100), so net profits are $13.70. Note that the rule puts one in the foreign currency at the start of the period, so, for example, a 10 percent rule yields zero net profits since one holds deutsche marks to the very end of the period. This procedure prevents us showing negative net profits when buy-and-hold profits are positive and the filter is so large that no transactions are made, that is, one never buys into the foreign currency.

Source: Dennis Logue, Richard J. Sweeney, and Thomas D. Willett, "The Speculative Behavior of Foreign Exchange Rates under the Current Float," *Journal of Business Research*, forthcoming.

FOREIGN EXCHANGE INTERVENTION BY THE FEDERAL RESERVE BANK OF NEW YORK: SOME QUESTIONS

Wilson E. Schmidt

Following several years of international monetary turbulence, capped by a massive international financial crisis, the leading nations, in March 1973, fell into a system of generalized floating of exchange rates. Under the new system, these nations did not fix the value of their currencies in terms of the dollar. In July 1973 the Federal Reserve Bank of New York began to intervene in the New York foreign exchange market to affect dollar exchange rates.

Federal Reserve Board intervention has increased sharply since then. From July 1973 through January 1974, the Fed's gross sales of foreign currency were $517 million. In the succeeding six months gross sales rose slightly to $527 million. During the next six months ending January 1975, gross sales grew to $724 million. And during the succeeding six months, February through July 1975, gross sales jumped to $1,045 million. Gross sales then dropped sharply to $106.5 million during the period from August 1975 through January 1976.

Alan Holmes, the executive vice president of the New York Fed, at a Treasury Consultant's meeting in June 1975 stated the purpose of Fed intervention: "As far as intervention policy is concerned, our current approach is to intervene solely to maintain orderly markets and not to achieve or maintain any particular rate." This purpose differs from Fed policy prior to August 15, 1971 (when the tie to gold was abandoned), because at that time intervention was designed chiefly to guarantee the value of dollars held by foreign central banks in order to ward off their exchange of these dollars for our gold. Holmes offers one justification for intervention:

> There are too many occasions in the foreign exchange market where purely transitory events—the bunching of exchange orders, the misinterpretation of a current news item—can cause disproportionate movements in the exchange rate, particularly if markets are thin or if market participants are uncertain about national policies as to exchange rates. Such movements are in no sense fundamental, but they can cause a great deal of trouble if they tend—as they often do—to generate other speculative movements of the bandwagon variety.

97

And Holmes clarified the concept of disorderly markets and what the Fed seeks to accomplish:

> Early this year, in January and February [1975], our activity was all one way as we sold foreign exchange to cushion in some degree a sharp decline in the dollar rate. At that time, as now, most commercial and central bankers felt that the dollar was undervalued—a view that I and my colleagues share. But other adverse factors, real or imagined, were enough to push the dollar down. Our intervention helped the market find its own footing so that reasonably good two-way trading could resume. Since that time our market activity has become more even-handed with market purchases and sales of foreign exchange about balancing out. While there have been occasions when sharp temporary rate declines necessitated support operations to maintain orderly markets, these operations were reversed at times when the dollar was strong, providing us foreign exchange to cut back our swap debt. While our net market purchases of exchange in the past three months were about even, we were able to repay swaps in a substantial amount through foreign exchange operations with our central bank correspondents.

The Mechanics

The mechanics of Fed intervention are simple. When the Fed wants to intervene, for example by selling German marks, the New York Fed instructs one or more commercial banks to sell a given amount of marks on its behalf. The commercial bank calls one or more brokers to place the offer; the broker then matches the commercial bank with a willing buyer. Since the inception of floating rates, all the deals have been in the spot market while none has been made in the forward market.[1]

The New York Fed serves as a manager, operating under a directive from the Board of Governors dated January 1, 1973, which provides very general guidelines for intervention policy. The directive, which is published in the Annual Report of the Board of Governors, is now being revised. There is daily telephone contact among the New York Fed, the Board of Governors, and the Treasury. In fact, the New York Fed seeks to contact the Board and the Treasury prior to any intervention. This may occasionally introduce some short delays in intervention when the

---

[1] The commercial bank that serves as the agent has to pay the Fed in Fed funds while the buyer pays the agent bank clearing house funds which in turn become Fed funds a day later. The extra cost, namely one day's interest on Fed funds, is compensated in the rate of exchange charged to the Fed.

appropriate officials cannot be reached. But, if the appropriate official cannot be reached, that does not necessarily hold up an intervention.

The Fed has two sources of foreign currency. The first is its own relatively small holdings which have ranged from a high of $423 million to a low of $1 million in dollar equivalent since July 1973. The second, much larger, source derives from a system of borrowing arrangements with foreign central banks (called swap agreements) which in principle allows it to obtain as much as slightly more than the equivalent of $20 billion in foreign currency for a period of three months. The funds can in principle be rolled over, though the general directive relating to Fed intervention obviously seeks to limit the total length of borrowing to twelve months. The swaps have in fact been reversed in one or two quarters.

The Fed can choose among a variety of methods or styles of intervention. Because the Fed has large resources under the swap agreements, a major factor determining the effect of Fed intervention is whether and how well it is known that the Fed is intervening.

Its styles range from highly public interventions, confirmed by a statement by the chairman of the Board of Governors, the secretary of the Treasury, or both, to highly secret interventions. Between these extremes, the Fed has some other options according to foreign exchange traders with whom I have talked.

The commercial banks are pledged to secrecy when trading on behalf of the New York Fed. They cannot exercise their own discretion in carrying out the transaction. The Fed may instruct the commercial bank to undertake the operations in such a manner as to make it fairly clear that the Fed has entered the market. For example, the bank can spread the Fed's offers among a number of brokers in the same amounts at the same quotations "all over the street." If foreign exchange dealers see offers in round amounts of, for example, 5–10 million marks at repeated rates, they suspect the Fed is in the market. By changing its rates, the Fed can cover its tracks. On the other hand, it can caution the commercial bank to operate very discreetly.

Although the Fed appears to rotate its intervention business among several banks, presumably to avoid charges of favoritism, it can fine tune the degree to which its presence is known by picking a bank that does not normally deal in large amounts of the currency it is offering. Alternatively, if it wants to keep its activities secret, it can choose a bank that is known to deal in that currency actively.

Another factor, which is again a question of style, is whether the Fed instructs the commercial bank to move aggressively, for example, by instructing the commercial bank to respond to every bid in the market, in which case it clearly has tremendous power to affect the market while it is operating. Less boldly, it could instruct the commercial bank to meet the bids at a certain level.

The highly public approach is easy to understand. With this approach the Fed relies on the "announcement" effect. This approach obviously does work on occasion. For example, on May 14, 1974, it became known that the United States, the Federal Republic of Germany, and Switzerland had informally agreed to engage in concerted foreign exchange operations. By the following day, in the "scramble"—to use the Fed's word—the mark and the Swiss franc had fallen 4.5 percent relative to the dollar. A similar announcement in early February 1975 caused the mark to fall 4 percent in two days.

Why would the Fed use the secret approach? It makes sense if the Fed wants to invest relatively little money in an operation and let the market believe that private market forces are driving the rate one way or the other. That is, if the market knew it was the Fed that was offering the small amounts, the market would not regard the Fed as being serious in its efforts to affect the rate. (This does not mean that small offers are of no consequence because some of the Fed's intervention is probably done to get the feel of the market.)

Another explanation for secrecy is that if the Fed were to become the dominant factor in the market it runs the risk of having its hand called. If the market believes the Fed is moving the rate in the wrong direction, the market will absorb all the foreign exchange the Fed has to offer, believing that when the Fed leaves the market, the rate will change sharply, providing buyers with handsome profits.

Some foreign exchange traders with whom I talked believe that it is difficult for the Fed to hide its presence. Certain patterns in the quotations from brokers, such as the same quotations for fairly large amounts from several brokers and their repetition, reveal the presence of the Fed. Traders sometimes call the commercial bank they suspect of intervening for the Fed to ask if they are doing so; the tone of the response provides information even if the words do not. Other traders call the Fed itself with the same results. These suspicions are hard to prove since no satisfactory records of the guesses are available to me.[2]

Another important factor determining the effect of Fed intervention is whether the intervention occurs in the morning or in the afternoon. In the morning the foreign exchange markets both in Europe (where it is afternoon) and in New York are open—providing a very broad market, whereas in the afternoon, Europe is closed so that the entire market is thinner. Thus a given amount of Fed intervention will have a much

---

[2] One person I interviewed claimed a 90 percent batting average based on records, but the period covered was too short to be conclusive.

stronger effect on rates in the afternoon than in the morning. The European market will often open the next morning at the New York closing rate.

Still another factor is how the market perceives the intervention. This seems in part to be a function of the amounts the Fed offers as well as its persistence in the market. What are thought to be insignificant sums will be disregarded. If, after a small intervention, the Fed leaves the market, the market pays it no heed. It is difficult to state what the market perceives as small because relative sums vary in importance with the condition of the market at a particular time. In a normal market, that is, one undisturbed by official announcements and neither a Friday nor a holiday, according to one trader, 250 million German marks would be a large amount while 50 million would be a small amount.

Important here are the traders' judgments whether or not the Fed is right in the direction of its intervention. If a trader thinks the market is saturated with dollars, he is apt to assume that foreign currency sales by the Fed will have no effect. Traders do not automatically assume that the Fed (or any other central bank) is right in predicting its own ability to slow or speed the movements of rates. When a trader senses that the Fed is in the market, he quickly evaluates the situation, perhaps widening his spread to protect himself while analyzing the situation. He may then help the Fed by doing whatever it is doing, or he may do the reverse, in effect trying to make money from the Fed. This includes the commercial bank selected to serve as the agent of the Fed. While the agent bank knows the Fed is operating in the market, and while the nonagent trader may be fairly certain the Fed is in the market, neither can know for sure the degree to which the Fed is operating. (The Fed sometimes sells foreign exchange in a sequence of deals and through several banks, and even the agent trader will have a difficult time guessing to what extent the Fed will go on any sequence or at any one time.)

Actually, the Fed has been right more often that it has been wrong. The substantial losses on foreign exchange transactions reported by the Fed for 1974 were probably attributable to losses suffered in repaying swaps dated before August 15, 1971. In 1975, the Fed made $16 million on its foreign exchange transactions, half of which it shared with its swap partners for a net gain of $8 million. In short, the Fed bought currencies when prices were low and sold them when prices were high. But its margin of profit, and thus its margin for error, was not very great. If I understand the Holmes-Pardee reports correctly, total intervention transactions must have been around $3 billion in 1975, suggesting a profit margin or margin for error of slightly above 5 percent.

Some Questions

Fed intervention in the foreign exchange market raises some interesting questions. What is the Fed trying to accomplish? Does it actually alter exchange rates? If so, should there be rules governing its intervention?

What Are Disorderly Markets? The notion of disorderly markets approaches the very core of intervention policy. From my talks with foreign exchange traders, the notion of a disorderly market is one in which there occur abrupt changes in exchange rates, where the market is only one way (supply or demand but not both), or that there are quotations without business being transacted. This suggests a very short-run phenomenon, prevailing only for minutes, for several hours, or at most, for a few days. The notion includes a widening of spreads between buying and selling rates. (It is perhaps ironic that such is one of the effects of Fed intervention reported above.)

I found no agreement among traders on the degree of abruptness in rate changes required to constitute a disorderly market. Nor do they agree that such markets occur only in the short run. Some private traders think markets are disorderly if rates swing widely over several months. Others think of such markets as only a very short-term phenomenon.

It seems clear from Alan Holmes's statement noted earlier, that the Fed views disorderly markets in terms of months as well as minutes. And it appears that other central banks agree. For example, the German central bank explains its policy as follows:

> In its intervention policy the Bundesbank's guiding principle is that interventions should be made only for the purpose of maintaining "orderly market conditions," and that fundamental trends in the markets should not (and cannot) be counteracted. However, interventions have not only served to maintain orderly market conditions and avoid hectic exchange rate fluctuations from day to day. Rather, the attempt has been made to moderate excessive fluctuations in the Deutsche Mark rate vis-à-vis the U.S. dollar over extended periods of time. This has been done not least also in the interest, and with the full consent, of the other members of the European currency bloc.[3]

There may be still another concept of disorderly markets. Judging from Fed reports on intervention it is obvious that the Fed considers it more important to inform the public when it bought dollars than when it sold them since the purchases of dollars are far easier to pinpoint in time in the reports than the sales. One wonders if the sales of dollars are not

---

[3] *Report of the Deutsche Bundesbank for the Year 1974*, p. 60.

made in smaller amounts and spread over a longer period of time than the purchases of dollars so as to have less effect on the market. Though the evidence is inconclusive, it is possible that the Fed may perceive purchases as being different from sales in respect to intervention, that is, that one constitutes intervention and the other does not. If this is the case, perhaps there is another concept, namely that disorderly markets exist when the Fed thinks the dollar needs support.

Obviously, there are significant differences among these concepts of disorderly markets in terms of whether or not intervention should alter trends. It is by no means clear which of the concepts prevails.

Does Intervention Have Perverse Effects? It cannot always be assumed that Fed intervention reduces disorderly markets. There is always a possibility of perverse effects.

The foreign exchange market is often rife with rumors, including rumors of Fed intervention when it in fact is not intervening. One foreign exchange dealer reported that on numerous occasions other dealers identified him as intervening for the Fed when in fact he was not. The Reuters ticker, a major source of information in trading rooms, often reports the rumors. Obviously, these rumors can make the market disorderly. Unfortunately, there is no way to determine whether the orderliness achieved by Fed intervention is larger or smaller than the disorderliness created by the rumors of intervention.

Another perverse effect may occur when the Fed withdraws from the market. Once the Fed ceases buying dollars, for example, those holding dollars may panic, fearing that their existing holdings of dollars will decline in value in terms of foreign currency, and therefore will sell them, driving the price down. According to traders this does in fact happen. The same phenomenon has been observed in the government securities market.

Also under the swap arrangements, the Fed must ultimately repay the foreign exchange it borrows, thus giving rise to another possible problem. In principle, the sale of marks today by the Fed should cause the value of the dollar relative to marks to fall in the forward market because traders know the Fed has to repurchase the marks sometime in the future. But since they do not know when the repurchase will occur, their uncertainty about spot rates in the future increases, thus increasing uncertainty in the forward market today.

Whether the perverse effects outweigh the positive effects of Fed intervention is extremely difficult to determine. After experimenting with several techniques of analysis, it is apparent to me that there is not enough public information relative to the timing of Fed intervention and to that of other central banks to draw strong conclusions.

Rules for Management? Recently efforts have been made to create rules for central bank intervention. These rules would call for intervention when reserves, exchange rates, or measurements of the balance of payments change by a certain amount or exceed certain norms. Upon reflection, it seems that the effort to establish rules is incorrect, both theoretically and practically.

The theoretical objection lies in the fact that a major justification for central bank intervention in the foreign exchange market is that the central bank has better information than the market. This better information is about the future. The past is known to all. Since all of the proposed rules are tied to changes from the past, they are embedded, one way or another, in the past. Rules calling for intervention prevent the central bank from using any inside information about the future that it has gained at the monthly Bank for International Settlements meetings of the leading central banks and from morning telephone calls among each other.

As a practical matter, it is not clear how much the authorities really do know about the future. In response to arguments for firmer management of the foreign exchange markets, Jack Bennett, who was involved in foreign exchange intervention under floating rates in his capacity as under secretary of Treasury for monetary affairs, stated: "I am convinced that would be a mistake. I have worked long enough as a bureaucrat to know that there is no special wisdom accorded officials which is not available to other market participants. Government intervenors would have no special powers of foresight...." [4]

Another practical objection is that no rule can be written which is automatically consistent with the exigencies of the marketplace. If the Fed is forced to intervene or forced not to intervene at a certain time because of a rule, that rule will become known through experience. If the market does not believe that the Fed's intervention under the rule is consistent with market forces, the market will wipe the Fed out, buying all the foreign currency it sells in anticipation of a subsequent rise in its value. When the Fed repurchases the foreign exchange at a higher price to repay its borrowing under the swaps, it will suffer losses which in turn will be borne by the American taxpayer since virtually all of the profits of the Fed are returned to the Treasury. Few would condone such taxation without representation for the benefit of speculators.

---

[4] Speech, Boston Economic Club, October 1, 1975 (mimeo.).

COMMENTARIES

Horst Duseberg

I think I should first refer to the use of the word "speculator." For many years I have been a practitioner in the market, and I never felt that my principal role was that of a speculator. I feel this is important to state because, for my taste, the word "speculator" has been used too often at this conference.

The participants in foreign exchange markets are primarily financial institutions which make this market liquid. In doing so, they provide a service to those who really need this market, the multinationals and all the other companies which have foreign exchange exposures. There is some discussion whether multinational companies are really hedging or whether there is speculation involved. This is often difficult to determine. By and large it seems their foreign exchange business reflects hedging of their foreign assets and liabilities as well as their commercial transactions.

Although banks do maintain some open positions, in many cases this is done for purposes other than speculation. It is done to have some kind of inventory in order to be able, even at a late hour, to accommodate customers who need to buy or sell currencies.

Let us take the particular case of the British pound. The pound was very weak recently, and a bank would have made the wrong trading decision if in the afternoon it had a long position, or even no position at all, in pounds. From experience, we know that much commercial selling can develop in the afternoon. In order to accommodate our clients and at the same time be competitive, we should have had a short position in the afternoon. Particularly in the late afternoon, interbank markets are extremely thin, and therefore there is no guaranty that a bank can sell a weak currency, in our case the pound.

May I now outline very briefly the problems that banks have faced since the general float began and also express my opinion on the way the foreign exchange market has functioned in the new environment. (My remarks refer in fact to Mr. Sweeney's paper on market efficiency.) There is no doubt in my mind that the advent of floating considerably increased the risk element in foreign exchange transactions. When the general float began, the market became exposed to extremely large fluctuations, particularly in 1973 and 1974. In this period, for example, the deutsche mark–dollar exchange rate changed by as much as 40 percent, and certain rates fluctuated by as much as 2 percent a day. Some market participants simply were not prepared for this new environment.

In fact, it was not surprising that some large losses occurred. As is very often the case, it took a serious crisis to prevent a bigger one. The Herstatt failure in 1974 forced market participants, regulatory agencies, and authorities to reassess market risks. This reassessment took place on three levels: the bank management level, the supervisory level, and the government level.

Banks had to decide whether to remain in the market as market makers or simply as order placers. Once the decision was made to remain active, many financial institutions moved to reduce their limits on overnight total risk positions, as well as on positions with individual trading partners. To the best of my knowledge, most U.S. banks, which traditionally have taken a conservative approach to foreign exchange dealings, did not find it necessary to cut back very drastically on their established trading operations. But they did install improved management control systems. Many institutions put a new high priority on the computerization of their trading operations. Supervisory agencies which, in the case of the United States, included the comptroller of the currency, the Federal Reserve Board, and state banking authorities began to pay special attention to foreign exchange operations. Out of this intensified foreign exchange supervision, auditors gained considerable experience and knowledge. Governments became so involved that, in Germany, for example, new legislative measures were taken to ensure sound practices, and in the United States, new reporting requirements were introduced by the Treasury and the Federal Reserve Board.

From the perspective of a practitioner, I am decidedly impressed by the efficiency and the depth of the market today. There is a healthy balance between professional arbitrage, on the one hand, and financial and commercial business, on the other hand. Exchange rate variations are, generally, much smaller, over an extended period of time, than they were in 1973 and 1974. Of course, there are a few exceptions, like the ones we experienced recently with the Italian lira and the pound. Moreover, the forward markets are functioning well for all the major currencies up to maturities of one year. The opinion that forward foreign exchange markets function well only for deutsche marks and Swiss francs is not correct.

There is, admittedly, a regrettable lack of quotations for periods in excess of one year, but this deficiency existed under the old system of fixed exchange rates as well. (I, personally, would like to see an effort by the leading foreign exchange banks to extend their future markets, up to five years. Many of our commercial clients would welcome such a development.)

Now, let us take a look at central bank intervention and at Professor Schmidt's paper. I refer particularly to the authorities' commitment to maintain orderly market conditions. Most market participants would applaud such action, but we have seen again and again that many central banks find it difficult to live up to their commitments. In all fairness, however, we must admit that it is difficult, even for central banks, to distinguish between movements in exchange rates arising from underlying economic conditions and those arising from speculative movements of hot money.

Sometimes, in order to maintain orderly markets, large drains on reserves are unavoidable. But central banks, particularly those with weak currencies, cannot afford this luxury. Intervention nearly always tends to be a one-sided affair. And small, but frequent, interventions will eventually add up to substantial reserve losses.

Italy offers a textbook case. For several days, markets had no semblance of orderliness despite modest official intervention. And it is questionable whether the full—and I emphasize the word "full"—extent of the lira's decline was a basic move.

The opposite situation exists in Switzerland. Without doubt, it is sometimes difficult for the Swiss National Bank to maintain orderly market conditions. Admittedly, disorderly conditions in the market for Swiss francs do not exist very often. But the intervention by the Swiss authorities usually is also a one-way street, leading to the accumulation of more and more foreign exchange reserves.

In the case of the United States, I wonder—and this is just an idea to be discussed later—whether it would not be beneficial for the Federal Reserve System to start accumulating reserves in foreign currencies. The increased involvement of the United States in foreign trade and finance would justify such a move and, at the same time, allow the Federal Reserve to be more active in the foreign exchange market. For instance, the afternoon markets in New York are often so thin that relatively small transactions influence the rates to an unwarranted extent. These movements could be ironed out through a more active participation by the Federal Reserve.

I have one additional suggestion. Instead of outright buying or selling of spot currencies, central banks should sometimes consider entering into swap operations, particularly when minor currencies are involved. By doing so, the authorities could influence the spot price by temporarily withdrawing liquidity in the currency which is to be supported.

We know that when the pound sterling was under pressure the Bank of England tried to buy spot sterling and to sell it forward. However, it turned out that the sterling market is so large that the amounts required to influence interest rates would have to be substantial. Although such a policy proved to be impractical in the case of the pound, it may be justifiable for some minor currencies.

I would like to finish with a brief question to Sweeney. He writes that some of the evidence to be cited suggests that there may have been imperfections in the functioning of the exchange markets, especially the forward markets.

I wonder whether he could elaborate on this statement. I do not agree with him. I think the forward markets are functioning very well.

Nicolas Krul

Like Horst Duseberg, I shall limit myself to stressing a few points—in my case, as a practitioner who is convinced of the disorderly nature of the exchange markets. I think a simple glance at the Swiss franc's behavior over the last few years fully justifies that conviction. The points I would make are mainly related to the impact of operational and other factors on the supply and pricing of forward facilities, whose repercussions on spot prices are evident. The objective of my remarks is to explain why exchange markets have not behaved as efficiently as many advocates of floating rates expected they would.

The first factor lies in the persistent unpredictability of exchange rates—or rather, in the change in their unpredictability from the pre-1973 period. Under the Bretton Woods system as it worked from 1949 to 1973, exchange rate forecasting was considered a relatively easy exercise. Under no-crisis conditions, premiums or discounts could be assumed to be a reasonable proxy for the measurement of tensions in the exchange market. It is true that under crisis conditions the arbitrage margin usually ignored the forward speculation market. But this could be forecast by a combination of judgmental appreciation and the traditional tools of disequilibrium analysis, more particularly through the real money supply, inflation rate, and balance of payments series. Consequently, as Paul Einzig frequently pointed out, exchange rate forecasting was an underinvested and precarious part of banking intelligence. After 1971, banks tended to adjust slowly, in part because fixity remained the objective of official policies, and it was often considered premature for banks to invest heavily in exchange rate research and management.

Nevertheless, the floating rate era started with great trading-room confidence in forecasting ability (and correspondingly vague and elastic notions at the management level). This confidence rapidly led to the quite amazing exchange losses suffered by some banks and multinational corporations. In turn, these losses led to a spectacular development of research—both in-house and by specialized institutions—and to a great deal of organizational innovation. However, little real progress has been made in the field of forecasting, as can easily be demonstrated by a comparison between the predictive power of discounts or premiums and the forecasting results of the various well-known (and costly) exchange rate forecasting services. There are, in my view, two main reasons for this lack of success.

First, the incapacity to forecast and measure leads and lags in a world where trade flows reach high monthly figures. Leads and lags have never been a popular subject for academic economists and, in addition, it was only quite recently that steps were taken to derive the statistical material necessary to measure leads and lags through balance of payments figures, trade credit, changes in foreign exchange covering arrangements or variations in banks' external assets and liabilities. However, the deficiencies in the (mostly delayed) statistical material remain very substantial indeed. It is highly doubtful whether they can ever be adequately remedied so as to integrate the data in question into a coherent economic or econometric presentation.

Second, the analysis of international capital movements remains rudimentary. Since the pioneering work of Tsiang and others, in the early 1960s, some progress has been made in the integration of hedging, covering, speculation, and interest arbitrage in both the spot and forward exchange markets. But in addition to some weaknesses which hamper its practical use, the theoretical work suffers from the inadequate treatment of expectations referred to by Willett and Sweeney. The Koyck-type distributed lag model (speculative capital flow as a function of changes in rates and speculative demand from the preceding period) has not adequately filled this gap since it relies on the past performance of a variable (the rate) proven to be only one among a number of variables.

The precariousness of existing forecasting techniques has exerted two consequences: on the *volume* of forward exchange facilities and on the *pricing* of forward facilities. Evidently, these repercussions on forward exchange rates have affected spot rates.

As to the supply of forward exchange facilities, we know that even before 1971 the potential volume of forward exchange was not the limitless quantity often taken for granted. Interest rate differentials played their role, and when prohibitive interest rates came to represent a negligible fraction of potential speculative profits, governments applied direct

109

control measures and intervened in forward markets. In addition, banks fixed limits beyond which they were not prepared to accept each other's names in interbank transactions. Since 1973, though, the volume of forward exchange has become subject to additional restrictive intra- or interbank rules and increased central bank regulation. As to the former, the increased risks (particularly after the Herstatt affair) have induced bank managements to intervene conservatively in the working of the exchange departments by (1) fixing (reducing) the limit on the total of forward commitments; (2) fixing (reducing) the limits on forward commitments in particular currencies and countries; (3) fixing (reducing) the limits on forward commitments entered in with particular banks or financial institutions; and (4) fixing (limiting) the forward exchange commitment schedule. The practical effect of these limitations is to put a degressive ceiling on the available volume of the forward market, a ceiling which, moreover, is not quantifiable since (1) banks never disclose the limits on the forward exchange commitments they fix in relation to each other; (2) the unreported involvement of unsecured Eurocurrency borrowings in forward contracts has recently lowered the ceiling to an unknown extent (as this practice increases the default risk from the mere exchange rate difference to the total amount of the contract); and (3) there seems to be some feedback from the activity of the more legalistic-oriented U.S. banks, even those working abroad (which have to cope with a U.S. bankruptcy law which does not exempt a victimized bank from honoring its own obligations in relation to the defaulter) on the formerly more relaxed attitude of European banks.

In fact, therefore, it is reasonable to assume that banks have come to err on the conservative side in fixing the volume of forward contracts and thereby have increased the likelihood that most of them may reach their limits in relation to each other. The very fact that an unexpected refusal might intervene (creating an awkward situation for the broker) is, of course, an additional limiting factor. (One may wonder whether this prospect of a cumulative contractional effect did not encourage the excessive early 1976 support by monetary authorities who expected that banks would soon be unable to undertake new commitments or to roll over existing ones.) Since 1973, government regulations concerning forward commitments have been substantially enlarged and refined. (The enlargement concerned practically all countries except Germany.) Notably, central banks have decided to impose controls on *net* commitments so that long positions could no longer be offset by short positions (the limit being SwFr 1 million or approximately $400,000 at the current rate per bank in Switzerland), to change monthly and weekly reports into daily reports so as to prevent positions between periodic reporting dates, to impose limits on the direction of exchange positions, and to coordinate between countries. Of course, these new regulations concern domestic operations and do not impede either Euromarket positions or the use of unregulated currencies as a proxy.

The price effect of declining supply is partly offset by the observed decline in demand, which is partly cyclical and partly structural, corporations having found other means of minimizing their exchange exposure. Nevertheless, most operators are of the opinion that supply conditions have had, and still have, a price and cost effect.

There has been much controversial discussion about perverse price formation—overshooting, bandwagon effects—in the exchange markets. The existence of such perversity I do not doubt on the basis of exchange rate variations in the European markets. In addition to the more sophisticated analytical arguments that indicate perversity, I may draw attention to two factors that became evident in 1975–1976. On the one hand, the closer management supervision of the exchange department has induced more reliance on past trends. In other words, the dealers are more reluctant then ever to contradict the "trend"—that is, to assume the risk of a "personal" forecasting error as opposed to an acceptable "general" or "common" forecasting error. As a result, the modification of a prevailing trend requires an above-average move of the forward quotation, not merely a return to the equilibrium rate. Failing such a move, trends tend to continue in the same direction. Examples can be found in the Swiss franc–dollar or Swiss franc–deutsche mark rates as well as in the exchange rate relations of the pound. On the other hand, price perversity occurs when exchange rates are expected to influence real conditions, either in the direction of contractive domestic adjustment to appreciation (the Swiss case), or in the direction of the exploitation of new expansionary possibilities opened by depreciation (Italy and the United Kingdom).

Scott Pardee

In holding a meeting like this, the U.S. Treasury and the American Enterprise Institute are providing a great service. For many years, academic people have been talking to academic people about foreign exchange, and market people have been talking to market people about foreign exchange, but neither group has talked very much to the other. This meeting is an opportunity to clear the air. We may disagree, but at least we will know more precisely the points on which we disagree. Now, my responsibilities are to conduct the foreign exchange operations of the Federal Reserve System. At this meeting so far, I have received a lot of free—and conflicting—advice on our operations. I would like to outline my view of the Federal Reserve's role in the exchange market.

The blunt fact is that the Federal Reserve is the only central bank in the world that does not have international reserves at its disposal. The Treasury holds the U.S. stock of international reserve assets, such as gold and IMF drawing rights, but these have been inconvertible since August 15, 1971. Moreover, neither the Federal Reserve nor the U.S. Treasury has shown interest in building up large foreign currency balances. Consequently, to intervene in the exchange market on any scale we must borrow foreign currencies. In this regard we have ample borrowing lines: the $20 billion of Federal Reserve swap arrangements with fourteen central banks and the Bank for International Settlements. These have been used very effectively, but all this is someone else's money: in effect, like anyone else in the marketplace, we are living by our wits.

Of course, we have several advantages over other market participants. We have the great advantage of being an insider in an insider's market. The exchange market, after all, is a money market. The Federal Reserve Bank of New York carries out foreign currency operations under the authorization and directive of the Federal Open Market Committee, which also sets domestic money market policy. Knowing what U.S. monetary policy is, and is likely to be, is a great advantage in evaluating conditions in the exchange market.

In view of the Treasury's responsibilities in international financial policy, we also consult closely with Treasury officials. The Federal Reserve System would not operate in the exchange market over Treasury objection. Indeed, the New York Federal Reserve has a more direct responsibility to the Treasury even than this, since we also serve as fiscal agent for the Treasury's Exchange Stabilization Fund in its foreign currency operations. Thus, we operate in the context of a broader range of U.S. international financial policies, beyond monetary policy as such.

Moreover, the Federal Reserve has close working relationships with foreign central banks, which have substantial information both about conditions in their money and exchange markets and about their own policies. This link with foreign central banks is especially important, since the major exchange market for every currency is not in New York but elsewhere. The more we know about conditions in those markets the better we can operate in the New York exchange market itself.

In addition, the Foreign Department of the New York Federal Reserve has close contacts with other participants in the exchange markets both in the United States and abroad. All those contacts and relationships allow us to gain a more complete picture of the situation at hand.

I might add that we also have at our disposal the immense data-collecting services of the U.S. government, again the Federal Reserve and the Treasury in particular. This gives us access to data which are not yet available—in their raw form not available at all—to other participants in the market. We also have the benefit of the economic research being carried out in these institutions. In some cases, to be sure, research economists give us numbers we do not need, such as weighted average exchange rates. (After all, the market deals in real money, not in weighted averages.) Moreover, research economists have a poor track record in forecasting certain developments in the international area, particularly on projecting the U.S. trade balance. Nonetheless, since market people tend to concentrate on short-run transitory factors, the longer-term perspective of the research economist contributes in an important way to our understanding of more fundamental developments.

Finally, the Federal Reserve has a valuable legacy from the era of Charles Coombs, who has recently retired to private life after serving as head of the Foreign Department of the Federal Reserve Bank of New York for some fifteen years. From the wide range of operations he undertook during those years, he has left us with ample resources, in the form of the swap arrangements, and a full arsenal of tested intervention techniques. As a master of personal diplomacy, he earned for us an immense measure of good will with our counterparts in other central banks. Because of this, when we do intervene we can be extremely effective.

I have stressed our advantages in the marketplace, but we also have serious constraints. Some of them are obvious. Central banks are occasionally obliged to intervene in a situation in which the economic fundamentals may be very unfavorable and a government may be weak or indecisive in resolving the problem. In such cases, central bankers do their best in what may be a losing cause. We are careful, however, to characterize such operations as "damage-control" or "rear-guard" actions.

Other constraints are what I will call simply "overriding considerations." One is the trade-off between domestic and international objectives of policy. In the Federal Reserve, domestic monetary policy objectives often hold sway over international objectives. Or the overriding considerations may arise from broader economic policy choices. At such times it is often forgotten that exchange market intervention by itself is not a policy solution. It is a signal that something is wrong; the bigger the intervention, the bigger the problem. To backstop or eliminate the need for intervention other policy actions are necessary.

For example, a great deal has been said here of the recent declines of the Italian lira, the pound sterling, and the French franc. In each case there was heavy exchange market intervention by the central bank concerned, but the intervention was not immediately supplemented by other policy measures. At least one participant in this meeting has drawn on these examples to suggest that central bank intervention in the exchange market is futile, if not perverse. But no one has mentioned the recent Belgian experience. The Belgian franc also fell under heavy speculation in early 1976, but the Belgian government responded forcefully and in an orthodox manner. The government issued strong denials of any intention to change the exchange rate. The central bank not only intervened massively in the market, it allowed this intervention to tighten domestic liquidity and even raised some domestic interest rates. Exchange controls were tightened and the budget was trimmed. This approach worked, and Belgium is now enjoying a significant reflow of funds. My point is that each situation should be analyzed on its own merits.

More broadly, there are times of clear governmental crisis when a central bank should make its presence known in the exchange market. The Federal Reserve's operations on November 22, 1963, the day that President Kennedy was assassinated, offer an example of effective intervention. On other occasions, however, political considerations may render exchange market intervention ineffective. Time and again in recent years the markets have been disrupted by loose talk about exchange rates by government officials and politicians.

For this reason, my first rule for floating would be in the form of a commandment to government officials: "Thou shalt not talk about the exchange rate in public." Anything said, even with the best of intentions, can backfire. Some of the wide volatility of exchange rates in recent years has reflected the market's response to statements and mis-impressions left by government officials. The cumulative rise of the West German mark and the Swiss franc against the dollar in late 1974 and early 1975 was such an instance. It took a firm stand by the Federal Reserve, the Bundesbank, and the Swiss National Bank through coordinated intervention in the exchanges to avoid what could have become a thoroughly disorderly market. Our part of that operation was financed by heavy swap drawings, eventually in excess of a billion dollars, which were subsequently repaid in full. Since that time the dollar has been generally steadier because—in some part at least—traders are now reassured that the Federal Reserve and other central banks will respond, forcefully if necessary, to counter disorder in the exchanges.

Finally, I believe that the widespread market skepticism about the Rambouillet Agreement is unfair. The major purpose of the communiqué was not so much to generate greater exchange market intervention for dealing with the current situation, as to seek means of resolving the fundamental disequilibria which are at the root of international monetary instability. Rambouillet has opened the way for increasing consultation among government officials of different countries. On that basis we will have a better chance to achieve more stable economic relationships among the major nations from which more stable markets can evolve.

To comment generally on the papers, I agree with Horst Duseberg that the role of the speculator is vastly overemphasized. The exchange market has many functions, only one of which is to serve as a vehicle for speculation. Even among the forces motivating exchange traders, speculation may not be particularly important. Fear of loss can be a more impelling force than desire for profit. Moreover, by focussing on the isolated question of the effects of central bank intervention, the papers tend to neglect the importance of broader economic policies for exchange rate determination. Also, the assumption of traders' rationality bothers me. Modern decision theory has shown that the assumption of rationality may yield misleading results in ambiguous situations—and the exchange markets are rife with such situations. Perhaps we should look into the recently developed "catastrophe theory" now being applied to "fight or flight" situations in behavioral sciences. This entails some highly sophisticated mathematics, but to me some of the results seem to fit more closely with actual behavior in the marketplace than do the models presented here.

Dennis Weatherstone

Before commenting on the papers presented in this session, I would like to refer to a market aspect that nobody has touched on specifically, and that is timing. It is fine to talk about trends and forecasts, to say that the market was wrong in not seeing what was going to happen in the "long term," but we should not forget that market exchange rates are determined daily by market makers—commercial banks—and that their accounts are determined monthly and published quarterly. It is not very satisfying, at the end of the month, to tell management that, though things look bad, everything will be all right in the long run—that it is the market that is wrong and does not understand the fundamentals. This is just one practical limitation on the so-called farsighted view that some scholars seem to expect of the market. The key is timing. There is little point in forecasting what rates will be in a year, or even in three months, unless such forecasts are revised frequently. The vast majority of our business in the market is based on settlement of commercial transactions that must be made in the near term. To us, what happens today, tomorrow, and in the ensuing month is more fundamental than the fundamentals.

We are market makers. We want to provide—as Duseberg said—a ready market, so that at any time our commercial customers can do their business, at spot or forward rates, at that moment in time at a reasonable price. We are not in the business of taking long-term views on currencies. As soon as we start to take long-term views about currencies, we can begin to use that much misunderstood word "speculator." And we have seen what happened to many banks who took long-term views. They have not generally been the true market makers, who have been fine tuning the rate day after day. Rather, if the dollar is oversold or overbought, they sit with it until proved right.

Turning to Rutledge's paper, the "speculator theme" has been almost worn out today. Bernstein is, of course, right in saying that it is not necessarily a dirty word. Economists, though, regard it differently, I believe, from the market and Congress. In New York, everybody is concerned about the use, or misuse, of that word, while in Washington people often talk about speculators as though they are helpful individuals, contributing to a good market. In New York clients frequently walk into the room and before relating their exchange problems feel it necessary to say for the record that they never speculate. Only once have I ever met a person who admitted to being a foreign currency speculator.

A word now on the bandwagon effect. We ask if there is or is not a bandwagon. I do not think one gets a true perspective from the West Coast. There is no doubt at all in my mind that, in 1973 and 1974, there was a bandwagon. We saw it operating, as big positions were being set up, and the market knew which banks were involved. If a bank or group of banks fairly clearly was moving $500 million, $1 billion, or $2 billion, how could a trader sit back and call that movement wrong? In the short run, he would trade the same way. Thereby he may make the currency movement exaggerated, but he is not there to lose money. Fighting the market majority can be an expensive luxury.

There was, then, a bandwagon market. How long it carried on is a little difficult to say. I believe, however, that the bandwagon was just one of the problems of 1973 and 1974. We had an exceptionally difficult time for determining proper exchange rates, with the imbalances created by the huge oil price increase, the oil embargo, the development of sharply different inflation rates, the International Equalization Tax, and the abolition of the Office of Foreign Direct Investment. All were unusual and major factors, making it impossible to guess which way rates should go, and how far.

The problem was magnified by the big speculative positions. I believe that the market is now in much better shape, and that this improvement is due only in part to the actions of central banks. The way to learn one has been wrong is to lose money, and painful lessons were learned. Look at the list of banks that lost money in 1974 in foreign exchange. The market learned its lesson and subsequently improved.

Professor Schmidt spoke of central bank intervention. I have little to add except that the last time we had a conference like this, I thought the sensible policy was to have a minimum intervention and to let the market decide the rate. When it was decided that intervention was appropriate, the central bank should be given maximum flexibility. I believe it well nigh impossible to formalize tight rules for intervention and have those rules be lasting. Today, we could say that we have worked out a fine set of rules for intervention. We have considered inflation differentials, interest rates, balance of trade, capital flows, and so on, and it would seem reasonable. But as soon as we walk out of the room, the rules may turn out to be wrong. Or perhaps in a week they may turn out to be wrong. A precise workable solution through rules is not possible. Let us therefore have a minimum of intervention. Let the market decide as best it can. Let us exercise judgment, have the central banks correct disorderly markets, and, when they do it, give them a good deal of scope and opportunity to do it properly.

Mr. Sweeney was talking about the forward market. Several of us have said that we do not consider the forward market to be deficient although it is not always what it appears to be when we are looking for quotations for the long term. There is a good market up to one year, and the market beyond one year is not bad either. My bank is willing to give quotations up to five years, in the Canadian dollar, the pound sterling, the deutsche mark, and the Swiss franc, and, three, sometimes five, years in the Japanese yen. These are currencies that are actively used in trade and investment, and there tends to be quite a good two-way interest in them.

We, however, prefer to make the market directly with our own commercial customers. We are a commercial bank, and we do not see much to be gained by putting our rates into the open market for those long periods if that only enables another bank to trade those currencies long date for their commercial customers. We would rather encourage as many commercial customers as we can to come directly to us. We think that our role as a major market maker well equips us to quote in the long-date market. Therefore, though it may be said there is no market, business can be done even if there is none in the accepted sense of the term. The other point is that those who say there is no possibility to do long-date transactions often mean they do not like the price, which is a different matter.

So much for comments on the papers. I referred a little earlier to the particular problems of 1973 and 1974. I would hope that those are behind us now, and I see no reason why they should not be. I think 1975 was a much better year in the exchange market; there was less movement in exchange rates and much more logic to the movements.

I can remember a commercial customer saying to me that he really did not know what to do. In 1973 and 1974 he started by hedging all his positions, and he lost money. Then he decided not to hedge any positions, because he decided he did not understand it sufficiently, and he lost money. He decided then to hedge half, and he still lost money. I said to him that in 1975 he must have made money, and he said that was exactly right. The explanation was that in 1975, there was a logical market, and his was a logical company. He did not make money in the illogical markets because he thought logically.

The New York market has become a better foreign exchange market. There has not been a rush, as there was on the continent after the Herstatt collapse and other incidents, to slap controls on the banks, inhibiting them from taking reasonable positions during the day and inhibiting them from making good forward markets. The system that has been adopted here so far has been to collect information on banks' positions. The banks in New York have been responsive to this. The authorities can now monitor the banks' positions, with the possibility of talking about them intelligently. The absence of rigid rules reflects recognition that there should be different rules for different banks with different abilities.

I am pleased to say that the system of flexible controls of foreign exchange activities has provided the basis for an intelligent administration of foreign exchange trading. It is a little like the system adopted by the Bank of England, which happens to have more specific controls to protect the exchange rate of the pound because there is a special problem with it. But the Bank of England has a flexible system for other currencies and wants to see a good foreign exchange market in London. The fact that the authorities here seem to have adopted a basically similar attitude has contributed to New York's becoming a better market than it was.

The market improvement extended into 1976, notwithstanding the turmoil within the European snake in the early part of 1976. I was disappointed that the decision on an exchange rate was again forced upon a country by a crisis. It looked from the outside like a case of insufficient forward planning. It was not really difficult to see that the deutsche mark–French franc relationship was going to come under pressure, and I had been hopeful that some plans for a change in that exchange rate would have been made in advance. But the opportunity for an orderly realignment was missed, and this was disappointing. It is certainly not easy to get everybody around a table to change the exchange rate. But difficulties notwithstanding, I was still disappointed because many of the problems could have been foreseen.

Nevertheless, the French have left the snake, and the market is not functioning well. With the better cooperation—possibly as a result of Rambouillet—it should improve upon its performance. Certainly I do not know of any new and better system, other than a gradual evolution of the present system with improved intervention policies, more intelligent management, and better disciplined banks. I do not want to sound too relaxed about it all, but we have come a long way from the float of 1973.

SUMMARY OF THE DISCUSSION

The lively exchange which followed the commentaries touched upon all major issues raised by the authors of the papers and elaborated upon by the commentators.

Rutledge's conclusion on the lack of evidence for any perceptible bandwagon effect in foreign exchange markets, challenged earlier by Krul, was also disputed by another representative of European investment bankers, Geoffrey Bell. A closely related issue of market efficiency was debated at length by Bernstein and Sweeney as well as other participants in the session. The very notion, and the usefulness of the concept, of market efficiency became a subject of intense controversy.

Schmidt's paper and Pardee's commentary sparked a discussion centering on the issue of feasibility and effectiveness of intervention policies. The possibility of official intervention in the forward markets was raised by Sohmen, and difficulties involved in its implementation were discussed by Pardee.

Then the discussion shifted to the problem of evaluation of intervention policies. Some alternative criteria for judging their social desirability were proposed and debated.

Finally, the roles of confidentiality and disclosure, as they pertain to the *modus operandi* of intervening authority, were reviewed and various opinions on this subject expressed.

Bandwagon Effects and Notions of Market Efficiency

Challenging Krul's assertion of foreign exchange markets often being dominated by speculative forces, John Rutledge remarked that one ought to be specific about who initiates a speculative run and why. He pointed out that, although jumping on the bandwagon may be a good strategy for any particular trader, such description of traders' behavior fails to provide an adequate explanation of the whole market outcome. If everybody joins in the rush, who is on the other side?

To this, Geoffrey Bell answered that the first thing one has to remember is that central banks have intervened quite frequently since

1973, and many of them did take losses. Besides, there is a long list of commercial and investment banks that have recorded substantial losses, not to mention privately held institutions, which are not subject to compulsory disclosure of their foreign exchange losses. So, Bell concluded, there *is* the other side. The reason for everyone's not getting on the bandwagon on time is that at some times various bankers succumb to the temptation of resisting the trend, in the belief that their own forecasting is better than that of the other side.

The presumption of the existence of bandwagon effects in the foreign exchange markets would indicate that the markets are inefficient. Referring to the results contained in his paper, Richard Sweeney pointed out that opportunities for making profits, as displayed by filter rule tests, lend some support to the view of market inefficiency. However, he called for caution in interpreting those results. First, he noted, the results are extremely sensitive to the period chosen. For instance, for the whole period of 800 trading days analyzed, some filter rules would enable a speculator to make profits in every currency except Canadian dollars. On the other hand, if the period were split into two halves, during the first 400 trading days the same filter rules would yield no profits anywhere except the United Kingdom. Moreover, Sweeney remarked, in all discussions about foreign exchange market efficiency it is necessary to distinguish between markets for the different currencies as well as between the spot and forward markets.

Wilson Schmidt interjected a remark questioning the usefulness of the tests conducted by Sweeney and others. He believes that the results are not particularly enlightening since the data on central banks' intervention are not known or cannot be isolated, so that it is impossible to tell whether the efficiency disclosed in a particular market is owed to stabilizing speculation or deliberate actions of monetary authorities.

Edward Bernstein devoted his remarks to analyizing the notion of market efficiency. He started by distinguishing between efficiency in the narrow technical sense and efficiency in the broader economic sense. Since, in general, transactions in the exchange market for dollars could be made promptly and discontinuities in prices were not occurring, one could say that the market has been efficient in a technical sense. However, Bernstein doubts that the market has been efficient in a broader sense of the term.

On his definition, a market is efficient if the traders can accurately foresee changes in supply and demand conditions that will occur in the future. In the commodities market efficiency means that a shift in supply because of a shortfall in the next harvest is fully taken into account by the buyers and sellers of future contracts. If such shifts are unanticipated by market participants prices will exhibit sharp fluctuations.

He referred to his own attempts at testing the efficiency of the stock and bond markets. On the stock market, he started by assuming that actual earnings over the last ten years could have been foreseen ten years ago. When the known earnings, appropriately discounted, were taken into account, the computed range of fluctuations of equity prices turned out to be about 25 percent of what it actually was. The bond market would be efficient, according to Bernstein, if the price of an outstanding government bond changes, say, in one year by exactly as much as the difference between the long-term rate on government bonds and short-term rate on Treasury bills over the same period. His findings indicate that although more efficient than the stock market, the market in (government) bonds is far from being efficient: it tends to exaggerate price movements.

In the foreign exchange market, large and reversible exchange rate movements, in Bernstein's view, imply that market participants were unable to foresee what the right rate should be in response to economic changes. On the criterion he proposed, the foreign exchange market was not efficient at all, notwithstanding its ability to provide traders with adequate buying and selling facilities.

Bernstein concluded by rejecting the argument that frequent changes in exchange rates were attributable to equally frequent shifts in the underlying trend. Saying that the market is always at the trend but the trend itself may change every day, he added, is equivalent to saying that the market is always right. He believed that such a concept is not particularly useful for any kind of analysis.

John Rutledge remarked that Bernstein's criterion of market efficiency is only relevant for a world of perfect foresight. In the presence of uncertainty about the future it is only natural that price fluctuations were bound to be larger than they would have been had the market been endowed with perfect knowledge of future developments.

Sweeney associated himself with Rutledge's objection. He emphasized that efficiency is an ex ante concept; it is an appraisal of how well, on the basis of available information, the market processes that information and sets prices it considers to be equilibrium prices. Differences between actual and hypothetical price variations computed by Bernstein can be regarded as an estimate of the sadness in life that we cannot foresee things as accurately as we would like to.

Next, Sweeney challenged Bernstein's views concerning the sterility of the concept of shifting trends. He pointed out that in econometric work the failure to take account of shifts in the mean will lead to biased results. It is known that the mean of the stochastic process of price changes displayed shifts in the bond market but appeared to remain stable in the stock market. It is quite likely that in the foreign exchange market the mean has been shifting, albeit not necessarily frequently, and, ideally, those shifts would have to be taken into account in analyzing the process of exchange rate changes.

Sweeney acknowledged that he is somewhat more inclined to impute inefficiencies detected in foreign exchange markets to central bank intervention than to credit central banks for making the markets efficient. He added, though, that in any case, unless official intervention is completely haphazard, the very fact that monetary authorities are active in the market does not invalidate conclusions about the efficiency of the foreign exchange market. Sweeney remarked that if a central bank's intervention sales and purchases are nonoptimal in some systematic, and hence predictable, way, other participants in the market ought to be able to make profits by anticipating official intervention. Thus, intervention does not render the tests for market efficiency useless, as Schmidt claims, although their design might have to become more sophisticated.

Feasibility and Effectiveness of Intervention Policies

Alan Teck was not convinced by Pardee's assertion that forceful intervention policy is bound to be effective in stabilizing the exchange rate. Readily acknowledging that, by and large, central banks have been performing well given the difficulty of their task of reconciling various objectives, Teck nevertheless challenged the opinion that exchange rates can always be stabilized by means of a forceful and credible intervention policy. He questioned the validity of the Belgian example invoked by Pardee, noting that the French and Italian authorities also intervened heavily and still were unable to prevent the fall in the external value of their currencies. First, he pointed out, the market for Belgian francs is much smaller than for the French francs or the lira, so that it was much easier for the Bundesbank to help support the Belgian currency than to support the other two. Next, the cost of auxiliary measures, like raising the interest rate, would have been higher for the French and the Italians, because of the sluggishness of their economy, than it was for Belgium. And, finally, Belgium has a two-tier foreign exchange market. While the authorities intervened in the commercial tier, the drop of the Belgian franc in the financial tier took a great deal of pressure off the Belgian currency.

In Teck's view the Belgian episode does not prove how good intervention policy can be, but rather raises the question whether it really was necessary. He doubted it was necessary. From the point of view of a company operating in or trading with a particular country it is hardly ever necessary. He reported that when currencies come under pressure his bank usually advises its corporate clients to hedge their assets denominated in that currency. No one need be particularly concerned whether the currency will be eventually devalued, as the French franc was, or not, as was the case with the Belgian franc. If assets of a risk-averting and protection-oriented company are appropriately hedged (on an after-tax basis), then, even if the anticipated devaluation does not materialize, what the company loses on its hedge it gains on its exposure. Of course, if the currency is devalued, the value of the company's assets remains protected.

Teck compared hedging to buying an insurance policy and pointed out that a sound exposure-management system is not contingent upon forecasting exchange rates with absolute accuracy; it is enough to sense the direction of pressures and have a good idea of the cost of taking protective action. His conclusion was that good exposure management by private parties is at least a partial substitute for official stabilization of exchange rates.

Schmidt concurred with Teck's opinion that it is difficult for the central banks to conduct an effective intervention policy while at the same time juggling a multitude of other economic policy requirements. However, associating himself with Weatherstone, he expressed his opposition to establishing rigid rules or formulas for official intervention. Any formula-dependent intervention policy sooner or later will result in some discernible pattern of central bank intervention, thus providing private economic agents with an opportunity to speculate profitably at the expense of the taxpayer.

Egon Sohmen, referring to Schmidt's mention of the Federal Reserve's having been exclusively in spot markets, questioned the rationale behind the apparent reluctance to intervene in forward markets. It would appear that, especially for the Federal Reserve System—a central bank that does not carry an inventory of foreign currencies—almost everything would speak in favor of (perhaps even exclusive reliance on) intervention in forward markets, letting interest arbitrage bring the spot market back in line.

Moreover, it has been mentioned that the longer-term forward markets, those beyond one year, are rather thin. Therefore, it might be a good idea for the Federal Reserve to build up more resilience in the forward markets for long maturities by intervening mostly or, perhaps, exclusively even in those markets which now almost do not exist as real markets. Sohmen stressed the point that the confidentiality requirements would especially speak in favor of intervening in forward markets, since this mode of intervention would make it unnecessary for the Federal Reserve Board to ask for, and for other central banks to lend, swap funds that are usually required for intervention in the spot market.

In a comprehensive response to Sohmen, Pardee acknowledged that the Federal Reserve System has not conducted any operations in the forward exchange market for its own account since the 1960s. At that time the system achieved its objectives and made handsome profits in the process. One can also find several examples of successful intervention in forward markets by foreign monetary authorities, an excellent example of successful forward market intervention being the Danish episode of 1972.

In 1972, on the eve of the referendum on the question of Danish entry into the European Economic Community (EEC), one of the subsidiary issues that arose was the necessity of devaluing the kroner if the "nays" should win. The kroner fell under heavy speculative pressure. The Danish National Bank, in order to relieve the pressure, launched a massive forward operation, knowing a date by which the operation would be complete and having a good guess about the outcome of the referendum. The referendum came out in favor of joining the EEC, the kroner did not have to be devalued, and the central bank made some $40 million in profits.

By no means, however, can all attempts at intervening in forward markets be considered success stories. In 1967, the intervention by the Bank of England in the pound forward market was a failure. The reason for that failure is clear; the authorities were using the forward market as a means of obtaining credit and, in the process, were providing an open-ended cover to the market.

Pardee emphasized the point that even when the forward market intervention is executed properly, unforeseen side effects often render it impracticable. In 1971, for example, the Federal Reserve carried out an operation in the forward market on behalf of the Bundesbank, who wanted to widen the discount on the mark so as to align it with the prevailing interest rate differential. In order to close just a portion of the gap between the discount and the interest arbitrage differential, the Federal Reserve was forced to sell forward very substantial amounts of marks. To its dismay it found out that those cheap marks were purchased to finance trade between third countries.

It follows from these examples that intervention in forward markets is more dangerous than intervention in spot markets; it requires drawing a clear picture of what the objectives are and what possible side effects may be produced. This does not mean, concluded Pardee, that intervention in forward markets is always undesirable; it means that so much caution has to be exercised both in its planning and execution that, for the time being at least, the Federal Reserve System prefers to limit its intervention to the spot market.

On Proper Criteria for Gauging Intervention Policies

Dennis Logue initiated a discussion on this subject with a reminder that intervention in foreign exchange markets is a type of intertemporal arbitrage. He suggested that a proper criterion for judging the effectiveness of intervention is whether the central bank makes profits in its efforts to lean against the wind, and, therefore, to minimize the variability of exchange rates. If the central bank correctly anticipates future events and correctly evaluates new information, on average it should end up making some profits. The Federal Reserve System made $18 million in 1975. However, what really matters is not the absolute magnitude of profits but the return on committed funds.

For instance, New York Stock Exchange specialists, during the late 1960s and very early 1970s, made between 25 and 100 percent on invested capital doing largely the same type of intertemporal arbitrage that the Federal Reserve engaged in. This invested capital included their office space, the value of the seat on the New York Stock Exchange (which, at the time, was about $450,000), and equipment. The performance of private intertemporal arbitrageurs can be used as a gauge for measuring the Fed's performance.

Pardee expressed strong opposition to the use of profitability of intervention operations as a basis for assessing the Fed's performance. He pointed out that if the system were in the market to make profits, it could do a very good job by deliberately creating disorderly conditions in the markets and then exploiting them to its own advantage. What the Fed is trying to do is to maximize the social welfare function which, in the present context, means to maintain orderly market conditions, not to maximize trading profits.

The Fed tries to run a technically efficient trading operation and wants to avoid losses. However, because of certain constraints on its actions (such as deadlines for repaying swap debts), the Fed may be compelled to endure interim losses, as it happened in the first half of 1975. Although the Federal Reserve System makes profits more frequently than it suffers losses, Pardee would not use profitability as the appropriate criterion for judging the effectiveness of its intervention.

Schmidt reminded us that in his paper presented earlier in the session he had defended the need for comparing the Fed's profit rate on intervention operations with the average rate of profit to private traders. He recognized, however, that Logue's comment covers a broader issue and opens up a different road of research on the question of intervention. He pointed out that funds invested by the Federal Reserve System ought to pay a social rate of return. Part of that return may well consist of removing or thwarting disorder in foreign exchange markets, but part of it is the cost of capital to the Treasury. Schmidt charged academic economists with neglecting this issue. He brought up the example of experts in the field of economic development who forced upon the World Bank and the International Development Agency methods of computation of the social rate of return that take into account both direct benefits and externalities. He appealed to research economists to approach the problem of intervention with a similar rigor and precision.

Jacob Dreyer remarked that the cost of supporting the dollar, and some other currencies, is borne not only by the Federal Reserve System but to a large extent by a number of foreign central banks. The total collective cost of intervention is not known, so that it would be extremely difficult to calculate the relevant rate of profit, let alone the social rate of return. Besides, if the cost of intervention to particular countries (especially West Germany and Switzerland) were known, their parliaments could set a cost limit on intervention. The point should not be disregarded that imposition of such a limit could be highly detrimental to the liberty of central banks to intervene (in support of the dollar, among others).

William Fellner agreed with the arguments behind what had been put forward by Logue and Schmidt. If the rationale underlying intervention policy is to support currencies that are too low in some reasonably definable sense and to depress the exchange rates of currencies that are too high in some reasonably definable sense, then profitability is, indeed, the proper criterion for determining whether a central bank is conducting its policy right or wrong. Moreover, the data on profitability of intervention operations should not be withheld from those who wish to appraise the effectiveness of central banks' policies.

Information and Disclosure

Fellner's last remark prompted an exchange, largely between Logue and Pardee, on the influence of confidentiality and disclosure on the behavior of both central banks and private participants in the market.

In Logue's view the variability of exchange rates is mostly related to the variability in government policy and the variability in expectations regarding future government policy. To the extent that the Fed largely makes financial policy within the country, it may very well be thought that its intervention in the foreign exchange market is a signal as to what that policy is likely to be.

If that is true, then it is not so much the intervention itself that makes a difference in controlling the volatility of the foreign exchange market, as it is the information conveyed by that intervention. It seems that the same goal can perhaps be achieved in a less costly way, by simply having the chairman of the Federal Reserve Board or the president of the New York's Federal Reserve Bank announce that they think the policy should be such and such—that is, removing the secrecy around the open-market-committee type of decisions.

Pardee argued that announcements contemplated by Logue are equivalent to reestablishing fixed exchange rates. He would prefer to have the market function on its own and to limit the role of the central bank to the provision of some guidance and reassurance of its presence in the market, of its resolve to resist a precipitous drop or a steep rise in the exchange rate. Detailed disclosure of policy targets would place monetary authorities in the center-stage of the market, where, according to Pardee, they do not belong.

Rutledge pointed out that making the public privy to the information available to monetary authorities should result in reduced volatility of exchange rates. The same information known to all market participants will, through the operation of the law of large numbers, secure the prevalence of average outcomes over extreme outcomes.

Logue expressed astonishment at Pardee's insistence on not disclosing certain information in the government's possession and on not disclosing its plans and intentions. He stressed the point that the foreign exchange market does not differ substantially from other markets—the market for goods, the market for corporate stock, the market for corporate bonds. Government policy has generally been to encourage the disclosure of material information pertaining to the values of those assets. The Department of Agriculture provides extensive crop reports, forecasts of crop harvestings; the SEC encourages corporate disclosure as to earnings or material events which have occurred within any company or, indeed, are likely to occur in the company. The presumption is that this makes for not only a more efficient but also, perhaps, a more equitable market. Logue thought it was somewhat counterproductive for the Federal Reserve System to pursue a policy which is in contradiction with other government policies.

Pardee disagreed that the foreign exchange market and other markets are similar in every respect. The main difference is that the major market for every currency is not in the United States; it is in foreign countries. Cooperation with other central banks is, therefore, absolutely indispensable if the Fed is to conduct its intervention operations effectively. But in order to secure close working relationships with those banks, the Fed has to maintain the same confidentiality they do. However, Pardee noted wryly, the United Kingdom has the Official Secrets Act and Canada has the Official Secrets Act, while the United States has the Freedom of Information Act. As a result the reporting responsibilities of the Fed to the Congress and the general public are much more extensive than those of other central banks to their legislatures and their people. Any more disclosure on the part of the Federal Reserve System would fail to accommodate the much more restrictive views on confidentiality of other central banks.

Concluding the debate, Schmidt voiced his doubts about the Fed's having special information not available to private traders. In support of his opinion he once again quoted a passage from a speech by a former under secretary of the Treasury for monetary affairs, Jack Bennett, who, in response to a suggestion that there be firmer management of foreign exchange markets, had said: "I've worked long enough as a bureaucrat to know that there is no special wisdom accorded officials which is not available to other market participants. Government intervenors would have no special powers of foresight." [1]

---

[1] Speech, Boston Economic Club, October 1, 1975 (mimeo.).

PART THREE

INTERNATIONAL TRADE AND INVESTMENT UNDER FLEXIBLE EXCHANGE RATES

THE ECONOMIC IMPLICATIONS OF EXISTING ACCOUNTING STANDARDS

With Special Reference to the New Standards for Multinationals

Joseph M. Burns

Existing accounting standards have been coming under increasing attack. The criticism has typically not been directed at the logic of the rulings of the Financial Accounting Standards Board or its predecessor, the Accounting Principles Board. Rather, the criticism has in general been directed at the relevance or realism of the rulings. Indeed, the reliance on generally accepted accounting principles, and consequently on the use of historical data, has become a source of great concern in the current environment of inflation and price uncertainty.

In an ideal state of accounting, all assets and liabilities—financial and nonfinancial—would be reported at their current value in end-of-period reporting statements, with adjustments by a general price index where appropriate. Such a system of accounting—economic value accounting—would ensure a perfect correspondence between accounting data and economic values.

Needless to say, for some assets and liabilities, this concept of accounting—economic value accounting—would be very difficult to implement. In particular, for fixed assets and inventories, *inter alia*, conceptual problems as well as measurement problems would exist. These problems are the primary reason why historical cost accounting for some items has persisted for so long.

Under existing accounting standards, reported or accounting values are not necessarily the same as the economic values to which they refer. Furthermore, and of greater significance, the expected accounting values

When this paper was written, the author, who is now director of research of the Commodity Futures Trading Commission, was deputy director of monetary research in the Office of Assistant Secretary for International Affairs of the U.S. Treasury Department. The views expressed are solely those of the author and are not to be attributed to the Commodity Futures Trading Commission or the U.S. Treasury Department.

This presentation is a summary of the paper presented at the conference. The conference paper has been incorporated as chapters 1 and 2 and the last two sections of chapter 3 of the author's study, *Accounting Standards and International Finance: with Special Reference to Multinationals* (Washington, D.C.: American Enterprise Institute, 1976).

are not necessarily the same as the expected economic values to which they refer. Indeed, as this study points out, it would be fortuitous if these values were the same. This discrepancy between accounting data and economic values (on both a realized and an expected basis) is likely to have some serious consequences—for the individual firm as well as for the national and international economic scene.

For the firm, the discrepancy between accounting data and economic values induces corporate managers to make wrong (nonoptimal) decisions. In addition, it impairs the ability of corporate directors to exercise effective control over the corporation. The introduction or enlargement of a discrepancy between accounting data and economic values by accounting standards—such as the new standards for multinationals— thus induces corporate managers to alter their decision making away from their optimal plan. The economic cost of discrepancies between accounting data and economic values has become increasingly burdensome.

For the international economy, investment by multinationals has likely been curtailed as a result of the new standards, and the allocation of resources for a given volume of investment has been distorted. In addition, the new standards have introduced a bias against a floating rate system. This bias is unfortunate in view of the greater benefits that multinationals realize under floating rates than they do under an adjustable peg system of fixed rates.[1]

The principal conclusions are: (1) the new accounting standards appear to have caused some serious economic problems; (2) the new accounting system with its uniformity of treatment may, nevertheless, be preferable in certain respects to the old system which permitted numerous standards to exist simultaneously; (3) the new standards are not capricious, but—taken as a whole—are rather carefully based on generally accepted accounting principles; (4) some of the generally accepted accounting principles appear to be outmoded in our current environment of inflation and price uncertainty; and (5) the introduction of economic value accounting appears to be the only way of mitigating the problems arising under existing accounting standards.

There are many difficult practical problems associated with economic value accounting. Despite the difficulties, and despite the fact that we are living in an age of uncertainty (indeed, largely because of that fact), it would be preferable to have figures which are reasonably accurate rather than to continue the use of figures which are assuredly wrong.

---

[1] My larger study analyzes the comparative advantages of fixed and floating rate systems, with special reference to the benefits and costs of hedging through futures markets. See Joseph M. Burns, *Accounting Standards and International Finance: with Special Reference to Multinationals* (Washington, D.C.: American Enterprise Institute, 1976), chapter 3.

EXPOSURE MANAGEMENT UNDER FLOATING RATES

Alan Teck

After discussing exposure management activities during and after the Bretton Woods period, this paper refers to selected aspects of the Financial Accounting Standards Board's Statement No. 8 and indicates how the exposure management practices of many multinational companies are likely to evolve in the future.

The discussion is devoted almost entirely to the activities of U.S. multinational corporations. Accounting principles, tax legislation, institutional arrangements, the regulatory environment and exposure management practices are significantly different in most other countries.

Early Bretton Woods

It seems appropriate to divide a discussion of exposure management under the Bretton Woods system into two sections: the first period includes all events preceding the devaluation of the pound sterling in November 1967; the second section deals with subsequent years ending in August 1971.

During the earlier period, the value of most currencies fluctuated within 2 percent of official exchange rates, with occasional parity changes. Exposed assets and liabilities denominated in foreign currencies were typically translated into the currency of the parent company at constant reference rates so that currency movements within the official limits did not affect the consolidated accounts. Exchange gains and losses on transactions were generally treated as ordinary income or ordinary expense because they were usually not large enough to warrant special accounting treatment.

Financial officers, to the extent that they were concerned with exposure management at all, typically extended their domestic cash management techniques to international operations. To reduce exposure, working capital was kept to a minimum by reducing float, collecting receivables as rapidly as the competitive situation would permit, and minimizing inventories where prices on finished goods could not be increased to offset losses related to currency depreciation. In countries with chronically weak currencies, many companies took more aggressive steps by borrowing the local currency whenever possible almost without regard to cost in order to establish net liability positions. Interest costs were treated as any other ordinary expense, and the financial officer could highlight the translation gains as extraordinary items. In developing countries with virtually no local capital markets, companies generally tried to convert their profits into U.S. dollars and to remit them to the parent company as quickly as possible.

During the early Bretton Woods period, the U.S. dollar was generally thought to be a strong currency. It was widely assumed that the U.S. balance of payments deficits, which became especially large in the early 1960s, were temporary and easily reversible, particularly in view of the Interest Equalization Tax, the Voluntary Credit Restraint, and the Office of Foreign Direct Investment programs that started in 1963 through 1965. Based on this assumption, many U.S. companies were willing to borrow abroad as the OFDI required, especially currencies such as the Swiss franc and deutsche mark which offered significantly lower interest rates than those available in the United States.

Exposure management for specific transactions was also less aggressive during the early Bretton Woods period than in the later era. Leading and lagging receivables and payables were not common practices, except for companies operating in countries with especially weak currencies. Credit terms were typically established in accord with the competitive environment, and payment schedules were followed to maintain good credit standings. When a foreign subsidiary or branch was permitted to build up intercompany payables, it was usually to finance foreign expansion rather than for purposes of exposure management.

Transactions for hedging in foreign exchange markets were also less common under the early fixed rate period than they would become subsequently. Most financial officers dealt only in spot markets, accepting small currency swings as a matter of course, although some astute treasurers with payments or receipts in particular foreign currencies would regularly buy or sell those currencies in the forward exchange market to take advantage of premiums or discounts. During this period, the foreign exchange trading departments of U.S. commercial banks were primarily service departments executing routine spot and forward transactions. Even during the years immediately preceding the sterling devaluation in 1967, most multinational companies spent more time adjusting to trade and capital controls than they did implementing the exposure management practices that were to evolve subsequently.

Later Bretton Woods

The sterling devaluation in November 1967 is often regarded as an important watershed in the Bretton Woods period. The 14.3 percent decline of the world's second most important trading and reserve currency was followed almost immediately by realignments of over twenty currencies and during the next two years by parity changes of the deutsche mark, the French franc, and several other currencies. It had finally become apparent that the resources held by private market participants and the ability of companies and banks to shift those resources rapidly among currencies could no longer be contained by prolonged central bank intervention, despite the sizable credit arrangements that had been developed.

The sterling devaluation made many financial officers aware of the need to become more concerned with the possible effects of currency changes. Those who had been properly protected did not want to be exposed to the possibility of subsequent currency movements, and those who had suffered losses did not want to lose again. This noticeable change in attitude was an important precursor of other developments in exposure management techniques.

First, the time devoted to exposure management tended to be significantly increased, and the areas of concern were broadened to include not only current exposure problems but also longer-term currency risks associated with foreign borrowing, budgeting, and offshore expansion.

Second, many financial officers began to consider alternative accounting procedures for defining translation exposure. During this period, companies began shifting from the current-noncurrent method to the net financial method (including long-term debt as exposed) or to the monetary-nonmonetary method (essentially including long-term debt and excluding inventory) to bring exposures into more balanced or into net liability positions. Some companies even began defining translation exposure differently for operations in different countries.

Third, the use of reserves for booking exchange gains and losses became increasingly common. Many companies adopted the conservative method of charging losses to income as they occurred and deferring unrealized gains until they materialized. However, it must also be noted that some companies misused their reserves by arbitrarily reducing them when additional profits were desired (explaining to auditors that the currency risk and, therefore, the need for reserves had diminished) and adding to reserves when profits were strong (arguing that currency risks had risen and that it was prudent to increase reserves).

137

Fourth, many financial officers began devoting more attention to international cash management as currency movements (mostly downward against the dollar during this period) increased the cost of maintaining excessive working capital at foreign locations. Such practices as reducing float with increased use of wire transfers and lock boxes, tighter control over receivables and inventories, and improved use of cash balances with netting and pooling systems became progressively more important as efforts were made to apply standard domestic cash management techniques to international operations. In addition, cash management activities that were uniquely international were applied more frequently. For example, many companies became sensitive to the desirability of denominating payables in weaker currencies and receivables in harder currencies. Leading and lagging became progressively more widespread. (Interestingly, some intercompany leading and lagging was done not by central direction but rather by profit centers trying to take advantage of other profit centers within the same company.) But for most companies the systematic application of international cash management techniques was still the exception rather than the rule.

Fifth, it became increasingly common policy to estimate the effects of possible currency movements when calculating the costs and risks associated with alternatives for foreign borrowing. Unfortunately, as proven by large exchange losses suffered on long-term debt denominated in Swiss francs and deutsche marks, these estimates were no better than the assumptions upon which they were based. Many treasurers began evaluating break-even matrixes to determine what currency change multiplied by the probability of its occurrence would offset the cost advantage of denominating debt in a particular currency. During this period, a few simple computer models were developed to make these calculations so the financial officer could rapidly quantify his expectations. In most cases, the computations were quite elementary, employing single point currency projections for particular points in time ("a 25 percent chance of a 10 percent devaluation in six months") rather than probability distributions or weighted averages for a number of future dates.

Despite these and other developments, most financial officers were still managing their exposures superficially and irregularly during the latter Bretton Woods period, ignoring exposures most of the time and rushing to hedge in the forward exchange markets during periods of crisis. Financial reports to the parent company were generally denominated in U.S. dollars rather than in the local currency; it was still a rarity to report separately on assets and liabilities in third currencies; exposure management responsibilities were still largely decentralized; and companies rarely considered tax effects when measuring their exposures or making hedging decisions. Although there was a growing awareness that costs and risks were associated with alternative protection strategies, systematically adjusting assets and liabilities or using the money markets for exposure management was still the exception. However, towards the end of the Bretton Woods period tensions were mounting rapidly, and by 1971 many financial officers considered exposure management to be one of their most important concerns.

After Bretton Woods

When the dollar was devalued in 1971, most U.S. multinational corporations were fortunate in having positive working capital positions in most or all of their foreign locations. They experienced windfall gains. Then, following the chaotic conditions of the Smithsonian system, most U.S. companies again experienced translation gains when the dollar was devalued in February 1973. Further gains were realized when the dollar continued to decline through mid-1973 as the currency markets were buffeted by the Watergate affair and other problems. Of course, companies with negative working capital positions experienced losses during this period; but these organizations were in the minority. Companies with long-term debt denominated in Swiss francs, deutsche marks, or other strong currencies ultimately incurred substantial losses; but at that time only a few companies included long-term debt as part of their defined exposure. Indeed, during that period it was still typical for companies to defer rather than accrue unrealized exchange losses related to long-term borrowing.

Although most U.S. companies experienced windfall gains from the parity changes in 1971 and 1973, these developments produced a sharply increased awareness of the problems associated with having assets and liabilities in foreign currencies. Many multinational companies accelerated activities that were already under way and considered new methods to improve their exposure management. Awareness of the problem was further increased in 1974 as the dollar began to rise as well as fall and to move in different directions against different currencies.

Some of the adjustments in exposure management practices that U.S. companies began making under floating exchange rates are discussed below, although the extent to which companies implemented these adjustments varied widely. Some organizations began altering their exposure management practices during the Bretton Woods and Smithsonian systems; others have started only recently; and still other companies have not yet made many of the adjustments.

One development that gained momentum during the Smithsonian period and early in the floating rate era was a significantly increased concern with translation (balance sheet) exposure. As previously observed, during the Bretton Woods period, exchange fluctuations had no translation effect as long as currency movements were within 2 percent limits. In most cases, the reference rates at which foreign currency accounts were translated into dollars remained stable. Gains and losses caused by parity changes were treated as extraordinary items. Also, the losses were often offset by gains on the protective exchange contracts.

By contrast, currency movements under floating rates were often substantial from one accounting period to the next. It was frequently necessary to change the reference rates with which accounts were consolidated, or to use current rates for translating selected assets and liabilities. For most companies, the *unrealized* gains and losses experienced when assets and liabilities denominated in foreign currencies were translated into U.S. dollars for consolidating financial statements far exceeded the *realized* gains and losses resulting from maturing transactions. In addition, the impact of translating sales at an average exchange rate and the cost of goods sold at either current or historical rates also introduced large fluctuations into the profits of each accounting period. These movements, combined with the realization that the value of the dollar might rise as well as fall, caused many companies to alter their definition of exposed assets in an effort to minimize the translation effect of currency swings. There was a noticeable shift from the current method to some variation of the monetary-nonmonetary method of measuring exposure. Typically, exposed assets were reduced or shifted into net liability positions by valuing inventory at historical rates and long-term debt, or that portion coming due within the year, at current exchange rates.

A second development was that many financial officers began to differentiate more explicitly between translation and transaction exposures. The former recognizes foreign exchange gains and losses in the consolidated accounts even though such gains and losses are not actually realized in the same accounting period, while exchange gains and losses on transactions are both recognized and realized in the period in which the transaction matures. When the cost of protection is considered unduly high, treasurers often accept the possibility of unrealized losses and cover only their exposure to the risk of incurring realized or cash losses.

A third development was that many financial officers began to broaden their concept of measuring exposure to include *anticipated* transactions. It was realized that currency movements would directly affect the dollar value of anticipated foreign currency receipts and payments, even though the gains and losses would not be explicitly recognized in the accounting statements as related to exchange rate movements. For example, some companies began to consider backlog of orders from foreign customers as part of their exposure when they knew that they would subsequently receive payment in foreign currency for merchandise to be produced and shipped. These companies recognized that exposure risk begins when the order is received, rather than when the receivable is booked, and continues until the foreign currency is collected and converted into dollars. Thus, many companies broadened their concept of exposure to include concern for protecting future profits rather than just the value of specific assets and liabilities.

A fourth development under floating rates has been the constantly improving ability of many companies to apply some of the more advanced techniques of exposure management. Even as recently as the early 1970s it was not unusual to interview a financial officer who followed an extreme philosophy of exposure management: "We always hedge all exposures because we are in the business of making and selling products and not of speculating on currencies," or "We never hedge exposures because currencies move up and down and these movements tend to even out in the long run." Virtually all financial officers subsequently abandoned these extreme positions in favor of making judgments about the degree of risk to be taken compared with the cost of protection. Some corporations have developed formal exposure limits, with exposures exceeding these limits automatically covered regardless of cost. Other companies are less formal, making separate judgments about each exposure, with one person or a committee monitoring the positions in view of constantly changing currency expectations and hedging opportunities. Needless to say, the hedging decisions vary widely depending on how conservative or aggressive the management is in accepting risks.

To make the necessary judgments for measuring and managing exposure most companies had to improve their reporting and forecasting systems. This improvement has been a major achievement during the floating rate period. As late as 1971, many corporations were still receiving their foreign financial statements denominated in dollars. Subsequently most of these organizations began requiring that the foreign accounts be denominated in the local currency. In many cases, it was an easy next step to request that all third currency assets and liabilities be appropriately reported. For many financial officers, the U.S. Treasury requirement that exposures in excess of $1 million be reported monthly and quarterly was a welcome opportunity to obtain compliance with

141

the type of reporting procedures that had been long desired but not achieved.

A fifth development under floating rates has been the persistent trend toward greater centralization of exposure management. Most companies, although certainly not all, have become aware of the benefits of an integrated exposure management program. Five years ago, many financial officers claimed they could handle exposure management problems "on the back of an envelope." However, most corporations soon became aware of the significant complications in measuring the worldwide *after-tax* exposure in each currency, the subtleties of analyzing risk in an uncertain currency environment, and the numerous protection alternatives to be evaluated. The "back of the envelope" approach began giving way to more rigorous measurement and analytical methods, particularly as younger analysts entered the field.

Although U.S. companies using Chemical Bank's Foreign Exchange Advisory Service may be more assiduous about solving exposure problems than are most multinational corporations, the following paragraphs refer to the more progressive methods that many companies use and which others will undoubtedly adopt in the future. Though the observations refer to two computer models, it is not the models themselves that are important but rather the educational processes that they embody. The model and the underlying analytical process make it apparent that many companies have come a long way in a comparatively short time under floating rates.

One Chemical Bank model permits a company to evaluate its worldwide currency exposures in either accounting terms (translation exposure), cash terms (transaction exposure), or both. The company can use either actual or *pro forma* data, and, of course, the exposures can be evaluated in different ways for different purposes and different periods of time. The analysis can be either pretax or after-tax, because the model has reduced to clerical proportions the exceedingly complicated tax aspects of measuring and managing exposures. For example, the user can consider: the tax impact from either the accounting or the cash flow viewpoint, or both; the different tax consequences affecting subsidiaries and branches; and the tax effects both locally and upon consolidation of a foreign location's exposures denominated in currencies other than the local currency. The company can also evaluate other information required for analysis of exposures and alternative protection strategies such as the local borrowing costs, spot and forward exchange rates, and outstanding foreign exchange contracts. Measurement of exposure and estimation of gains and losses can be accomplished in conformity with the standards established by FAS No. 8.

With respect to the currency outlook, the user can indicate his "most likely" as well as his most optimistic and pessimistic currency forecasts for the periods being evaluated. A company can use Chemical Bank's currency projections, its own, or anyone else's projections. Regardless how numerous or involved the exposures may be—many companies have hundreds of exposures—the computer quickly indicates the company's consolidated, worldwide after-tax exposure in each currency. These numbers are of primary concern to a centralized exposure management system, although, of course, the user can look at individual transactions or locations if desired. The model then indicates the expected gain or loss in each currency from that day's spot rate or a reference rate to the "most likely" rate forecast for each currency. The risks associated with the exposures are also quantified by indicating the maximum possible loss that could be incurred at various confidence levels after considering the amount of each exposure, the most pessimistic currency forecasts, and the correlation of movements among the currencies. In other words, the user can anticipate the most likely gains or losses as well as the most pessimistic outcome that could occur if he leaves his exposures unprotected. Under floating rates, many companies have moved from reviewing exposures in terms of single-point currency forecasts to evaluating alternative currency forecasts and quantifying the risks associated with each.

If the user decides that either the "most likely" losses or the related risks are too great, strategies can be simulated to compare after-tax advantages, costs, and risks of remaining exposed with the alternatives of buying and selling currencies in the forward market, or of altering foreign assets and liabilities by using leads and lags, local borrowing and investing, or a wide range of other financial possibilities. The model indicates which simulated strategies provide the greatest protection at the least cost and minimum risk. In brief, the user can anticipate gains and losses and the after-tax effects of protective strategies using the standards of FAS No. 8 or any other criteria that his company might consider relevant.

As previously noted, however, for the purpose of this discussion the analytical process is more important than the model itself. It indicates that many of the underlying concepts—viewing exposure from a central focus, measuring exposure in different ways for different purposes, evaluating the cost of protection after taxes, explicitly considering risk, and comparing a range of alternative protection strategies—have been gaining more general acceptance.

Another increasingly important concern is how to evaluate long-term funding possibilities denominated in foreign currencies. When the

143

OFDI regulations were in effect, many companies borrowed Swiss francs and deutsche marks, which later appreciated very substantially against the dollar. Many of these loans are now maturing, and borrowers are no longer as naive about exchange risks as they were a few years ago. When evaluating options for refinancing these loans, financial officers explicitly consider exchange risks along with interest rates and other costs.

It is too early to know whether FAS No. 8 will discourage companies from using foreign financing that may otherwise have been desirable. FAS No. 8 requires that long-term debt denominated in foreign currencies be carried at current exchange rates, while the fixed assets that such borrowing often finances be carried at historical rates. As an example of how at least some companies are evaluating the effect of expected currency movements on the cost of long-term debt, the following paragraph refers to Chemical Bank's computer model called ALTDET (Alternative Debt Evaluator). Again, it is the analytical process rather than the model itself that is important.

ALTDET permits the user to compare borrowing options denominated in U.S. dollars or in other currencies for any number of time periods. The user can enter any takedown schedule, any payback schedule, expected interest rates and other costs, tax assumptions, and any exchange rate forecasts. For each borrowing alternative considerable information can be obtained including net cash flow by period, costs by period, and the overall cost of each loan based on the derived internal rate of return. Sensitivity analyses may be performed to evaluate alternative exchange rate and interest rate forecasts.

A sixth development during the floating rate era is that many companies, while improving their exposure management techniques are exploring and implementing other aspects of international cash management. In most cases, this involves integrating well-known domestic cash management techniques with the additional considerations required by different national regulations, institutional arrangements, and currency risks. However, although considerable advances have been made in exposure management practices, most companies have yet to develop their international cash management activities to the fullest extent. These activities can be expected to receive considerable attention in coming years.

As requests for foreign exchange and exposure management advice have increased, so has the supply of advisory services. Many corporations, in addition to developing their own expertise, have turned increasingly to commercial banks for advice. Most banks have responded by assigning foreign exchange traders, economists, or territory officers to handle inquiries and requests. Realizing that foreign exchange traders typically have a short-term perspective, that economists have a longer-term perspective, and that territory lending officers often have no specialized foreign exchange training, some banks have developed groups of specialists to deal with technical exposure management problems that require an intermediate- as well as a longer-term outlook.

Currency forecasting services have also proliferated, ranging widely in size and ability. Most recently, a number of organizations in the United States and abroad have been using econometric models to produce currency forecasts. Although most of these models, despite the claims of their creators, have yet to produce useful results, the best are potentially capable of providing interesting insights into the forecasting process. These services will undoubtedly continue to increase, and the best of them will help improve the ability of corporations to operate under floating rates.

Recent Developments and Attitudes

The results of a questionnaire recently sent to 400 U.S. multinational corporations by Professors Michael Jilling and William Folks, Jr. in the Department of Economics at the University of South Carolina shed light on a few recent trends in exposure management.[1] They also underscore the tremendous diversity that still exists in the attitudes, concepts, and practices of companies in relation to managing their exposures. The following paragraphs comment on a few of the findings.

A fifteen-page questionnaire was sent to corporations defined as having multinational company status (MNC): equity positions of at least 25 percent in companies located in six or more foreign countries. The questions are organized into six broad categories: company characteristics, exchange rate forecasting, exposure definition and analysis, design and evaluation of defensive strategies, implementation of defensive strategies, and an opinion questionnaire.

Highlights of the company characteristics section indicate that of the 107 responding corporations, 50 had annual sales exceeding $1 billion, 32 had sales between $300 million and $1 billion, and 25 between $90 and $300 million. About 25 percent are "old MNCs," having satisfied the definition before 1960, with the rest having become MNCs since that date. The ratio of foreign-to-total sales is under 20 percent for one-quarter of the respondents, between 20 and 40 percent for about half, and over 40 percent for the rest.

---

[1] Michael Jilling and William R. Folks, Jr., *Foreign Exchange Risk Management Project: Working Paper #1* (Center of International Business Studies, College of Business, University of South Carolina, May 1976).

The paper reports three interesting findings relative to company characteristics: first, over 40 percent of the respondents claimed that their exposure management responsibilities have become more centralized during the past five years. In fact, only two corporations indicated less centralization. Second, although this survey was taken many months after the Financial Accounting Standards Board's preliminary draft of statement No. 8 had been circulated, and just a few months before the final statement was released, only 5 percent of the respondents indicated that they were using the temporal accounting definition for measuring exposure. Moreover, over 65 percent replied that current rates were being used for consolidating inventory. Third, most of the executives responsible for exposure management claimed to be devoting less than 25 percent of their time to this function; although the questionnaire does not indicate how much staff time was being spent on this activity. Although the responses have not yet been analyzed in correlation to corporate size, the experience of Chemical Bank's Foreign Exchange Advisory Group has been that most intermediate and large companies devote more than 25 percent of one person's time to exposure management.

Among the interesting findings is that almost all respondents felt that foreign exchange risks had become more of a problem in the past five years and could no longer be ignored. Almost half thought that the dollar devaluations of 1971 and 1973 aroused their senior management to the need for currency forecasts, and over 60 percent indicated an increased commitment to exposure management since 1970. Though most recipients (67 percent) claimed to have gained increased expertise in exposure management since 1971, less than half (42 percent) felt that they had become more skilled in currency forecasting. Almost half thought that currency forecasting was still the weakest link in their exposure management program. In most companies the fear of loss from foreign exchange fluctuations greatly exceeds the hope for gain, and 73 percent of the respondents concluded that exposure should be reduced to acceptable levels before a decision is made about whether the remainder should be covered. These responses complement other studies indicating that virtually all companies view exposure management from a defensive rather than a speculative standpoint.

The questionnaire reports that almost all of the companies make exchange rate forecasts for each currency in which they have exposure. More than half make these forecasts either monthly or quarterly: 37 percent forecast direction only, 30 percent a point estimate for one or more future dates, 8 percent a range, 2 percent a probability distribution, and 13 percent use a combination of methods. Though only 42 percent thought that they had become more skilled at currency forecasting, half considered themselves either "satisfied" or "strongly satisfied" with their forecasts since 1971.

Questionnaire responses relative to defining and analyzing exposure and implementing defensive strategies reflect a wide range of activities. For example, though about 70 percent of the companies computed their exposures monthly or quarterly, almost half of the respondents indicated that they *never* considered more than balance sheet exposure when evaluating their operations in foreign currencies. Questionnaire replies relative to defensive measures for periods exceeding six months indicate that although a wide range of strategies was employed, the most satisfactory way to reduce exposure was to adjust current liabilities in foreign currencies. Among defensive strategies for periods of less than six months, using forward exchange markets, adjusting remittances to the parent company, and altering local currency borrowing were considered the best techniques. These measures are among the easiest to implement rapidly. However, since only 40 percent of the respondents reported that they compared the cost of altering their assets and liabilities with the expense of forward cover, it is clear that the majority does not do so. Well over half observed that they "seldom" or "never" hedge transactions denominated in foreign currencies.

The 27 percent response to the questionnaire, a particularly large response in view of its length and complexity, suggests a high degree of concern with exposure management and a widespread awareness of the central problems. And the replies generally indicate that the knowledge with which companies of all types and sizes approach their exposure problems is probably greater today than ever before.

Financial Accounting Standards Board's Statement No. 8

FAS No. 8 has further increased the concern of management, shareholders, and the investment community over the impact of currency fluctuations. For many companies, this standard increases the volatility of reported profits, results in prudent actions being mislabeled "speculative," and causes management to take action for accounting purposes that is contrary to good business judgment. Unfortunately, some of the distortions created by FAS No. 8 will probably be mistaken to be difficulties of adjusting to floating rates. Three points illustrate the type of problems that have been created.

First, by prohibiting the use of reserves for absorbing exchange gains and losses, FAS No. 8 introduces greater volatility into reported profits. With the investment community preferring relatively stable and predictable growth, the increased volatility often results in reduced price-earning ratios and lower security prices. This, in turn, increases the cost of capital for many companies. In addition, many financial officers tend to incur otherwise unnecessary expenses to avoid gyrations in reported profits that might be difficult to explain to senior management, shareholders, and security analysts. A high disutility is often attached to maintaining exposed positions even when remaining exposed might be the appropriate strategy. It would probably have been less confusing and certainly less costly to the business community to permit the continued use of reserves for smoothing unrealized exchange gains and losses, with the flows into and out of reserves being thoroughly disclosed in the accounting statements.[2]

Second, hedging against the risk of exchange losses related to having an *expected* payment or receipt denominated in a foreign currency is an example of how FAS No. 8 can cause prudent actions to be viewed as "speculative." For instance, if a company has plans to sell a warehouse in Germany at the end of the year and prudently uses the forward exchange markets to sell the deutsche marks that it expects to receive, auditors interpreting FAS No. 8 are likely to deem the exchange contract to be "speculative." According to FAS No. 8, gains and losses on the exchange contract must be booked in each accounting period, while in the same accounting period there would be no offsetting entries for the expected transaction. This treatment of anticipated and off–balance-sheet exposures increases swings in quarterly profits and tends to discourage defensive actions.

Third, perhaps the best example of how FAS No. 8 can make profits more volatile while discouraging prudent activity and accentuating differences between accounting and economic decisions is found in the treatment of assets and liabilities appearing in the financial statements at the exchange rates in effect on the day they were acquired. Probably the most discussed asset in this category is inventory, although there are similar problems with fixed assets.

By requiring that inventory be booked at historical exchange rates, FAS No. 8 creates a situation in which exchange gains and losses related to inventory are passed through the income statement over time through

---

[2] Other countries that have followed the U.S. lead in developing more uniform accounting standards for transactions in foreign currencies and for the translation of foreign financial statements have permitted greater flexibility in defining exposures and in permitting the use of reserves in certain situations. For example, see "Exposure Draft 21: Accounting for Foreign Currency Transactions," issued by the Accounting Standards Committee of the Institute of Chartered Accountants in England and Wales, and "Financial Accounting Standard on Consolidated Financial Statements," issued by the Business Accounting Deliberation Council, Ministry of Finance, Japan.

cost of goods sold rather than being reflected during the period in which the exchange rate changes occur. The logic of accounting for inventory at historical rates (at the lower of cost or market) is based on the assumption that if the value of a foreign currency declines, a company can raise its prices on finished goods to offset the effects of the devaluation. However, many companies cannot raise prices on finished goods just because a foreign currency has depreciated, either because of the competitive environment or because of local regulations. For these companies, inventories denominated in foreign currencies are exposed to the impact of a depreciation. The parent company's income is reduced even though the loss is not explicitly recognized as a foreign exchange loss under the definitions of FAS No. 8. A company faced with this situation must decide whether or not to include inventory in its definition of exposure, and whether or not to protect that exposure against anticipated losses.

Although the ultimate cash effect on profits is the same regardless whether inventory is booked at current or historical rates, the treatment of inventory Statement No. 8 increases the volatility of reported profits and influences management decisions in at least two ways: when sales are translated at average exchange rates and the cost of goods sold at historical exchange rates, the result gives a misleading impression of operating profits in each accounting period. Based on translated financial statements, it is virtually impossible for management to compare the profitability of different locations and different product lines. In many cases, an additional set of financial records must be provided in which both sales and cost of goods sold are booked at the same exchange rates. Similar distortions occur when depreciation is recorded in the income statement at historical exchange rates.

A financial officer who anticipates a decline in the value of his inventories when translated into the currency of the parent company, and expects that the loss cannot be recouped by raising prices on finished goods, might consider it prudent to hedge the exposed inventory using the forward exchange markets. However, FAS No. 8 deems such exchange contracts to be "speculative" and, therefore, tends to discourage protective action. Gains or losses on the forward exchange contract pass through the income statement each month with no offsetting gain or loss on the inventory being covered. Recently, the Financial Accounting Standards Board "Interpretation 17" underscores how far the board has removed inventory from the effects of currency changes. "Interpretation 17" states that if currency movements require inventory to be written down to market value, the reduction is to be treated as an unusual charge to "other expenses" rather than as a foreign exchange loss.

FAS No. 8 has undoubtedly increased the concern that U.S. multinational companies have with regard to their foreign exchange exposures. But whether that concern will produce more appropriate exposure management strategies remains to be seen. Because FAS No. 8 highlights the accounting effects of unrealized exchange gains and losses, the initial result has been to shift attention away from the underlying cash effects of exchange rate movements. However, many financial officers are already directing their attention back to the possible cash effects related to having receipts and payments as well as inventory and fixed assets denominated in foreign currencies. This trend toward renewed emphasis on the cash effects of currency movements appears likely to continue.

Conclusion

The huge and increasing amounts of liquid resources held by private market participants and the many methods by which these funds can be shifted rapidly between currencies make a continuing system of floating exchange rates inevitable. Although intervention by monetary authorities can mitigate currency movements for brief periods, shifting exchange rates will continue to be the predominant characteristic of the currency environment as long as the business cycles and external accounts of different nations continue to move at different rates.

Most U.S. multinational companies have already made considerable progress adjusting to floating exchange rates, despite a wide diversity of attitudes and practices. Even with the difficulties posed by FAS No. 8, recent trends suggest that the ability to define currency exposures comprehensively and to obtain protection against the risks associated with floating exchange rates is likely to continue improving.

INTERNATIONAL TRADE AND INVESTMENT UNDER FLOATING RATES

The Reaction of Business to the Floating Rate System

James Burtle and Sean Mooney

After spending more than three years on the sea of floating rates, it is time to evaluate the experience of business under this system, particularly to ask whether businessmen are now all experienced sailors on a smooth sea between the Charybdis of depreciations and the Scylla of appreciations—or whether they remain a group of seasick landlubbers searching for a haven of fixed, or at least viscous, exchange rates.

The impact of floating exchange rates on the international trade of goods and capital might be evaluated in three different ways: by direct empirical research of trade and investment development following the establishment of floating rates in March 1973; by directly surveying businessmen; and by determining the relative costs of doing business under the new system versus the costs incurred under the Bretton Woods system.

Empirical Analysis of U.S. Trade and Investment

The present flexible rate system has not been in effect long enough to test adequately the results it may have for international commerce. Since March 1973, when widespread floating began, there have been extraordinary upheavals on the international front, such as the OPEC oil price hikes, the commodity boom, followed by a sharp decline in commodity prices, and the world recession. These factors have made it difficult, if not impossible, to determine by direct empirical inquiry the impact of a single factor, in this case the increased volatility of exchange rates, on international trade and investment. Econometric evidence that exchange rate variability has, in fact, not seriously affected world trade is provided by John Makin, but his results are not conclusive.[1]

---

[1] John Makin, "Eurocurrencies and the Evolution of the International Monetary System," in Carl H. Stern, John H. Makin, and Dennis E. Logue, eds., *Eurocurrencies and the International Monetary System* (Washington, D.C.: American Enterprise Institute, 1976).

Surveys of Business Executives

Because data on trade and investment patterns are inconclusive, we turn our attention to the more direct but less objective survey approach. Four surveys have been conducted on the attitudes of businessmen toward floating exchange rates—by Norman Fieleke of the Federal Reserve Bank of Boston,[2] by the Conference Board,[3] by Folks and Jilling of the University of South Carolina,[4] and by the National Association of Manufacturers (NAM).[5]

The general conclusion of these surveys is perhaps best summarized by the National Association of Manufacturers.

NAM has conducted a survey of nonbank corporate experience with floating exchange rates on the basis of a small but representative cross section of U.S. industry. Findings, though not fully analyzed, seem to reflect a positive evaluation of floating. Compared with realistic alternatives, it was recognized by the majority to be the only viable system.[6]

This statement does not, of course, say that companies favor floating rates. On the contrary, most respondents to the Conference Board survey report that floating exchange rates have made it more difficult to conduct international business.[7] The Conference Board study is frequently quoted as supporting the view that business is not in favor of floating rates. The study definitely stresses the uncertainty caused by floating exchange rates. "Uncertainty of exchange rates makes planning particularly difficult," and "Uncertainty about future currency parities also complicates decisions on sourcing."[8] These are examples of expressed reservations about floating rates. They do not, however, appear to trans-

---

[2] Norman S. Fieleke, "The Hedging of Commercial Transactions between U.S. and Canadian Residents: A View from the United States," *Proceedings of Conference on Canadian–United States Financial Relationships*, Federal Reserve Bank of Boston, September 1971, pp. 171-191, and "Exchange Rate Flexibility and the Forward-Exchange Markets: Some Evidence from the Recent Experience with the German Mark," *New England Economic Review* (May/June 1972), pp. 2-10.

[3] Michael G. Duerr, "Protecting Corporate Assets under Floating Currencies," *Research Report of the Conference Board*, New York, 1975.

[4] William R. Folks and Michael Jilling, information provided as a preliminary result of the Foreign Exchange Risk Management Project, Center of International Business Studies, University of South Carolina.

[5] National Association of Manufacturers, Washington, D.C., statement provided by Peter M. Clark on preliminary results of NAM survey. This survey and the one by Folks and Jilling have not been published, and permission to quote from the results of these studies is gratefully acknowledged.

[6] Ibid.

[7] Duerr, "Protecting Corporate Assets under Floating Currencies," p. 2.

[8] Ibid., pp. 3, 6.

late into opposition to the system. The panelists consulted for the Conference Board survey present an encouraging vision of the adjustment to floating rates and to the attitude of getting on with business. The study concludes: "while many executives decry the volatility of exchange values, they have accepted them as a current challenge to managerial ingenuity in preserving corporate assets." [9]

James Green of the Conference Board, who analyzed the survey's results, concurs with our own interpretation of those results, that is, while the respondents were not prepared to be evangelists for the new faith, they were at least willing to be converts.

In the Folks and Jilling survey there are no questions addressed directly to the issue of businessmen's preferences between fixed and floating rates.[10] Table 1, however, shows that 52.3 percent of the respondents to the survey would prefer a fixed rate system because such a system facilitates forecasting—thus implying a narrow preference for a fixed rate system.

Fieleke's surveys were directly concerned with the possible interference of floating exchange rates with international trade. There were no affirmative answers to the first question of his 1971 survey that refers to the experiences of companies following the floating of the Canadian dollar in June 1970: "After June 1; 1970, did you at any time decide against entering into a transaction with a Canadian resident on the grounds that it would be too expensive or difficult to buy Canadian dollars forward?"[11] In the same study, Fieleke found no evidence that flexibility interfered with trade or that there was any lack of efficient hedging facilities.

In a second survey, published in June 1972, Fieleke deals with the floating of the deutsche mark between May and December of 1971. Again, none of the 113 respondents to the survey decided to forgo a transaction with a German resident because of greater difficulties in securing forward cover. Although Fieleke's surveys were limited to particular episodes of floating and restricted to two currencies, the unanimity of the respondents provides strong support for the view that floating did not affect trade-related business decisions.

Our own conversations with business colleagues have reinforced the opinion that although floating exchange rates have not been welcomed with open arms, they are appraised realistically as a better alternative to the fixed rates that were vulnerable to big parity changes, such

---

9 Ibid., p. 42.
10 The information presented here is a preliminary result of the Foreign Exchange Risk Management Project, under the direction of Professors Folks and Jilling, Center of International Studies, University of South Carolina.
11 Fieleke, "The Hedging of Commercial Transactions," p. 173.

Table 1
Preference Ranking by Forecasters of Exchange
Rate Standards, 1975

	Percentage of Responding Firms[a]					
	Ranking of exchange rate standards					No response to question
Exchange Rate Standard	first choice	second choice	third choice	fourth choice	fifth choice	
"Clean" floating rates	22.4	10.3	14.0	9.3	0.9	43.0
"Dirty" floating rates	0.9	2.8	12.1	27.1	0.0	57.0
Crawling peg	17.8	26.2	8.4	0.9	0.0	46.7
Fixed rates (subject to formal parity change)	52.3	7.5	6.5	3.7	0.0	29.9
Others[b]	0.9	0.0	0.9	0.0	0.0	98.1

Note: Ranking is based on the anticipated relative ease of forecasting exchange rates under various exchange rate standards.

[a] Based on 107 completed questionnaires.

[b] Fixed rates for currencies within a currency bloc; joint floating of bloc currencies against other currencies.

Source: Calculations provided by Professors William R. Folks, Jr., and Michael Jilling as a preliminary result of the Foreign Exchange Risk Management Project, Center of International Business Studies, University of South Carolina.

as those that occurred in major trading countries between 1967 and 1973. Choosing between floating rates and parity-vulnerable fixed rates is like choosing between ulcers and apoplexy. Under floating rates, each day brings a new pain that can be ameliorated by defensive measures, but can never be eliminated. Under fixed rates, except when the probability of a rate change is low, each weekend brings with it a new terror of a large devaluation. This distinction is not clear-cut, however, because the present system, fulfilling its reputation as a "dirty float," has at times (for example in February and March 1976), displayed the worst characteristics of both fixed and purely floating rates.

The deutsche mark and the Mexican peso are useful illustrations of these points. In the spring of 1976, corporations with short positions in deutsche marks have been subject to constant tension whenever the deutsche mark showed an appreciation—seemingly every second day. On the other hand, potential apoplexy was a fair description of the mental health of many holders of long positions in Mexican pesos over the 1976 Easter weekend. Mindful of the fact that it was on the Easter weekend in 1954 that the peso was last devalued, and with discounts on the peso as large as 20 percent (annualized), individuals or corporate officers responsible for exposed Mexican assets had a very uncomfortable holiday.

Further evidence that the float has met with acceptance is that there has been no noticeable lobbying effort against it. When business has a problem, people in Washington are usually the first to know about it. Major business organizations indicate that they have had no complaints about the floating rate system. Indeed, it is revealing that the Conference Board and the National Association of Manufacturers found it necessary to ask business executives whether they had problems with floating rates, rather than having had the executives knocking on their doors.

Increased Costs under the Flexible Rate System

Costs of operating abroad have risen in three areas for U.S. based companies under the flexible rate system: an increased overall demand for cover; higher unit costs of forward cover of exposure to exchange rate risk; and higher internal costs of managing a company's exposure, that is, higher expenses associated with information gathering, processing, control, and decision making.

Increased Demand for Cover: Higher Volume. The new system is generally regarded as having increased the demand for forward cover. Under the Bretton Woods system, particularly from 1958 to 1967, forward cover was rarely needed. In addition, when cover was required—for example, when fears of a sterling devaluation became widespread in 1967—the support operations of the central banks frequently prevented a large increase in the cost of cover, and many companies actually ended with a realized net gain following a depreciation. Under the flexible rate system, exposure in most currencies is risky and consequently there is a greater demand for cover—either through the forward market or through borrowing. However, an expanded demand for cover has not always resulted in a higher cost to business. For example, if a currency falls 6 percent and a company has a contract at a 3 percent "cost" (the discount between the forward and the spot rate at the time of the contract), then the company has a realized gain.

Unit Costs of Cover. Unit costs of cover may be divided into hedging costs and transaction costs. In our experience, forward premiums and discounts have on the average reflected interest rate differences as a result of the interest arbitrage mechanism. Therefore "hedging costs" (the premium or discount on forward versus spot rates), are essentially the same as they were under the Bretton Woods system.

A convenient measure of the transaction cost of cover is the difference between the asking price and the price bid. It has been asserted that the costs of cover have risen appreciably because the bid-ask price spread for both spot and forward exchange has widened, following the introduction of the flexible rate system.[12]

A wider spread means one gets fewer units of foreign exchange than before when selling domestic currency, and fewer units of domestic currency when selling foreign exchange. Put another way, the cost of a theoretical round trip at the same moment from dollars to sterling and back to dollars rises as the bid-ask price spread widens.

Some observers attribute the increase in the price spread to the New York foreign exchange market's unwillingness to automate and thus reduce its cost of doing business.[13]

The increase of the price spread does not, however, significantly increase a company's cost of doing business. Relative to the fluctuations in the market, the bid-ask price spread is small. On an average day, even with relatively quiet markets, an exchange rate will change by about 0.25 percent (figure derived from daily quotes for deutsche mark–U.S. dollar rate in February 1976) whereas the bid-ask spread is usually lower than 0.1 percent. Thus, we do not believe that the increase of the price spread changes our conclusion that the unit costs of cover in the present system are essentially determined in the same manner as they were under the Bretton Woods system, that is, by interest rate arbitrage, and that the costs of cover have risen or fallen only insofar as interest rate differences have risen or fallen.

Internal Costs of Managing Floating Exchange Rates. A more serious but less tangible determinant of increased costs has been resources devoted to the internal management of a company's accounts. Under the Bretton Woods system, specific management of a company's international accounts manifested itself only in crisis situations. Information as to a company's foreign exposure was needed only when there were widespread fears of a devaluation or revaluation.

---

[12] For evidence on the widening of the spread, see Charles Pigott, Richard James Sweeney, and Thomas D. Willett, "Some Aspects of the Behavior and Effects of Flexible Exchange Rates" (paper presented at the Conference on Monetary Theory and Policy, Konstanz, Germany, June 1975), Table 7.

[13] Chris Welles, "The Computer Assault on New York's Foreign Exchange Market," *Institutional Investor,* international edition (March 1976), pp. 68-74.

Under flexible rates, however, efficient management requires an up-to-date and comprehensive reporting system relative to the corporation's exposure, as well as reliable forecasts on likely movements in exchange rates. These operations use up man-hours both in the company's subsidiaries and at corporate headquarters. No estimates of these indirect costs of the flexible rate system are available to the best of our knowledge, but we believe they are significant and should be considered in any full evaluation of the total costs of different exchange rate systems.

Overall Evaluation and Outlook

In summary, when information on costs is combined with survey responses, we come to the tentative conclusion that while the cost of doing business internationally has increased, this increase has not led to any serious cutback in the international operations of U.S. companies.

Because business has generally accepted the flexible rate system, it is of interest to consider the changes and trends in international financial management that have occurred in the last few years. For example, decisions on foreign exchange management are becoming more centralized. Buying forward cover at the local level is a phenomenon from a simpler and perhaps more romantic past. Eighty-four percent of the respondents to the Folks and Jilling study report that exposure defense responsibility is centrally organized (see Table 2). Forty-three percent indicate that they became more centralized in the 1970–1975 period, and only 1.9 percent say they became less centralized (see Table 3).

Most panelists in the Conference Board survey report that their companies make decisions about foreign exchange coverage at corporate headquarters, and several companies indicate the pendulum is swinging toward further centralization.

Parenthetically we may note that this movement toward centralization runs counter to the general management doctrine of decentralization of control and the establishment of profit centers, and thus creates internal conflict within a corporation both strategically and operationally.

Central organization allows for the balance of assets and liabilities of different subsidiaries within one country, thus reducing the overall need for cover. Moreover, in the halcyon days of the European joint float, a further offsetting practice was to manage the firm's total position in the float currencies rather than manage accounts in separate currencies. But those days are over and the possibility of a breakup of the

Table 2
Centralization of U.S. Multinational Corporations for Exposure Defense, 1975

Extent of Centralization	Responding Firms	
	Number	Percentage
Completely centralized organization	53	49.5
Centralized organization	37	34.6
Decentralized organization	6	5.6
Completely decentralized organization	3	2.8
No response to question	8	7.5
Total	107	

Note: Centralization refers to the extent to which foreign exchange risk management programs are organized centrally, with a top officer exercising responsibility across divisional and national boundaries.
Source: Folks and Jilling, Foreign Exchange Risk Management Project.

Table 3
Trends in Management Centralization for Exposure Defense in U.S. Multinational Corporations

Trend	Period			
	1973–1975		1971–1975	
	Number of firms	Percentage	Number of firms	Percentage
More centralization	43	40.2	46	43.0
Less centralization	3	2.8	2	1.9
No change	46	43.0	40	37.4
No response to question	15	14.0	19	17.8
Total	107		107	

Source: Folks and Jilling, Foreign Exchange Risk Management Project.

snake or of a realignment of the float currencies does not allow financial managers to cancel long and short positions in different float currencies.[14]

---

[14] The balancing of intercountry exposure may frequently leave a company open to the charge of speculation in foreign exchange markets. For example, if the Dutch guilder and the German mark were expected to appreciate in tandem, a short position in guilders could be balanced by purchasing a long contract in deutsche marks. (In the wider deutsche mark market, contracts are easier to obtain than in the guilder market.) To an outside observer, however, this may be construed as speculation in German marks and, to avoid such charges and the nuisance costs involved in refuting them, corporations may refrain from such transactions.

COMMENTARIES

Donald Kirk

There is a great deal of criticism of FASB No. 8, much of it focusing on the volatility of quarterly reported earnings that has resulted from applying the standards set forth in that statement. The principal reason for that volatility is floating exchange rates.

One might wonder why there is criticism about reporting fluctuating earnings when there are floating exchange rates. The reason is that companies dislike reporting unstable or volatile earnings. Rather, they see a consistent reported-earnings trend as being more easily explained and a favorable factor in determining the market price for a company's stock. Thus, when the Federal Reserve does not intervene enough in the market to quell erratic swings in exchange rates, accountants are expected to distinguish the "real" rate changes from those that are only temporary in order to use the "right" rate of exchange for reporting purposes. Unfortunately, no one has yet developed a method for distinguishing such rate changes—except for hindsight. Therefore, many would have us simply defer recognizing exchange gains and losses.

The Financial Accounting Standards Board has been asked to make various revisions in FASB No. 8 in order to dampen the swings that changing exchange rates cause in the earnings of companies. However, the board does not perceive that smoothing fluctuations in reported earnings should be a function of accounting standards, and Statement No. 8 explicitly reflects that view. There is no question that FASB No. 8 has increased the potential for volatility in earnings. That was a conscious decision made by the board.

FASB No. 8 changed the accounting measurement of balance sheet exposure for many companies—that is, they are now asked to measure their balance sheet exposure in a standardized way. However, FASB No. 8 emphasizes that that balance sheet exposure is not the entire economic exposure of a company, and the statement requires companies to explain and disclose, if practicable, other effects of exchange rate changes—the effects other than reported exchange gains and losses, namely, the effects on revenues and costs when measured in dollars.

159

With regard to balance sheet exposure of foreign currency monetary items, FASB No. 8 requires recognition of exchange gains and losses whenever exchange rates change. In other words, changes in dollar measurements that result solely from rate changes are recognized at the time the rates change. For other assets, those carried at cost, value changes, including the effects of exchange rate changes, are generally not recognized until such assets are converted into monetary items. That is in accord with the so-called historical cost accounting model that is the foundation of our current system of accounting.

Granted, FASB No. 8 does not cause all the economic effects of a rate change to be recognized at once. It therefore creates timing differences by recognizing the effects of rate changes on monetary items as each rate change occurs, but deferring recognition of the other effects of exchange rate changes on the value of nonmonetary items—for example, inventory—until such assets are sold or consumed in operations. FASB No. 8 has been accused of improperly measuring balance sheet exposure. For most companies, long-term debt is the principal monetary item. Because foreign currency debt is a monetary item, gains or losses, measured in dollars, will occur when rates change from the time the debt is incurred until it is repaid. It is only a question of when the effects of exchange rate changes should be recognized. The board chose to recognize those effects when rates change and not to spread or defer those effects until the debt is paid or rolled over, or until a company is liquidated. Although the historical cost accounting model mandates the use of historical exchange rates to translate inventory carried at cost, FASB No. 8 in no way implies that inventory, or any other nonmonetary asset, is not exposed to an economic risk should exchange rates change. However, that exposure is dependent on the asset's selling price—not its historical cost. The responsiveness or nonresponsiveness of local currency selling prices to rate changes determines the economic effect of a rate change. Under the historical cost accounting model, the selling price of inventory is not recognized until its time of sale. The fact that the rules of FASB No. 8 do not require recognition of an exchange gain or loss on nonmonetary assets at the time of an exchange rate change does not alter, or deny, the fact that they may be exposed assets.

Joseph M. Burns, in his study on accounting standards and international finance, directed much of his criticism at the "historical cost accounting model" rather than at FASB No. 8. He expressed hope that an accounting system based on current value would be developed and that such a system would better measure an entity's economic exposure to exchange rate changes. However, it is my opinion that there are major implementation problems in adopting a current value system—a fact acknowledged in the study. Further, current value accounting will not eliminate the volatility of earnings attributed to FASB No. 8. In my opinion, current value accounting would create even more volatility in earnings during periods of floating rates because it would generally increase a company's accounting exposure to rate changes. Rather than its net monetary position being considered exposed, a company's entire net worth could be exposed.

Some people question whether there is an alternative to using exchange rates for purposes of incorporating foreign operations into U.S. consolidated financial statements. Theoreticians have offered hypotheses to that effect. However, for purposes of financial reporting, multiplying deutsche marks in a West German bank by something other than the current exchange rate results in a number which cannot be meaningfully consolidated with other cash balances denominated in dollars.

Some have suggested that FASB No. 8 causes managements to take uneconomic actions. It cannot be denied that FASB No. 8 can affect certain business decisions. In fact, it probably has already affected certain decisions made by some companies. If the stock market is as efficient as Burns believes, some of those actions were possibly uneconomic and unwarranted. But is that sufficient reason for not issuing an accounting standard? Without standards, accounting has its own efficient market. Ways can be found to cope with (or obscure) problems through a variety of alternative accounting practices. (Alan Teck mentioned in his paper that laissez-faire accounting—that is, "creative accounting"— came to the rescue in the early 1970s.) Some people have said that the Financial Accounting Standards Board has now imposed too much discipline on accounting practices. However, if there were not at least some degree of standardization in financial reporting, nothing would be available but what may be described as creative accounting.

Admittedly, change creates confusion, but there is hope. Certain security analysts' reports dealing with FASB No. 8 have been very thoughtful. They have reflected an understanding of the distinction between the balance sheet adjustment effect (the exchange gain or loss) and the continuing effect of exchange rate changes on the results of operations. There is also evidence that analysts are *not* being misled and are *not* misinterpreting those effects, as Alan Teck has implied.

The result of FASB No. 8 is to bring accounting practices up to date with the floating exchange rate environment. Floating rates do have an economic effect on a company's results of operations when measured in dollars. Therefore, if rates are volatile, then there should be a volatile effect on reported earnings.

Geoffrey Bell

Anyone operating in the market tends to work from a limited sample, and my comments are based only on my personal view of what goes on in the foreign exchange markets. Although working simultaneously in London and New York, spending a lot of time in Caracas, and criss-crossing the Atlantic, I know in real depth the problems only of those institutions I advise.

I would like to make one or two remarks about foreign exchange markets before commenting on particular papers. First, it is my impression that exchange rate volatility over the last few years has been gradually diminishing. The lira and pound are rather special and not indicative of an interruption of the trend to reduce the ups and downs in exchange rate movements.

One reason for this trend is that institutions are taking reduced outright positions in foreign exchange as compared with the earliest years of floating exchange rates. Bankers have become less confident in their forecasting abilities, and they, or at least the exchange dealers and the directors in charge of the departments, have realized that the risk-reward ratio in the promotion stakes within the institutions generally does not favor speculation—that is, being right about exchange rate movements does not always fully compensate for being wrong. Most banks have learned the lesson that the normal position is to be safe and to let others take the risks.

But, that was not the case in the early years of floating rates, mainly because in the fixed exchange rate world it was not very difficult to make substantial profits in the exchange markets. In 1967, it was unlikely that the pound would appreciate in value, or that the deutsche mark would depreciate in value a year or two later. Now under floating rates there are differences in points of view about the future behavior of some currencies. The relative stability of the dollar–deutsche mark relationship, for example, has been impressive despite the significant volume of activity in that market. I would also comment about the supposed lack of forward cover at the present time. In fact, if one searches hard enough, cover in most traded currencies can usually be found. But as Dennis Weatherstone has pointed out, cover is available, but most people do not like to pay the price. Consequently, institutions search for other means of covering their exposures.

Another topic worthy of discussion is investment policies under floating exchange rates. In this context, an important development is a closer relationship between Eurodollar interest rates and domestic interest rates in the United States. Investors—and not simply commercial banks—have shown a great deal more confidence in the Euro-dollar market, causing a good deal of arbitrage to take place between Eurodollars and domestic U.S. dollars. On occasion, the net result has been that the premium for Eurodollar deposits virtually disappeared. One reason for this return of confidence was the decision at the Bank for International Settlements meeting in September 1974 by major central banks to recognize their collective responsibility for the super-vision of operations by commercial banks in the Eurodollar market. The awareness of the "lender of last resort" role played by central banks in the Eurodollar market has helped greatly to reassure depositors about the safety of their funds.

One of the advantages of the change from the fixed to the floating rate system is that new knowledge is gained and then can be used to advantage. Alan Teck pointed out that this is a new area of operation, especially for bankers. It is a source of new business and of future revenues.

Both Teck and Mooney have established the fact that companies are much more concerned about their foreign exchange exposure than they were prior to the establishment of floating rates. Earlier, many companies did not recognize, or chose not to recognize, the degree to which they were taking foreign exchange risks. Some companies ap-peared to consider a change in the exchange rate as an act of God. Thus, one of the benefits of generalized floating rates has been the concentration of the attention of companies on foreign exchange expo-sures, thereby leading to the creation of proper reporting systems, regular decision making meetings, and so on. At the same time, there is no question that more and more companies are finding their exposure posi-tion to be an area of concern and are looking to bankers to help them.

In this context, many companies are somewhat disillusioned about the efficacy of forecasting future exchange rates. Most companies, how-ever, seem to be interested in findings ways to minimize exposure by means other than taking outright exchange positions. By the same token, it has been noted that the demand for forward cover is great. But, I found that a number of companies use the forward exchange market more as a last resort, because they recognize that it is necessary to cover exposure twice because of tax. Therefore, there is more emphasis on matching assets and liabilities within the different countries in which companies have foreign exposure. And with the help of bankers they can find ways to achieve this end. For example, there is more use of back-to-back or parallel loans at present—that is, finding a company in one's own country to lend a foreign currency in return for its borrowing in the domestic currency.

Also of interest is the fact that, at least to some degree, companies have learned a lesson from unhedged borrowing, particularly in deutsche marks and Swiss francs. They were tempted originally by the low interest costs but then adopted the mistaken notion that if they could renew the loans at maturity they would not be taking any exchange risk. Although this attitude seems to have changed, large amounts of money were borrowed in 1975 by non-Swiss companies through the Swiss franc private placement route. It may well be that these companies were using the Swiss franc as a proxy for the deutsche mark, in which some of their assets were denominated. But it may also be a case of once bitten not necessarily twice shy.

In conclusion, the introduction of floating exchange rates has not made investment any more difficult than before. Exchange rates have always changed, and the fact that they are now moving continuously has not made investment decisions that much more difficult. Currently, most large-scale investors look at the major investable currencies—that is, U.S. dollars, deutsche marks, Swiss francs, and perhaps even Canadian dollars—then decide to acquire those assets for structural reasons. Markets for marks and Swiss francs are, of course, much narrower than those for U.S. dollars, Canadian dollars, and the pound sterling. But, again some of the arguments about the thinness of nondollar markets tend to be exaggerated. For example, some investors have found it difficult, or have alleged that it is difficult, to buy West German bonds. That may be true, but their problem may also reflect the fall in interest in West Germany and, therefore, reluctance by the banks to sell these bonds.

Most participants in the investment business also look at another group of currencies on a more or less periodic basis. It is quite interesting to note, for example, that the French franc comes into demand every so often. The demand for French franc bonds has at times been extremely strong. It follows that when one talks about investment under a floating exchange rate regime, one has to be quite careful to separate the effects of floating rates from other factors that are affecting the breadth of capital markets.

Dennis E. Logue

According to many papers in this session, the recent accounting rule changes that affect the reporting of international operations may lead firms to engage in foreign financial transactions which are not justified on economic grounds. Some firms probably make such decisions for the sake of their reported financial statements; form often takes precedence over substance. But beyond this concern with corporate behavior are two more fundamental issues. First, do uneconomic decisions that make financial statements more attractive affect corporate valuation? And second, how should firms behave with respect to foreign exchange hedging operations?

Regarding the effect of accounting practice on corporate valuation, the evidence is quite strong that the security markets, where corporate values are determined, effectively pierce the "veil of accounting."[1] Prices in these markets on the average reflect true corporate value, the discounted stream of future dividends. The account or financial reporting differences among corporations do not have any substantial systematic or persistent effects on share valuation. Choice of accounting methods cannot obscure poor or wasteful management. Accordingly, firms that engage in more foreign exchange transactions than are optimal will not achieve any real payoff from this activity besides incurring the cost of these operations.

Security markets and, perhaps more important, their information-gathering and processing functions are competitive. Uncovering previously unknown information relative to the valuation of shares can produce huge profits for the analyst. Because profits may be earned by reading behind the accounting numbers, analysts have every incentive to do so. This competition among analysts to discover new facts about firms ultimately leads to market valuations of these firms that are not systematically incorrect. Because returns over time to security analysis are on average competitive, it may be inferred that no one analyst or small group of analysts has any monopoly access to new, economically relevant information concerning the "correct" value of a firm's shares.

Security analysts tend not to be fooled by misleading accounting information gathered over any appreciable period of time. Accordingly, it appears that firms which engage in foreign exchange transactions simply to provide window dressing for their periodic financial reports to the public are not only behaving inappropriately but are also expending funds on activities for which there are no benefits.

Normative work on the subject of how firms should behave has generally been supported by accounting criteria. Many models of optimal foreign exchange hedging behavior have focused on the reported balance sheet and income statement impacts of exchange rate changes. As implied above, this makes little sense. Other models of optimal behavior have assumed that future foreign exchange rates are predict-

---

[1] For a careful review of the literature on this subject see Thomas R. Dyckman, David H. Downes, and Robert P. Magee, *Efficient Capital Markets and Accounting: A Critical Analysis* (Englewood Cliffs, N.J.: Prentice-Hall, Inc., 1975).

able. If the foreign exchange market itself is, however, an efficient market where all available and economically relevant information is already incorporated in the observable market prices, then robust and potentially supraprofitable predictions of future foreign exchange rates are not likely. In this case, the best predictors of future spot exchange rates tend to be current forward rates, and, as it turns out, actions based on these observable rates do not yield the firm any systematic excess return. It is only when ultimately accurate predictions diverge from the expectations influencing market prices that large profits could be made or large losses avoided. If exchange markets are efficient, however, as is suggested by a growing body of evidence,[2] firms should not devote extensive resources to prediction of future exchange rates. Thus, it appears that hedging models based on prediction of future exchange rates simply lack value. What, then, should firms do?

In making investment or even most tactical financial decisions, indeed any decisions that will increase risk to the firm's capital (including decisions concerning investing abroad and foreign exchange hedging), the corporation must decide what is the appropriate opportunity cost and develop a "hurdle" or "screening" rate that is a required rate of return for investments falling into a particular risk class. The firm must ask how much yield it demands from a particular investment.

Corporations have grappled with this problem for a long time; it is, in essence, the cost of capital problem. To help resolve this problem, financial economists have developed a "Capital Asset Pricing Model." [3]

This model provides a functional relationship between the required return on an asset and its degree of *relevant* risk. The issue of how risk is measured is an important one, and this model distinguishes between two types of risk. The riskiness of returns has been defined as variability, and this variability has been split into two components: "systematic" risk and unsystematic or "specific" risk.

The systematic risk is that risk which cannot be avoided when one does business in a particular economy. It reflects aggregate or market risk. The unsystematic component of risk is firm specific and, in essence, unpredictable or random. This dichotomy can be extended to an international setting. If a firm operates in several different national economies, whose aggregate economic fluctuations are not perfectly correlated, the systematic risk of the firm will be functionally related only to the variability these economies share or have in common. To be more

[2] See Dennis E. Logue, Richard James Sweeney, and Thomas D. Willett, "Speculative Behavior of Exchange Rates during the Current Float," *Journal of Business Research,* forthcoming.

[3] See, for example, William F. Sharpe, *Portfolio Theory and Capital Markets* (New York: McGraw-Hill Book Co., 1970), for the development of this model.

concrete, in a two-country world a multinational firm would bear the risks of each economy in proportion to its output in each economy. However, to the extent that fluctuations in one economy were countered by opposing fluctuations in the other, the level of systematic risk borne by the firm would be reduced.

Let me offer a specific domestic example. If a businessman were considering the purchase of a machine, the expected returns on that machine—the number of "widgets" that would be sold times the per unit price, less the costs of production and variable overhead—would depend upon the condition of the general economy over the life of the investment. The returns would represent a return for bearing systematic risk or broad economic risk. Normally, in investment decision making, unanticipated factors—such as a possible power failure which shut down the machine for a week or an unanticipated high rate of productivity by the machine operator—would not be considered an alteration of the investment screening rate. These latter factors would be examples of unsystematic risks, that is, unpredictable or random factors. Finance theory suggests that, in general, one should relate the required return on a particular investment only to the systematic factor, and one should ignore the unsystematic factors, at least in setting screening rates.

Similarly, portfolio investors, when making investment decisions, tend to view only systematic risk—or the contribution to overall *portfolio* risk to the particular financial asset which they are holding—rather than unsystematic or unanticipated risk, as being relevant.

This assertion is based upon capital market theory and has given rise to a whole array of portfolio diversification strategies. Moreover, it turns out that in actuality, investors are not rewarded for bearing unsystematic risk, except, of course, when they have inside information about the potential value of the asset.

Investment rewards are a function of systematic risk, or more precisely *expected* investment returns are solely a function of systematic risk. And if an investor happens to be rewarded in a particular period for bearing unsystematic risk, that is accidental and not predictable for future periods.

The required rate of return (the hurdle, or screening rate) that a business firm might use in making its real asset decisions, and the screening rate or anticipated return that an investor may use in making portfolio decisions, is a function of the systematic risk, that is, the variability of the entire economy and the asset's relation to the economy.

Research done by Sweeney, Hughes, and myself showed that multinational corporations and purely domestic corporations seemed to be priced very similarly in terms of their forming part of a potential international portfolio.[4] The implication of this research is that investors, at least at the margin, are evaluating both domestic and multinational firms in an international context, and that the systematic risk of financial assets issued by purely domestic firms is being assessed in the context of holding a perfectly diversified international portfolio.

Where does this leave us in terms of practical decision making? Essentially it leads us to believe that firms, when deciding upon the criterion rate of return, can use the systematic risk of an asset and not consider exchange rate variability.[5] Investors, because they are rewarded for bearing only systematic risk, seem to ignore exchange rate variability. Such variability is unpredictable in an efficient market and ostensibly is neutralized in a diversified international portfolio.

If there were two countries in the world, "Bombia" and "York," and if the exchange rate of one currency fluctuated relative to the other, and if 50 percent of one's wealth were invested in one country and 50 percent in the other, there would be no diminution of that wealth, no matter which currency went up and which went down; moreover, this example generalizes to any number of countries.

At the margin, it can safely be assumed that the average investor does hold a diversified portfolio; if he does not, he is not being rewarded for bearing diversifiable risk. In practice, if a portfolio involves, for example, ten multinationals, it is close to being completely diversified.

Of course, there certainly may be a diminution in real wealth as a result of the general level of inflation in both countries, but a properly diversified portfolio protects the investor as much as can be done. In setting hurdle rates, multinational firms making foreign investment decisions and domestic firms making domestic investment decisions theoretically can safely look at only the systematic risks of the particular investment. So long as they seek to maximize shareholder wealth, they can ignore—at least in setting their hurdle rates—potential exchange rate fluctuations, because netted across the whole world, this variability sums to zero.

Relaxing the assumptions of the theory, however, leads to the notion that firms may be ill advised to adopt this sort of perfect market view as to how investment decisions should be made, primarily because there always exists the threat of insolvency. Though in theory the threat of bankruptcy can be ignored, actual bankruptcy or default on the out-

---

[4] John S. Hughes, Dennis E. Logue, and Richard J. Sweeney, "Corporate International Diversification and Market Assigned Measures of Risk and Diversification," *Journal of Financial and Quantitative Analysis* (November 1975).

[5] For an elaboration, see Robert deBakker, Richard S. Bower, and Dennis E. Logue, "Capital Budgeting for Multinational Firms" (unpublished manuscript, June 1976).

standing loans of the firm carries with it costs—such as the cost of idle productive capacity, legal costs, and so on.

Consequently, the investment theory that has just been outlined, while providing a measure of how firms might make asset commitment decisions at the margin, requires a few modifications before it can be made operational.

One possible supplement to the theory is some sort of modest hedging strategy. The positive theory as outlined suggests only one generally acceptable type of hedging strategy, that is, minimizing the impact of exchange rate fluctuations on the firm's cash flow.[6]

In choosing locations for factories, firms do not have optimally diversified international portfolios. Factories are lumpy investments, and certainly a single firm, when it decides to become an international firm, does not evenly distribute its factories around the world. A firm, for example, may build factories first in England, then in Germany, then in France, and then stop expanding. Firms, then, do have to consider exchange rate variability, but only insofar as it affects the probability of bankruptcy for a particular firm.

The firm can also employ portfolio concepts in developing an appropriate hedging model. Indeed, the portfolio concepts would tend to lead to a strategy which would minimize the variance of total cash flows due to exchange rate fluctuations. This would be an appropriate way to hedge, because individual investors, aside from the potentiality of bankruptcy, really are able to hedge against the broader fluctuations in cash flow due to currency fluctuations. Once this notion of bankruptcy has been accommodated, there is no reason for a firm to go any further in its hedging decisions.

On the basis of the ideas reviewed here, there seems to be little reason for firms to hedge substantially in foreign exchange markets, notwithstanding accountants' suggestions as to how they should keep track of their international economic activities. The artificial attractiveness of financial statements has no persistent effect on corporate valuation; and hedging in excess of the amount necessary to keep the risk of bankruptcy at acceptable levels may not yield any positive benefits for the firm.

---

[6] For the complete development of this model, see Dennis E. Logue and George S. Oldfield, "Managing Foreign Assets when Foreign Exchange Markets Are Efficient," *Financial Management,* Summer 1977.

SUMMARY OF DISCUSSION

The discussants focused their attention principally on two subjects. The first, accounting methods employed by multinational companies under floating exchange rates, was developed in great detail in the paper presented by Joseph Burns. The discussion centered on one particular aspect of this problem, that is, the effects of accounting rules and procedures on the behavior of the multinationals. Participants in the discussion manifested considerable differences over the influence on corporate decision making of new accounting rules for multinationals.

The second subject dealt with the broader and more diffuse problems related to the consequences of the risk averting tactics of economic agents. More specifically, the discussion focused upon the real costs associated with increased volatility of exchange rates and their probable impact on corporate decisions, and, hence, upon international trade and investment.

Accounting Problems under Floating Exchange Rates

Robert Roosa opened the discussion by remarking that no matter which accounting standard is adopted, floating exchange rates are bound to make it difficult to evaluate the performance of multinational companies. He acknowledged that most firms may welcome the unification of rules implied by adoption of the guidelines contained in the Financial Accounting Standard Board Statement No. 8. He said that universally accepted accounting rules will make it easier for investors to compare changes in companies' positions that are caused by movements of exchange rates.

Roosa noted, however, that restating balance sheets in accordance with the rules of FASB No. 8 is likely to cause considerable difficulty for companies trying to distinguish between the effects of their operating efficiency and the effects of exchange rate changes; that is, the new accounting standards would make it difficult for companies to discriminate between different sources of earnings volatility. He said that FASB

171

No. 8 did not make it easier for the management of a multinational company to judge the performance of its foreign subsidiaries.

Roosa said that the ruling has also created new problems for securities analysts attempting to assess the proper value of a company. While it is true, he said, that many analysts have begun to learn to incorporate the effects of the accounting practices recommended by FASB No. 8, their acuity is frequently impaired by a lack of relevant data. For such data to become available, however, companies would have to reveal what they regard as proprietary information in a competitive environment.

Roosa pointed out that greater frequency of reporting reflects an even greater volatility in reported earnings, and thus means greater difficulty in discerning the level of profits yielded by actual operations. Moreover, he said, considering that the manner in which a firm manages its foreign exchange exposure reflects upon the overall performance of its management, it is not clear whether changes in earnings due to changes in exchange rates should be disregarded by analysts. However, he said that FASB No. 8 does not provide a framework within which the evaluation can be done impartially, that is in a manner corresponding to the standards of probity and accuracy that characterize accounting for purely domestic operations.

Donald Kirk asserted that, in formulating the Statement No. 8, FASB attempted to allow a great deal of latitude relative to ways in which balance sheet adjustments and other effects could be disclosed. He said the board pointed out that, in certain cases, concentrating exclusively on the balance sheet adjustment could be misleading, because there are other significant effects that should be disclosed. Kirk said the board recognized the need for guidance relative to how best to display the transactions and events of a year, and even more so, of a quarter, and that it is aware that FASB No. 8 is of little current use to the companies in their attempts to portray what has happened. He also noted that creating a set of accounting rules that would perfectly reflect the results of a company's performance will be a long and difficult process.

Elaborating on Roosa's point about the separability of the effects on earnings of actual operations and of exchange rate changes, Kirk acknowledged that the management of foreign exchange exposure could be of legitimate concern to outsiders. He noted, however, that in many cases separating the effects of balance sheet adjustments from the effects of operations is artificial and unwarranted, though he agreed that in the case of long-term debt those effects might be argued to be separable. But so many balance sheet adjustments are nothing more, he said, than corrections of previously reported revenues and expenses. Balance sheet numbers, once figured into the income statement, he said, are always subject to adjustment until the items are repatriated, or invested in a way that they become invulnerable to exchange rate changes.

At this point Horst Duseberg suggested that companies could use footnotes on their balance sheets to explain the effects of accounting rules on their profits and financial positions. He reported that a number of companies had already begun to use footnotes for this purpose in their quarterly income statements.

Roosa promptly replied that footnotes would hardly resolve the problem. He said that in order to describe the developments that had an impact on a company's earnings, footnotes would have to be several pages long. Also, he said that it is quite possible that auditors will not give an unqualified endorsement to such an income statement and that the threat of a qualified endorsement imposes an effective constraint on directors' freedom in trying to supplement their company's financial reports with footnotes.

Joseph Burns, expanding the scope of Roosa's remark, noted that FASB No. 8 permits the inclusion of additional information relative to the effects of exchange rate changes. It mandates, however, the clear reporting of the methodology employed to reach conclusions concerning those effects. Burns noted that the effects of exchange rate changes are not limited to the particular quarter, but extend over a longer period of time. He said that the effects on future revenue and on cost streams are extremely important for appraising the value of a business at a given point in time. While FASB No. 8 does not specifically prohibit consideration of the effects of exchange rate changes expected in subsequent quarters, it does not require that either. It only specifies that the effects discussed in a quarterly income statement are to be related to that particular quarter.

Duseberg said that the type of accounting methods embodied in FASB No. 8 had been previously implemented by Swiss multinational companies. The Swiss experience indicates that any appraisal of the operating performance of a corporation, either on the basis of the balance sheet or the income statement, is entirely unreliable. Current valuation methods of accounting, he said, result in the enormous sensitivity of profits to variations in exchange rates. He noted that foreign assets and liabilities, when translated into domestic currency at today's exchange rates, may mirror a healthy situation, but when translated at yesterday's rates may indicate a disastrous overall performance.

Wilson Schmidt expressed puzzlement at the rather ominous implied real effects perceived by Burns, Teck, and others as a consequence of FASB No. 8. Schmidt referred to the results of research, suggesting that changes in accounting rules do not affect the value of a company as long as its tax position remains unchanged. The market tends to disregard changes such as, for instance, switching between LIFO and FIFO, as has been discussed by Logue. Schmidt believed that since FASB No. 8 does not seem to have an effect on companies' tax positions, the stock market is likely to penetrate the accountant's veil and note the reality of companies' operating performances.

Burns agreed that the markets were efficient in the manner described by Schmidt. But he indicated that corporate managers were concerned with reported earnings even though the stock market appeared to be concerned only with real earnings. One reason for this attitude may be that bonuses are often given on the basis of paper performance and not for real performance. Another reason, he said, may be that corporate managers feel that stockholders are primarily concerned with the level and stability of reported, that is, accounting, earnings.

If corporate behavior is influenced by reported earnings, the manager can be expected to react accordingly. However, various measures designed to protect the stability of reported earnings—be they financial measures or real hedges—are costly departures from the economically optimal decisions. The market efficiency argument compounds this problem, he said, because the market understands that what corporate managers are doing is harmful to the firm; that is, that these hedging adjustments are uneconomical. Because the market is efficient, it values the shares of such companies at a lower price; therefore, the price-earnings ratio falls, the cost of borrowing goes up, and these increases in the cost of capital have a further adverse effect on the companies.

Burns proceeded with the following illustration. The new standards embodied in FASB No. 8 will tend to move firms in the direction of increased net short exposure in the accounting sense. Firms are concerned about this kind of exposure. They would like to be able to reduce it without affecting their real positions. Yet, most hedging opportunities, once taken, alter the firm's accounting exposure and, at the same time, alter its real exposure. In order to deal with the problem, companies resort to what Burns calls the accounting straddle—selling an asset to yourself. Such a transaction, he said, creates a long position, since it serves as a hedge against the short accounting exposure. Although the accounting straddle probably represents the least-cost adjustment technique, it still entails a pure and unadulterated waste of resources for the sole purpose of neutralizing the inevitable consequences of adhering to the accounting standards of the Financial Accounting Standards Board.

Sean Mooney concurred with the opinion that accounting rules may have an effect on the behavior of multinational firms and, consequently, on the pattern of their production and investment decisions. He strongly challenged Logue's view that rational behavior of multinationals would imply a disregard for the possible effects of exchange rate changes on their international portfolios. Logue's contention was that whatever capital loss is incurred through the depreciation of one currency is offset by a capital gain enjoyed as a result of the appreciation of another currency. Mooney countered that U.S. multinationals are based in the United States, their shareholders are mainly American residents, and the value of their stocks, their earnings, and their dividends are denominated in dollars. Those multinationals show, Mooney contended, an understandable concern with the probable effects of exchange rate changes on their assets and earnings.

Effects of Floating Rates on International Trade and Investment

Robert Heller expressed his surprise at the discussants' neglect of the problem of costs resulting from the reallocation of real resources. He pointed out that exchange rates give signals to decision makers on the basis of which they make investment decisions. He voiced disbelief at the acquiescence of a business community subjected to large and abrupt changes in exchange rates. He found this acquiescence even more surprising, since proposed tariff changes of 2 or 3 percent will be enough to cause threatened groups to lobby for federal subsidy programs, special allowances, and other forms of support.

Nevertheless, changes in exchange rates do entail real costs, stressed Heller. Therefore, even though appropriate market exchange rates presumably determine efficient resource allocation patterns, the increased efficiency has to be balanced against the costs of exchange rate changes. For instance, in the case of the dollar-mark exchange rate, the long-term trend for the last three years has been flat. Therefore, Heller found it difficult to understand why short-run fluctuations around that trend improved the long-term efficiency of resource allocation.

Teck, in a direct response to Heller, remarked that volatile changes in exchange rates do not lead automatically to changes in production patterns. If firms perceived the changes in rates as transitory, he said, they would not seek new contracts or expand production, but would instead cling to their share of the market by adjusting their profit margins.

Moreover, Teck contended, this problem is not limited to volatile changes in exchange rates; it arises whenever the market is subjected

175

to some sort of shock. He said the situation was not qualitatively different under fixed exchange rates, because, then, in order to maintain those rates, governments had to apply temporary controls, tariffs, subsidies, deposit schemes, and other measures of a similar nature. As a result, some industries benefited periodically, while others endured temporary hardships, just as is the case under the present regime of floating rates.

Gretchen Greene offered another potential explanation for the acquiescence of the business community already described by Heller. She said that the most substantial depreciation of the dollar occurred in 1972–1973, a seller's market period when companies could pass the higher prices of imported products on to consumers, who then bore the burden of dollar depreciation. That is one reason why, she said, there is not nearly as much business or labor criticism of floating exchange rates as of quotas or import duties.

Roosa amplified Greene's explanation by pointing out that the depreciation of the dollar in 1972–1973, coinciding with the worldwide economic boom, contributed to increases in companies' posted earnings. Under such circumstances American business had no reason to complain about floating exchange rates.

Mooney noted that, although Heller's concern with the welfare implications of floating exchange rates is legitimate, not enough work had been done in this area for any definite conclusions to be safely drawn.

Turning to the question of business firms' alleged passivity regarding the issue of floating rates, Mooney remarked that, in addition to increased earnings in the wake of the dollar depreciation, most U.S. companies had long positions abroad and, therefore, saw the dollar value of their total assets rising as well. He concluded that lack of opposition to floating rates in the past does not presage similar passivity in the future. FASB No. 8 rules—which make earnings more volatile the more erratic the exchange rate movements—may contribute to a growing resistance to floating rates in the future. More important, he said, with dollar exchange rates periodically rising, entire industries may suffer, giving rise to the possibility of a future lobbying effort.

Logue said that too much attention was being paid to the effect of exchange rate volatility on trade and investment. He pointed out that exchange rates had been considerably less volatile, even during periods of the most hectic trading activity, than were the interest rates that relate directly to the firms' cost of capital. He recognized, however, that businesses do not drastically alter the way they conduct current operations when faced with what they perceive to be transitory changes in interest rates. Neither do they change drastically their long-term investment strategy. They may postpone an offering, delay the building of a factory, but they still do not scrap their plans. He said there is no reason to expect their responses to transitory changes in exchange rates to differ substantially from their reaction to transitory changes in interest rates. Besides, Logue noticed, the cutting edge of the argument about the sensitivity of firms' responses to exchange rate changes becomes dulled as those changes become smaller. Since the variability of exchange rates has diminished demonstrably, he said, there is no danger that relatively small fluctuations in the rates will bring about large and unnecessary adjustments in the pattern of production, investment, and trade.

Given differing rates of monetary expansion in various countries, Heller argued, the proposition that inflation rates may be reduced in individual countries under flexible exchange rates implies widening differentials among the rates of inflation among countries. He juxtaposed this notion with the observation of Logue and other discussants that exchange rate variability has been declining for some time, wondering if this apparent paradox could be explained.

Thomas Willett suggested that Heller's seeming paradox could be caused by a matter of timing. When exchange rates were first allowed to float, their flexibility in an environment that was highly inflationary allowed an increased divergence between national rates of inflation. More recently, he noted, conscious efforts by a number of governments to reduce that divergence has led to the more stable behavior of exchange rates.

Commenting on Willett's answer, Roosa remarked that such was the case for those countries that imposed upon themselves the discipline entailed by adherence to the snake agreement. That discipline has exerted considerable continuing influence on the economic policies of those countries that managed to remain in the snake. In contrast, the exchange rates of the pound, the French franc, and the lira—all currencies of the countries that failed to bring down their inflation rates to the levels prevailing in the snake countries or in the United States—continue to show rather high variability.

Dirck Keyser advanced the hypothesis that exceptionally high volatility of exchange rates at the beginning of the floating exchange rate period was due to institutional factors. He conjectured that the banks, being unused to the idea of free operation of the foreign exchange market, were reluctant to allow their trading rooms enough capital or authority to take or to carry sufficiently larger trading positions. The greater stability of exchange rates in the second half of 1975 can be, he suggested, traced to more power in trading rooms, manifested in the greater resiliency of the market.

Teck and Duseberg rejected Keyser's conjecture. Teck's impression was that with the advent of floating rates, some banks had become more, rather than less, prudent. An awareness of the riskiness of dealing in currencies, he said, causes many banks to reduce the limits available to their traders.

Duseberg added that Keyser's hypothesis is indicative of a widespread tendency to overestimate the importance of banks in the foreign exchange market. Multinational companies, he said, are quantitatively very important participants in that market. The companies, he said, have learned how to operate in the market more efficiently, and have contributed to a greater stability of exchange rates.

Concluding the discussion, Robert Slighton expressed the opinion that the most important issue discussed—that is, the one related to the welfare implications of variable exchange rates—had not been precisely formulated. Slighton considered the issue to be so crucial, in fact, that he found it worthwhile to reformulate the question of the real costs of exchange rate variability as originally raised by Heller.

According to Slighton, the real costs associated with increased exchange rate variability are three: (1) inefficiencies due to the difference between the expected price upon which allocation decisions were made often turns out to be different from the actual price; (2) inefficiencies due to the more risky environment caused by floating rates (if private willingness to bear risk becomes less than social willingness, fewer risky decisions will be made than is socially desirable); and (3) inefficiencies due to increased transaction costs.

It was Slighton's impression that most discussants dismissed the importance of these costs. He said that it appeared from their remarks that, as compared with the par value system, the system of floating exchange rates had not introduced much uncertainty with respect to expected prices, especially with respect to expected prices over a reasonably long period. Regarding the greater short-run volatility of exchange rates with increased differences between expected and realized prices, corporate managers appear ready to bear the increased risk associated with this volatility rather than curtail the scope of production and investment. He said, finally, that transaction costs, although clearly greater than under the par value system, are not great enough to alter corporate managers' attitudes towards major production and investment decisions.

PART
FOUR

INTERNATIONAL GUIDELINES
AND PRINCIPLES FOR
NATIONAL FINANCIAL AND
EXCHANGE RATE POLICIES

INTERPRETING THE RAMBOUILLET AND JAMAICA AGREEMENTS

Edwin H. Yeo III

I would like to talk about the Rambouillet and Jamaica agreements, and what they mean. Rambouillet involved considerable compromise and considerable adjustment of positions, and some of the post-Rambouillet rhetoric might not be entirely descriptive of what was actually agreed to.

Political people have a need to present their constituents with an image of gradual change, even though the change might not be so gradual. The thinking that went into the Rambouillet and Jamaica agreements involved, first, a very limited concept of the role of intervention; second, a major emphasis on the role of underlying economic and financial factors as determinants of exchange rates over any sustained period of time; and third, in conjunction with the financial factors cited above, the concept of the role of capital flows. As a matter of fact, in the understanding at Rambouillet, there was a significant section on the role of such flows. In general, the analysis was that the increased mobility of financial capital, of portfolio capital, was, in part, a function of the way we had financed the inflation of the past ten years through the accumulation of short-term assets by the private sector. This accumulation had provided the wherewithal, had provided the base, or had contributed to the provision of the base, for significant capital flows.

In that section, it was noted that domestic price stability, if we were able to achieve it, would provide the basis for a funding operation, an extension of maturities of those liabilities. And that, it was thought, would probably contribute more toward a diminution of capital flows than any other single thing that we could do as policy makers.

I would like to read one sentence regarding intervention: "The individual central banks, in the consultations, would decide whether market conditions were disorderly and, thus, destined to be described by the phrase 'erratic fluctuations.' "

These remarks were delivered at the conference by Under Secretary of the Treasury Yeo as a luncheon address, on April 21, 1976.

That reminds me of the first day of deer season in Pennsylvania with people going out in search of erratic fluctuations. They only exist stuffed, ex post. It is impossible to distinguish them ex ante.

And that is why this phrase was written just the way it was written. Disorderly conditions are destined to be described by the phrase, "erratic fluctuations" ex post only. So underlying the Rambouillet Agreement was the concept of a world in which, first, stability could not be produced by a superimposed mechanism, but only by proper management of underlying economic and financial factors; and second, the role of financial capital flows is growing. By inference, that concept of the world explicitly entails a very limited role for intervention.

I would like to report about what has been going on in my particular group since the conclusion of the Jamaica Agreement.

The consultation mechanism is still on an informal basis, but it is quite extensive. There is a degree of understanding of various positions that, to the best of my knowledge, has not existed for a number of years. That does not mean to say that there is an agreement on what a position ought to be, but there is an increased degree of understanding of other points of view. That can be interpreted to mean that mistakes in interpretations of viewpoints have been reduced very, very substantially.

It is an example of the power of ideas, to watch the discussions as they have proceeded, and to see the shifts in attitudes regarding exchange-rate variability, especially the shifts in attitudes regarding the role of intervention.

One manifestation of these shifts is a sharp step up in time and resources devoted by treasuries around the world to economic and financial analyses of other countries, practically an explosion of that kind of activity. Another manifestation of the concept of underlying economic and financial factors is a much more frequent and meaningful exchange of topical information, near-market information among national treasuries.

In the last two months particularly, attitudes regarding the role of intervention have become more congruent. The tuition, in some cases, has been rather high, but I think there are many today who have a different concept of the appropriateness or inappropriateness of various types of intervention.

There is a general realization of the danger of officials locking into a market structure that has initially developed an equilibrium. By locking into it and attempting to hold it, by suppressing the natural equilibrating forces, an officially designed disequilibrium will be produced that ultimately is manifest in an unnecessarily sharp variation in exchange rates.

Our own adjustments in the U.S. Treasury involve a substantial step up in our economic and financial research on a country-by-country basis. There has been a considerable expansion of our monitoring of market developments, not just in the narrow sense in terms of foreign exchange markets, but also in terms of the money market as a whole, one component of which is the foreign exchange market.

One of the things that has been very interesting in the last three months has involved different philosophies, different concepts of intervention. Despite the danger of appearing a little too loose, a little too general, I am going to talk about one particular approach, which I would call the right rate or target approach.

This is the antithesis of the phraseology that was agreed to at Rambouillet and is implicit in proposed Article IV. It involves the concept of determining an appropriate rate and intervening to maintain the relationships represented by that rate. Frequently, in the last several months, it has assumed the manifestation of analysis supported by trade-weighted averages, and it is to this analysis that I would like to address myself.

I take as given the fact that trade-weighted average analysis can be very useful; it is something that we must follow and examine very closely, and we do so at the Treasury. However, I fear that in its present form that analysis does not make much sense analytically, and the approach itself is not of any great practical usefulness.

I am bothered by this particular approach to intervention for two reasons. First of all, we have the problem of weights—bilateral weights, multilateral weights. Second, we have the problem of the appropriate measure of rates of change in prices. Should we use rates of change in prices? Ought it not be rates of change in costs, to eliminate compression of relative profit margins?

There are some people who believe—I am happy to report, a very limited number—that this sort of analysis can lead one to the right rate. First of all, this totally ignores the fact that the right rate, even on trade in goods, is a function of price elasticity and income effects. In other words, it simply measures the prices, ignoring income effects. But more important, this analysis ignores financial or portfolio capital movements and neglects direct capital flows.

I find it very disappointing at times to encounter people who are attempting to deduce the right rate by looking at a small portion of the total flow of transactions that are being handled by the foreign exchange market. It is almost as if we could turn the clock back to a world in which capital flows were minimal, or as if we could pretend that we do not have highly variable capital flows, not only in terms of portfolio capital but also in terms of direct investment flows, which, as you all know, are highly variable.

So that for all of these reasons, given the present technology, I am reluctant to endorse the described method of deducing the right rate. There are two other reasons why I have difficulty with the approach. The less important is that all of this analysis, even if it were comprehensive, deals exclusively with ex post phenomena when, by definition, the right rate is a combination of what has happened and what people think might happen.

But the bottom line, for me, is the kind of system that this produces. Imagine a group of people sitting around, each member of the group being a political official. Each official has a constituency made up of steel producers, furniture producers, wine producers, and Lord knows what, and each haggles over what the right rate is because, understandably, each analysis leads to *the* right rate. What it amounts to, at least in its ultimately degenerate form, is daily renegotiation of a par value system. That hardly represents the basis for much of a system. As a matter of fact, to me, it is the epitome of a nonsystem.

I would not want to suggest that this approach, in terms of haggling officials, is in the ascendancy; rather, I would like to report that this type of activity is probably declining, although it was in the ascendancy several months ago. But those "right" rates of several months ago turned out to be the wrong rates. Since then, a congruence has been developing in terms of attitudes regarding this particular approach.

That is why, in Rambouillet and Jamaica, the very limited concept of countering disorderly market conditions was used. It is manifest in several forms. One is the language that I described, and another is the language in Article IV, Section 7 (iii), namely "avoid manipulating," which is the reciprocal, in a sense, of the concept of countering disorderly market conditions.

I am personally convinced that, under the general aegis of countering disorderly market conditions, we have the greatest opportunity for constructing the kind of symmetrical system that we must have. In such a system, rates must be able to move both up and down, with the permission of officials for that type of rate action.

Next, I would like to address myself to the notion that there is a lack of discipline in the present system. I have to start by saying that I am personally a little concerned that the system is perhaps too disciplinary.

Let us start with the problem of liquidity, without dwelling on the difficulty in defining liquidity. The concept has become quite elastic. In an approximate sense, I tend to think in terms of base sources of liquidity and borrowed liquidity, official and unofficial, and in terms of how much leveraging can be put on top of base liquidity. I would like to point out that the ability to borrow liquidity has been proven since 1974 to be limited—not infinite, but limited.

In other words, there are limitations to how much a given balance sheet can carry in terms of borrowed liquidity. In several cases, we are approaching those limits in terms of borrowed liquidity obtained in the private market.

As countries exhaust their capacity to borrow liquidity, or exhaust their capacity for intervention in the foreign exchange market, at least two things happen. One is an adjustment in rate, usually quite substantial, reflecting the suppressed disequilibrium that had been growing for some time; and the other, which ultimately happens in almost every case, is an adjustment process. Ironically, this is an adjustment in internal policies to deal with the underlying disequilibrium whose external manifestation has been financed for a number of years. I think that, in some cases, that is happening.

We have several concerns in this connection. First, the way in which this discipline works is quite abrupt. This is in part because of the institutional arrangements in the private banking sector, the tendency for heavy syndication of loans, which tends to inhibit discriminatory lending. Once the door closes, it is closed, and it is very difficult to reopen.

A second factor that concerns us is our limited ability to provide what we would call transitory financing, official financing, during a period of adjustment, from here to here, in J-curve terms. It is one of the reasons why we are working very hard to gain additional support for the Financial Support Fund.

The present system does have a discipline. At times the effects of this discipline may be even too abrupt, not gradual enough. But the discipline inherent in the system eventually will compel adjustment. To the degree that it reveals suppressed disequilibrium, it will involve substantial rate adjustments which ought not to be associated with the functioning of the system as a whole, but should be addressed to the individual situations which have produced that phenomenon. Specifically, we could not take the case of the Italian lira and ascribe the recent market performance of the lira to the functioning of the system.

A word about the International Monetary Fund's role in the kind of system that we see developing. First, the Fund, in our view, will play an increasingly important role as a lender of last resort, as a provider of official transitory financing, and as a provider of assistance for adjustment. It is one of the reasons we fought so hard for the maintenance of conditionality in Jamaica.

The Fund will be pulled into its role as an adviser, and a conditional lender, as I view it, when private sources are exhausted, or nearly exhausted, and when adjustment has to begin. From our standpoint, this places a tremendous burden on the Fund and puts it in a pivotal role, where it ought to be able to count on our support.

Second, according to proposed Article IV, Section 3 (iii), the Fund will assume a large role in terms of discerning or reviewing practices designed to manipulate the system. Thus, in the writing of Article IV, the Fund is put in the role of arbiter. This is a huge responsibility. Article IV provides only the foundation; it does not provide the superstructure.

Concluding my review of the evolving monetary system, I would like to report that I think it *is* a system. I think it has enough built-in disciplines, perhaps being even too disciplinary.

In terms of progress recently achieved, we are moving, in my opinion, toward a more congruent view of what is appropriate intervention. I suspect that it will come quite close to the language that I read as part of the Rambouillet understanding.

I can also report that there is a perception of the need for supplementing the present transitional official financing capacity. Moreover, despite the variability in exchange rates which we have all observed, officials are cooperating far more than had been the case, and I suspect that the history of the last three months would have been substantially different, had it not been for that cooperation.

Finally, there is the potential for a framework of what might be called stability among hard currencies. One of them would be the deutsche mark bloc, and another, the yen. The Japanese recently tried to internationalize the yen to the extent that it is starting to assume the role of a reserve currency. At the top of the triangle, I would like to see the dollar.

If we want an effectively functioning system, I suspect that our handling of the dollar and, in particular, the success or failure of our domestic policies will be pivotal. We are not likely to have a functioning system, or to achieve the results we desire, in the absence of more effective public policies in the United States.

THE ROLE OF THE IMF UNDER THE AMENDED ARTICLES OF AGREEMENT

Sam Y. Cross

I have been asked to discuss the institutional setting for the future evolution of exchange rate arrangements—first, by describing some aspects of the Jamaica Agreement and the proposed amendments to the IMF articles and, second, by describing the role of the Fund under the amended exchange rate provisions.

The new exchange rate provisions reflect the understandings reached initially at the time of the Rambouillet summit. As many in this audience will certainly know, the main point of those provisions is that true exchange rate stability can be achieved only by attaining underlying economic stability. The principal focus of attention must be on sound economic policies in the member countries, rather than on actions to peg or manage exchange rates. In my view, the matter is as simple as that.

The proposed Article IV thus retains the basic objectives of the Bretton Woods system—the promotion of an open and expanding world economy, international financial and economic stability, cooperation, and so forth—but stresses achieving stable underlying conditions rather than attempting to prescribe a specific exchange rate regime.

Thus, instead of attempting to specify that one particular exchange rate arrangement, namely, par values, must be applied, the new provisions set forth certain general obligations and recognize that these obligations may be met through a variety of exchange arrangements.

The focus is more on the things a nation does than on the techniques and means by which they are done.

The amended Article IV establishes a broad requirement that members collaborate with the Fund and with each other to ensure orderly exchange arrangements—by undertaking (among other things) to direct their economic and financial policies toward fostering orderly growth with reasonable price stability, to promote orderly underlying economic and financial conditions, and (very important) not to manipulate the exchange rate system either to avoid adjustment or to gain unfair competitive advantage.

Within this general framework, the new Article IV does a number of things; it effectively legalizes the current exchange rate practices, including floating; it provides wide latitude for individual countries to adopt specific exchange arrangements of their own choosing, so long as the country fulfills its general obligations; and it provides a flexible framework for the adaptation of the exchange arrangements over the future.

Provision is made for decision by the Fund by an 85 percent majority vote for the establishment of general exchange arrangements, leaving scope for individual countries to adopt specific arrangements of their own choosing, so long as they are consistent with the Fund's purposes and with the member's general obligations.

No attempt is made to prescribe a list of the possible general exchange arrangements which could evolve in the future; the future decisions may reflect the evolution of the monetary system. Provision is also made for possible future adoption—again, by an 85 percent vote—of a system based on stable but adjustable par values. A decision to introduce general par values would require a determination that certain specified conditions exist in order to ensure that a system would be workable—conditions related to the existence of stability in the world economy, effective inducements for adjustment, adequate sources of liquidity, and other factors.

In addition, important changes have been made—improvements in my view—over the kind of par value provisions which were in the Bretton Woods arrangements. One such change is that individual countries would not be required to adopt par values and could choose to maintain or adopt other arrangements. While there would obviously have to be a sufficient number of countries in a par value system to constitute a critical mass, so that the par value system could operate, this does not mean that every country would have to maintain a par value.

Moreover, a country would be free to terminate a par value it had adopted unless the Fund objected by a 85 percent majority. The par values under the new Article IV would be somewhat more flexible than former par values. They might be changed more readily, for example, to prevent the emergence of—as well as to correct—fundamental disequilibria. The Fund is enjoined to discourage the maintenance of unrealistic par values.

Another change from the original Bretton Woods par value arrangements is that the amended article provides wider exchange rate margins as well as the power to change those margins. Also the Fund is authorized to terminate a par value that a member is not maintaining, thereby freeing other members of any obligations toward that par value. And an important—in fact essential—aspect of the new exchange-rate provisions is that the Fund is provided with clear authority to oversee the international monetary system, to assure its effective operations, and to oversee the compliance of each member with its obligations. The Fund is to exercise what the article calls "firm surveillance" over the exchange rate policies of members and is to adopt specific principles for the guidance of all members with respect to those policies.

Development of the principles underlying the new article will undoubtedly be a subject for the IMF directors and for the Interim Committee while the amendments are under consideration in legislatures in the period ahead. The IMF Board of Governors is currently voting on the final text of the amendments, and has already approved a resolution on the proposed quota increase. Legislative action is required in most countries (including the United States) following completion of the governors' vote, before the amendments can be ratified and the quotas increased.

The package of amendments must be accepted in their entirety, and they will come into effect only after three-fifths of the members, or seventy-seven countries, having four-fifths of the voting power, have accepted them. This process could take one and a half to two years.

There have been some who have criticized the absence of detailed and limiting exchange rate provisions in the article, and the consequent scope for flexible adaptation, as leaving a vacuum, or the appearance of a system without its substance. Others have questioned whether the new monetary arrangements represent an advance over the Bretton Woods or other systems, pointing to the recent exchange market disturbances.

For the most part, the questioning reflects in some sense a misreading of the agreements that have been reached. The focus on achieving underlying economic stability does not mean a promise of instant stability in the exchange markets. Differences in economic conditions between countries in inflation rates and in recovery certainly remain substantial. The process of reversing the pattern of heavy reliance on short-term financing—so characteristic of recent years—has not been completed.

In these circumstances, it would seem that no monetary system can deliver on the promise of stability. Furthermore, the new arrangements, in my view, could not be expected to guarantee that governments will follow the appropriate policies. No system can really ensure that all government policies will be appropriate. Systems may provide the proper focus, may start us down the right track toward stability, and may provide a framework of operating principles, but, clearly, we are just at the beginning of this process.

Perhaps I should comment on the Fund's experience with principles or guidelines in the two years after the IMF took the first steps in this direction, with the adoption in June 1974 of a set of guidelines for the management of floating exchange rates.

The concept underlying this endeavor, which was to develop a benchmark against which to judge countries' policies, remains valid. But it would seem to me that this approach requires major revision and reorientation to take account of accumulated experience and the new arrangements. For example, the 1974 guidelines deal only with IMF members regarded as having floating rates. This brings up a difficult question of terminology. Under those guidelines only a relatively few countries were regarded as "floating" even though in some sense it could be said that all currencies are floating. Perhaps this reflected a difference of view whether floating was a kind of temporary aberration or a transitional measure to facilitate changes in fixed rates, or a freely available option or even the norm for the system.

The guidelines are not ideally suited to a system of exchange rates where floating is an acknowledged alternative. For example, they do not effectively deal with actions to peg a rate to avoid adjustment, although such action would, in my view, not be consistent with the new Article IV.

The guidelines also tend to encourage official intervention. From my viewpoint, they are intervention oriented, rather than having an orientation towards the justification of intervention, and this is an important distinction.

The guidelines are influenced by the view that there can be a medium-term target zone or target rate for an exchange rate that can be defined and discovered, and that intervention should be directed towards achieving or maintaining this rate. There are strong doubts about this whole role of zones.

There are, of course, elements in the present guidelines that are useful and that can be carried forward and strengthened. The good things are that they discourage restrictive trade action; they recognize that the exchange rates are a two-way street; and they recognize that the United States has an interest in the impact of intervention in dollars undertaken by other countries. But major elements of the present guidelines would, it seems to me, have to be adapted to accord with the new Article IV. Just how they will be adapted is a question that will occupy the Fund for quite a while.

We shall be working on this in the Fund and elsewhere over the period ahead. We must develop the arrangements necessary to enable the Fund to carry its functions of surveillance over members' exchange rate policies and over the system to assure that members are not manipulating exchange rates to the disadvantage of others.

COMMENTARIES

Thomas de Vries

I should like to make a few remarks on the way in which the crucial change to greater exchange rate flexibility came about, on its consequences, and on some measures that seem necessary in present circumstances.

First, I should like to call attention to the almost unbelievable tenacity with which most policy makers during the late 1960s and early 1970s stuck to the par value system. This attitude continued to exist after it had become quite obvious that the par value system could no longer function under the prevailing circumstances, and, even more remarkable, after that system had finally and completely collapsed in spite of stubborn efforts to maintain it. After the considerable disturbances of the 1960s, it took three speculative waves of unimaginable proportions, with the counterpart of billions of dollars moving from one country to another in a single day, sometimes in a single hour, to move the world in March 1973 towards a more flexible exchange-rate regime for an "interim period," after which par values were to be gradually reestablished according to the thinking or the hope of many authorities concerned.

Thus the par value system was abandoned and greater exchange rate flexibility adopted not as a result of *reform*, but as a result of *breakdown*. The fact that a fundamental change in the international monetary system came about in this way has serious consequences. It means that no agreed view exists on how the new system is to be operated. It also means that the authorities, having lost control over the evolution of the international monetary system, have become reluctant to take up the urgent tasks that await them in regard to managing and improving the system.

It is a remarkable and curious fact that the Committee of Twenty, which witnessed this basic reform of the exchange rate regime during the early months of its existence, chose to ignore it in most of its subsequent work. This occurred although the Committee was charged with reporting on ways and means of bringing about a comprehensive reform of the international monetary system. But although the change to a more flexible exchange rate system meant that *the most important and pressing reform had in fact taken place,* the Committee continued to work on a system based on "stable but adjustable par values," even though that system had collapsed in the meantime. As a result the documents produced by the Committee of Twenty contain very little analysis of the question how to operate a flexible exchange rate system. We have therefore moved to a basically different system without any clear rules for the member countries on how to behave under the new system. The task of evolving such rules, even much of the preceding analytical work, still has to be carried out.

I do share the conviction that the new system does need to have internationally agreed guidelines and principles for exchange rate policies, if it is to work satisfactorily. And it is here that we enter uncharted waters.

One approach would be to establish target zones or reference rates, with the actual exchange rate expected to approach these rates in the medium term. Such a system necessitates the determination of balance of payments aims, most likely both on current and on capital account, at least for the main countries.

Many countries do have balance of payments goals. They may not always be very explicit, but discussions with officials of a country usually show that they do have, at least implicitly, rather clear notions about the appropriate balance of payments structure of their country.

These balance of payments goals of the main countries are often quite inconsistent with one another. Obviously, the current account position of all countries taken together must add up to zero. Hence, one country's surplus must find its counterpart in a deficit somewhere else, which often is far from welcome.

As long as we had fixed exchange rates, it did not matter so much that countries had inconsistent balance of payments goals for the current account, because they lacked the instruments to reach them. But variations in the exchange rate constitute an instrument to bring about desired changes in the current account balance. Hence, these balance of payments goals, sometimes explicit, will be one element that in the future will guide countries' exchange rate policies—at least to some extent.

Therefore, if the Fund were to make any headway in giving guidance in the field toward establishing desirable medium-term reference rates, it would first have to determine a desirable medium-term balance of payments position and structure, at least for the major countries. Then, as a second step, it would estimate the reference rates that would bring about these payments positions.

This difficult task has been rendered even more difficult by the OPEC surpluses. For this means that the Fund would have to develop a view on how the corresponding current account deficits should be distributed. Before the explosive rise in the oil price, the task was less difficult. The combined current account surplus of the industrial countries was equal to the combined deficit of the developing countries; its magnitude was determined by the amount of real resources the first group was willing to make available to the second group as development aid in real terms.

Given the enormous difficulties—analytical, political, and practical —of determining a set of reference rates under these circumstances, this approach seems over-ambitious, at least at the present time. Many officials would tend to treat the reference rates as a kind of par value, especially as long as the basic change in exchange arrangements is not fully digested.

Fortunately, there is an easier approach. Taking most exchange rate relationships and balance of payments positions as given, it is possible, if the case presents itself, to isolate one or two exchange rates which either are seriously out of line or are moving in that direction. Attention should then be focused on these cases of clear-cut deviation from equilibrium, and corrective action should be sought. It seems important for the Fund to develop this approach at an early date and to start putting it into practice at once. In this way, a certain experience and tradition will be available when the proposed Second Amendment of the Fund's Charter becomes effective, and the Fund will be charged with the important task of exercising "firm surveillance over the exchange rate policies of members" (Article IV, Section 3(b)).

Another reason why it is imperative for the Fund to make an early start with surveillance of exchange rates is that there exists a serious misunderstanding or disagreement on the role of monetary policy in exchange rate management.

Mr. Cross has implied and Mr. Yeo has said explicitly that the basic concept of the Rambouillet Agreement underlying the new Article IV on exchange rates is that "exchange rates should be set by market forces." This seems to me a seriously misleading, if not outright erroneous, statement, given the fact that the active monetary policy of

193

the authorities in all countries has a direct and forceful effect on those market forces and the resulting exchange rates. So direct is that effect that it is often only a matter of tactics that determines whether a desired change in the exchange rate will be brought about by official intervention in the money or in the exchange markets.

Indeed, so elusive is the idea that the price of an asset (the national currency) which is produced and regulated by the monetary authorities is to be "set by market forces" that only one interpretation of that statement seems to carry any concrete meaning. That is that U.S. monetary policy will be set exclusively in the light of conditions in the domestic economy, and that the U.S. authorities are ready to accept any exchange rate for the dollar that may result. But this means that exchange rate relationships will not so much reflect the underlying economic conditions, about which there is so much talk, but rather the temporary and quickly changing relations between short-term interest rates for various national currencies, which are the result of continuously changing monetary policies. That is in fact an important part of what we have seen so far.

A first rule, therefore, which the Fund should lay down, should be that monetary policies pursued with internal aims in mind should not be carried to a point where they seriously distort exchange rate relationships. This implies a greater reliance on budgetary policy for the purpose of demand management.

A second rule should be that trade and payment restrictions maintained for balance of payments reasons should be terminated, and be replaced by an appropriate change in the exchange rate. With greater exchange rate flexibility the justification for such restrictions has further diminished. The Fund, which has followed a somewhat lenient policy in this field up to now, should under the new circumstances take a stronger stand.

I should like to close by emphasizing a point that seems to me of crucial importance. In spite of a lack of concrete results, all countries have during the turmoil of the past years as a matter of course accepted and desired a large measure of international cooperation. This is a very striking difference from the situation prevailing in the 1930s. Sometimes it seems by far the most important difference.

It was the desire to cooperate that led to the creation of the Bretton Woods institutions and the agreement on their charters. The forbidding and voluminous document to which Professor Haberler referred earlier embodies the desire to continue that cooperation.

J. J. Polak

It is not easy to find one's way through the exchange rate provisions of the amended Articles of the International Monetary Fund, even though they are relatively short. Perhaps the main reason for the difficulty is that there are two possible answers to the question, "What is the heart of these exchange rate provisions?" There is the philosophical approach, which was expressed for example by Under Secretary Yeo, to the effect that stable underlying conditions make for stable exchange rates, and that we cannot have the latter without having the former. And there is the operational approach, which is also contained in the article.

The philosophical approach contains rather vague injunctions, telling members "to endeavor to direct their policies towards the objective of fostering orderly economic growth," and to "seek to promote stability by fostering orderly underlying economic and financial conditions," and so on. But the operational provision obliges members to "avoid manipulating exchange rates . . . in order to prevent effective balance of payments adjustment." In my opinion, this is the heart of Article IV. This provision, which derives from the basic lesson learned from the failure of the Bretton Woods system, became the major conclusion of the reform exercise. Incidentally, this provision was not contained in the version of Article IV that came down from the summit at Rambouillet but was inserted by the Fund's directors.

This provision implies the obligation of the Fund to develop principles for the management of exchange rates. One tends to slip and call them "principles for intervention," but that is not the central point. These principles must differ from the guidelines that were developed two years ago, in part because they must apply to all currencies and not just to those that call themselves "floating." The distinction between floating and other currencies has proved to be of little use in categorizing countries. To mention one example, Italy made a most important policy change in 1976 by moving from a so-called floating rate to a genuine floating rate.

The injunction of the new Article IV against rates that "prevent effective balance of payments adjustment" must, to my mind, refer to avoidance of a rate that is economically incorrect. Yet I heard Under Secretary Yeo proclaim that the concept of the "right exchange rate" is the antithesis of the new Article IV. The way I heard what he said, there were quotation marks around *right exchange rate*; that is, what countries a few months ago thought was the right rate might not be what they say now is the right rate. What surely is the antithesis of

195

Article IV is the maintenance of a rate when it has become the wrong rate.

As I see it, the main objective of Fund surveillance over exchange rates, apart from the avoidance of erratic fluctuations, it to make as sure as one can—which is not very sure—that members stick to something like a correct rate for their currency or, when necessary, move to such a rate. The two aspects, "stick" and "move," are equally important. This is a major change from what we had before. And I think we do have a general notion of what we mean by a correct rate. It is a notion that is not new but was developed some time ago, namely, that a correct rate is a rate compatible with balance of payments equilibrium over the medium term. Admittedly this produces quite a number of gray areas in questions of application.

Let me mention a few points, not to indicate that we know the answers, but to indicate the areas where we have to look for the answers.

When we talk about the balance of payments over the medium term, we do not mean the reported balance of payments for the most recent quarter. We mean recent balance of payments data corrected for all kinds of cyclical and other factors. I think we are reasonably capable of making these corrections.

When we talk about an exchange rate in a situation where all rates are fluctuating, we mean some kind of an average exchange rate. We need an approach to a definition of weights appropriate for this purpose. Again, this is a difficult question, but it is not insoluble in principle. We mean an average weighted in such a way that if the weighted average does not change, the country's balance of payments does not change. We have, I think, a reasonable approach to such a set of weights in the Fund's multilateral exchange rate model. Of course, we cannot say that exchange rates should remain stable, only that they should adjust to the changes in underlying conditions. As Gottfried Haberler emphasized, we cannot assume for the purposes of this exercise that we have stable underlying conditions.

A subject attracting great attention recently has been differential rates of inflation. It is fascinating how the purchasing power parity theory, which went out of fashion in the mid-1920s, is suddenly blooming again, is being touted all around as an explanation of exchange rates—with all the inaccuracies and all the lack of qualifications so correctly criticized about fifty years ago.

Finally, we must pay more attention to the question of interest rates, in particular in connection with the great recent interest in purchasing power parity. Insofar as exchange rates adjust on the basis of differential rates of inflation, corresponding differential rates of interest are needed to keep exchange rates from diverging from their purchasing power parity levels by anticipation. Actual interest rates do not always meet this test. The countries with the highest rates of inflation do tend to have higher rates of interest than the countries with the lower rates of inflation, but not correspondingly higher.

Armin Gutowski

Even if having a set of international guidelines and principles for national financial and exchange rate policies is considered desirable, such guidelines or principles cannot be dictated by some countries and imposed upon others: they must be negotiated, and each country must feel that it will gain some benefit from them.

First of all, I want to point out that, in principle, there is no necessity to have an international agreement on specific guidelines for each country under the regime of floating exchange rates so long as all—or, at least, the major—countries direct their national policies at restoring the stability of medium-term expectations.

I should like to explain what I mean by considering the West German example. The West German Council of Economic Experts has, in its annual report, expressed the opinion that restoring stability of medium-term expectations was of utmost importance, inasmuch as investment was to be increased again in order to ensure an adequate rate of growth of the production potential and to restore a high level of employment.

The Council believed that exclusive reliance on expansionary monetary and fiscal policy would not be sufficient to attain these goals, since ad hoc demand management had come close to the limits of its effectiveness. Expansionary policy was indispensable in the early phase of the business cycle, but to be successful it had to be accompanied by policies which would reestablish confidence of investors and consumers.

In particular, this implies (1) a monetary policy to bring down the rate of inflation gradually; (2) a fiscal policy that (given the monetary policy) will not crowd out private investment when the economy approaches full employment again because persisting public structural deficits have made long-term interest rates too high; and (3) an incomes policy that will have a high probability of preventing minimum wage unemployment.

There is little use in merely proclaiming these policy objectives. Proclamations have been made in the past—for example, in the European Community—and failed. Therefore, the means had to be spelled out by which those objectives could be reached.

197

For several years now, the West German Central Bank has announced in advance a rate by which it will expand the corrected monetary base over the next twelve months, thereby showing the (decreasing) limit for the rate of price level increase still compatible with a particular growth of the production potential and its use. A clear-cut monetary policy of this sort is probably the most important national guideline for stabilizing medium-term expectations.

It is necessary for the government to show—in its budget for the next year and in its medium-term fiscal plans—which expenditures it will cut, which taxes it will raise, in order to make the structural deficit vanish within the time needed to reach the full employment level.

Most difficult is the formulation of an adequate incomes policy. In a free society in which wage contracts are autonomously negotiated by trade unions and employers' associations, it is both difficult and undesirable to establish binding guidelines on the rate of wage increases. The current wage round in West Germany, however, suggests that workers and employers will limit wage increases when the monetary authorities remain committed to a pre-announced rate of monetary expansion directed at gradually pressing down the inflation rate.

Of course, let me say that on the side, the battle for income distribution will not be won in this way. A change in income distribution has to be achieved, mostly, by other means than nominal wage policy; for example, by profit and loss sharing.

No doubt, economic and social conditions in West Germany are especially favorable for implementing such policies. Countries with high rates of inflation and long conditioning to accelerating inflation will probably have to be much more careful in bringing down the rates of price increase. However, this should not prevent them from setting up guidelines (even more or less ambitious ones) for their monetary and fiscal policies directed at these objectives, even though it must take them much longer to reach those objectives. If all major countries established credible national guidelines, medium-term expectations would be stabilized.

What would be the consequences for the movements of exchange rates? Our discussions have strengthened my belief about one important cause of erratic exchange rate fluctuations. That is the high degree of uncertainty over the medium-term development of basic economic variables, as a result of the uncertainty over policy decisions in various countries.

Medium-term expectations as to the development of basic economic variables change rather often as a result of these uncertainties. It is not surprising, therefore, that both spot and forward exchange rates, though differing according to interest differentials, move upward because of some policy decisions which let people expect more stability in the future, but reverse the direction of their movement as soon as something happens that casts new doubts on the firmness of stabilization policies.

Establishing national guidelines in major countries that people believe will be followed would remove the most important source of volatility of exchange rates. Thereby misallocation of resources associated with such volatility would be prevented. Unfortunately, we know from past experience that mere understanding of these interrelationships can hardly be expected to bring about the discipline in national policies necessary to stabilize medium-term expectations for exchange rate movements.

Here international guidelines and principles could be helpful. By international guidelines I mean an international agreement on national goals for monetary and fiscal policies for each country participating in the agreement. Clearly, those goals would differ from country to country, according to their different rates of inflation and unemployment at the outset, as well as their different ability to follow stabilization policies. The only necessary condition would be a pre-announced binding policy that does not allow the rate of inflation to rise. Of course, at least in the longer run, policies should be aimed at gradually bringing down this rate.

Mere international agreement on specific guidelines for national monetary and fiscal policies for each country would not suffice. The international agreement would have to contain claims on national discipline in adhering to the agreed-upon guidelines and principles. It would also have to contain provisions for international solidarity in extending credits to countries needing help in meeting the guidelines and principles they had agreed to observe.

Those provisions for national discipline on the one hand and for international solidarity on the other have to be balanced against each other carefully. The trouble with the Bretton Woods system—and even more with the experiment of getting a monetary union in Europe underway by fixing exchange rates among the participants—was that the provisions for national discipline were too ambitious and the claims of the weaker nations on the solidarity of the stronger ones could not be met. The arrangements were therefore bound to break down.

The guidelines ought to be such that, for the weaker countries, the disadvantages of observing them would be light compared with the disadvantages of not being entitled to the solidarity of the international community. For the stronger countries, there would also be an incentive for coming to such an agreement, inasmuch as these countries could expect that exchange rates would behave in a less volatile manner and (probably more important) that the danger of more trade and capital controls would be reduced.

Even if an international agreement on specific guidelines for national financial policies were reached, medium-term exchange rate expectations of private money holders and investors could temporarily run counter to the expectations of governments and monetary authorities that follow the international fixed guidelines and principles. In this case, official interventions beyond those of smoothing day-to-day fluctuations would be desirable. International guidelines for national exchange rate policies, if they are necessary at all, would have to be derived from the international guidelines for national monetary and fiscal policies.

In other words, there would have to be a set of consistent guidelines for national financial and exchange rate policies. Guidelines for interventions or even obligations to intervene in the foreign exchange markets make sense only if there are national monetary and fiscal guidelines which lead to diminishing (or at least not rising) rates of inflation, and which seem likely to be observed. If such international guidelines for national financial policies cannot be made to work—and the European guidelines do not make me optimistic—then I see no rationale for guidelines concerning exchange rate policies only, except those intended to smooth out day-to-day fluctuations and to prevent competitive depreciations.

Exchange rate fluctuations stemming from uncertainty over the trends of basic economic variables must be accepted as unavoidable, even though they might distort resource allocation. In my opinion, the monetary authorities cannot know which way the underlying economic variables will turn. Therefore, official interventions might bring about greater distortions of resource allocation than the exchange rate fluctuations that would occur if there were no intervention.

Fred Hirsch

I would like to start with a few brief reflections on assessing the Jamaica agreement as it relates to exchange rates, because this is obviously central to the future development of the guidelines for exchange rate policies. I am struck by the extraordinarily wide range of interpretation and assessment that has been given.

The best way I know of encapsulating the point is to make up or recount book titles for the many books that are being written about this. I happen to know the title of one which is being written by my colleague, John Williamson, which is going to be called, "The Failure of World Monetary Reform 1971–1974." At one time there was a rumor that Jeremy Morse might be writing a book, and the title of that, of course, would have been, "The Triumph of International Monetary Reform." And then, the last one—with some sort of apologies to Messrs. Salant, Kindleberger, and Despres—would be something like, "We Didn't Just Do Something: We Stood There This Time—We Really Did."

This is not meant in an entirely flippant way. When I read the new Article IV, it did seem to me an incomplete document, taken by itself. It was a kind of an agreement to have a cease-fire, an agreement to accept the *fait accompli* on the cease-fire line. The peace treaty that says on what basis the peace is to be kept will be worked out later. If this is a correct interpretation, it provides some explanation of why one can have conflicting views about the strength, durability, and significance of the accord.

On the exchange rate, there is a rather fundamental change from the earlier system. I am not saying whether it is a change for the worse or a change for the better, but it is a fundamental change, and this is in line with what Sam Cross was saying. Rather than laying down certain specific obligations for countries, certain specific procedures they are expected to follow, the emphasis is on intent and on outcome. The intent is to avoid manipulating exchange rates, and to avoid an unfair competitive advantage as an outcome. All this is to be done without specifying a norm to which these aspects can be hooked.

It is quite consistent with this interpretation—and maybe this underlies what Sam Cross said—to say that the system could give the international community much closer control over what countries do and what actually happens than had been the case when there were specific rules for countries to follow. And it is quite fair to say that out of this, the ideal world exchange arrangements could come.

But the point that strikes me forcefully is that in this view one is really putting an extraordinary load on the authority of the international umpire.

An analogy can be made to a tennis game. In the old system, we had certain rules—people were expected to stand outside the baseline, to serve in a certain way, and so on, and the umpire called out when the rules were not met. In the new system, we have a much more sophisticated tennis game. It is recognized that players of different sizes have different needs—for serving in different positions, for different tennis shoes, and all that. And on the whole, we can play this game as we like, provided first that we do not hit the ball in a nasty manner; and, second, that our opponent is not put in an unfair position upon receiving it. If these things happen, the umpire will blow the whistle. To be sure his whistle is not in particularly good working order and he still has to work out the principles upon which he is going to blow it, but in time the problems will be worked out.

The facetiousness will stop there—but I do think the analogy emphasizes both the strength and the weakness of the new system. Clearly, to have totally discretionary—one might almost say subjective— principles of surveillance of this kind, the umpire must have much stronger authority than he has had. One must give the umpire a much greater degree of discretion. The question becomes whether countries are willing to do this. In this connection, those of us who were critics of the par value system ought to recognize a secondary function that a set of specific rules can provide, the function of providing leverage for those who survey and oversee a system. Thus, specific obligations—whether in a par value system, or in a pegged system, or in a system of managed floating—ensure that countries in certain circumstances will be tripped up by *specific* transgressions so that there will be a clear-cut case for exercising international influence over them.

In fact, even in the decaying phase for the par value system, but certainly in the earlier 1960s, one did have a number of cases of this kind. Often, the actions that were taken were undesirable. West Germany financed its surplus, rather than getting rid of the trade surplus, and to some extent Japan did also. Nonetheless, we need to recognize that we did have some basis for international consistency, and unless we are willing to abandon consistency, we must find some substitute for this leverage.

I am not arguing that we should go back to the old type of leverage, but simply that it is especially important to develop a system of international exchange management based on something more than a mere agreement to cooperate.

This brings me to the more specific question of surveillance of exchange rates. The underlying philosophy is that international surveillance of some kind is desirable on two grounds: (1) that the market does have inadequate information, not least in relation to the policy objectives of the authorities, and (2) that countries do, as Thomas de Vries was saying, have views, whether implicitly or explicitly, about desirable balance of payments structure. But what ought to be the way for applying that philosophy? I think in principle, there are three ways.

The first is to rely, in effect, entirely on process, to say there are certain specific things countries must not do in exchange rate intervention, and maybe also (though this is more difficult to specify), in money market policy. They must not push the rate down when it is already going down. I suppose that an outright prohibition of exchange restrictions would come under this head. The second is to develop certain norms for exchange rate equilibria. These must obviously be based on success in the prior task of working out a consistent set of balance of payments patterns and targets.

The third way, and this, I suppose, is in a sense in the spirit of the IMF guidelines, would be a weak mixture of the first two, based mainly on process, with some background view about the desirable structure of exchange rates. The second element would be secondary, and at present not operational, and this third way would come down to tracking the pace of movement, rather than really having a deliberate view about the movement of rates.

In my view, the first system, the reliance on process, is so weak that it differs little from the mere central-bank smoothing implied in the Rambouillet agreement. Moreover, I am probably in a minority here in questioning whether that system can be stiffened by a tight system on exchange restrictions. Frankly, such a tight system would be inconsistent with the new philosophy—and with the old philosophy as well.

If a country—perhaps the United Kingdom—decides that as a matter of policy it wants to impose capital controls in order to prevent an outflow of capital, I do not see—given the general philosophy that countries should have responsibility for their own system—how it is either practicable or desirable to rule out this imposition of capital controls.

It follows, then, that the third system would be weak for the same kind of reason as the first. What I come down to is that if one is serious about putting any kind of force into international surveillance at all, one must try to hammer out certain kinds of exchange rate norms.

Finally, I will indicate a rather controversial rough sketch of the form in which this hammering out might be done. I want to emphasize that this is not a forecast, because it is unlikely to happen.

To begin with, an official high-level body—it may be Working Party III of the OECD or the IMF Executive Board—should start with the relatively familiar task of having meetings with representatives of major countries. They should indicate their expectations for their balance of payments outcome and structure, and the different sets of numbers should be reconciled.

At the level of policy confrontation, the burden of justifying an objection must lie with the objector. Each country's expectations would be accepted unless there were clear reasons for objecting to them. The two reasons for objecting to them could be an undesirable structure or a structure that is unacceptable to other countries in the group, and non-performance on earlier expectations. Fred Bergsten mentioned that Japan, for example, appears to be developing a large trade surplus balanced by large capital movements. If those capital movements appear to be unsustainable or undesirable, or leading to excessive reserve accumulation, that would be open to objection. Policy confrontation exercises such as these would include a certain scope for pressure for remedial policies.

On a lower level, the professionals in the business, the secretariat of the Working Party III and the IMF staff, having heard the arguments presented on the higher level and knowing the outcome of negotiations, would translate the amended balance of payments expectations into estimated exchange rate norms—normally, of course, on a cyclically adjusted basis. Those norms would have a status akin to parities without margins—that is to say, they would be an estimate of the equilibrium rate, but with no absolute commitment to defend the rate at any point.

We all know the technical difficulties in a route of this kind. Obviously, one of the biggest difficulties lies in the scope for professional differences of view on the various stages of translation to be carried out, from balance of payments expectations to exchange rates.

Moreover, governments are unwilling to leave the decision on what rate is going to be published in the *Financial Times* to somebody about five levels down in some organization. The publication of the IMF exchange-rate calculations after the U.S. suspension of gold convertibility in the famous leak of August 1971 was a troubling experience. If there is only one set of numbers, and if that set of numbers is published sporadically, then the speculative dangers would be significant. The best solution would be to try to take some of the authority out of these numbers by getting two—at least two—technical secretariats to do them. If the two come out with different results, that would be fine. I think this is the only way in which one would ever manage to take the drama and apparent final authority out of such numbers. Publishing the numbers in a range is another possibility, but a range is not much better than a single number, because people tend to look just at the limits.

There should be a certain amount of confrontation over policy, combined with rather open technical work based on that confrontation. Rival numbers should be published, and anyone who does not like the result can say that the estimated elasticities are wrong and ought to be changed. As far as possible, the technical aspects of the discussion should be published, following the Federal Reserve Board policy on the minutes of its meetings.

In this way, one would be doing something dear to the heart of the free market advocates—that is, supplying the market with more and better information, although the best information will not always be unique information from one source only. Beyond that, some leverage would be gained for exerting international influence over a country that was felt to be going for either an inconsistent or undesirable target.

What Armin Gutowski has suggested is, I am sure, by far the best way of getting to exchange rate stability. That is not really what I am talking about, of course; I am talking about consistency. I think the difficulty is, as he indicated, that exchange rate stability is dependent on countries' accepting international discipline to move towards a stable domestic financial structure. In fact, we have to live in a world where this will not always happen.

Obviously his system would be the most desirable if the underlying conditions were there, but what I do not see is why, if those underlying conditions are absent, one cannot take the second best system—going for exchange rate consistency and attempting thereby to avoid the worst of the fluctuations without full coordination of internal policies. In other words, I think that Gutowski's plan, while not returning to the notion of putting heavy weight on full coordination as in a par value system, is getting fairly close to it. The main problem, in my view, is finding the second best system.

Rimmer de Vries

We have had comments on the triumph of monetary reform and on the failure of monetary reform, but the entire process looks to me more like the struggle for monetary reform. It is clear that this process is far from being completed, and on the question of exchange-rate management I would like to make three propositions.

My first is that exchange rates are sensitive to and will tend to respond to a variety of factors. These include (1) inflation differentials; (2) capital flows, which are in part the result of interest rate differentials and in part of differentials in capital availability; (3) trade and current account developments, which would reflect both cyclical and structural changes; (4) political developments; (5) general exchange-market sentiment; and (6) official intervention and exchange rate policies. These are the main areas from which the pressures on exchange rates will rise.

It is of course difficult to generalize about the significance of each of these factors at any particular moment. The significance will vary from time to time and from country to country. In Britain, for instance, the development and expectation of inflation differentials, the first factor, appear to be the most important sources of pressure on the pound. Any news—whether dealing with wages, money supply, or the exchange rate itself—or any new expectations on the inflation differential between the United Kingdom and other countries will tend to have an immediate impact on the exchange rate of the pound.

On the other hand, in Canada, it is the second factor, the capital flows, which appears to be of overriding significance. The enormous amount of borrowing abroad is the principal determining factor behind the current strength of the Canadian dollar—in fact, it overrides the impact of the inflation differentials, which would call for a much weaker Canadian dollar. An example of the third factor, trade and current account developments, may be found in the Netherlands, where the large natural gas exports have overshadowed adverse price influences on Dutch competitiveness and, consequently, on the trade balance, and have kept the guilder a strong currency. And in Italy, it is the fourth factor, the political situation, which has been of primary importance. One would have to be an expert in Italian politics in order to forecast the exchange rate of the Italian lira. The lira at 900 does not reflect relative prices or interest rate factors but rather political conditions.

From time to time general exchange-market sentiment can influence a currency completely contrary to rational economic expectations and thus can become an autonomous factor by itself. We have seen several important examples in the last few years, involving the dollar (early 1974), sterling (spring 1976), and the lira, where the market moved a currency far away from levels that make sense from a price and interest rate point of view. My task as a commercial bank economist is to identify the significance of these various pressures on the key exchange rates and to judge what their relative strengths are and in what direction on balance they are going to work on the exchange rate. I hasten to add that one must be very flexible inasmuch as if one were to focus exclusively on one factor—say, inflation differentials—and come to the conclusion, say, that the Canadian dollar should be moving from 102 to 98 to the dollar, one might be dead wrong. Other factors could be preponderant and could be moving that currency in the opposite direction. One must look at an entire range of factors, all of which may be of great significance in exerting pressure on the exchange rate. Commercial banks and dealers, in taking positions and in giving advice to their clients, should assess the relative strengths of these factors and not focus on one particular factor.

The same applies to central banks. If a central bank or treasury were to look exclusively at inflation differentials and decide that on the basis of relative prices a particular rate would be the most appropriate, stabilizing it in accordance with that judgment and ignoring all other factors, intervention could at times be very heavy. In the case of Canada, for example, it could mean that the Bank of Canada might have to take into its reserves most of the heavy foreign borrowing by the various Canadian entities, if the authorities took the view that, say, 98 or 100 would be the right rate for the Canadian dollar. But this would not be a sensible policy; it could indeed prove to be very expensive in reserves losses if there were downward pressures, and very inflationary with heavy capital inflows.

We must recognize that many factors may have an influence on the rate, and that the significance of these factors can change quickly, sometimes in a matter of three months. I was asked the other day about the importance of these various factors in relation to the dollar. For some time, trade figures had a large influence on the dollar, then it became fashionable to watch the federal funds rate and money supply data. Swiss bankers and exchange dealers visiting New York would always ask one question: "What is the federal funds rate going to be tomorrow?" In a period like this, relative interest rates are clearly of overriding significance. Recently, however, inflation differentials have become a more important factor.

The second point I want to stress is that governments should be concerned about their exchange rate. This seems to be a controversial issue. Countries with very large external trade sectors obviously must be attentive to their exchange rate. Changes in the rate have an immediate impact on domestic prices and will tend to affect employment as well. The United States—because it is less foreign-trade oriented than many other countries—probably can afford to be somewhat less concerned about its rate. However, as Sam Cross has mentioned, the United States should at least be indirectly concerned, because it is affected by the actions and policies of other nations. To be sure, some U.S. officials, including Under Secretary of the Treasury Yeo, have correctly pointed out that we should not be *actively* concerned, because we really do not know what the right exchange rate is. It is indeed difficult to determine, and impossible to prove, what the right rate is, just as it was difficult to specify during the Bretton Woods era what fundamental disequilibrium was. But the issue does not end here.

As Marina Whitman notes, it is helpful sometimes to arrive at a judgment in a negative way. We may not know what rate is right, but we have a good idea when a rate is clearly wrong and out of line. For example, if today, on the basis of current cost relationships, the mark were at 2.00 or 3.50 to the dollar, rather than 2.55, most of us would agree that it would not make much economic sense. Even the U.S. Treasury, I suspect, would be rather concerned if, with the present structure of prices, such a rate were to be brought about by exceptional capital flows set off by political developments or expectations. The U.S. authorities certainly should be upset if the Smithsonian devaluation of the dollar were to be unwound irrespective of cost or price developments. I strongly suggest that governments, including the U.S. government, should have an interest in the levels of their exchange rates, even under a system of floating. Although we cannot determine and pinpoint the right rate, we probably can set a broad range within which the rate makes good economic sense. And if the rate moves outside that range, governments should examine various policy alternatives to correct rate movements.

The third point is that exchange rate adjustment should be carried out mainly through the markets. This is the main reason for the interest in, and the continuing discussion on, the efficiency of markets. Heavy reliance on markets assumes that these markets are efficient and will reflect fundamental underlying economic trends. If markets are the most efficient and impartial medium through which adjustments should be brought about, then the authorities should inform them as well as possible. Perhaps markets know best *how* to bring about adjustments, but they do not know best how large the adjustments should be. They want to know best. They are always guessing and searching for information. Governments should refrain from secrecy and should improve the information stream. If exchange rates are to reflect fundamental factors in an economy, such as inflation differentials, information about these differentials should be readily available. However, the compilation of comparative price data is still quite difficult. Many countries do not have adequate price statistics, particularly wholesale price statistics in manufacturing, and those statistics available are frequently dated. But market knowledge of appropriate data on prices, costs, trade, current accounts, and balances of payments is vital if the market's judgment is to reflect fundamental factors. Let countries and the various international organizations such as the Organization for Economic Cooperation and Development and the International Monetary Fund improve and publish the data and the raw material from which the market must derive its judgment. I would not, however, advocate that these organizations be made responsible for regularly expressing their views on the appropriateness of exchange rates.

What should we do when markets are not efficient and do not reflect fundamental economic factors? There is wide agreement that central banks should correct disorderly and inefficient markets. The way in which this matter is phrased is significant because some central banks probably would prefer to maintain orderly markets than to correct disorderly markets. I sympathize with them because they may have nothing to do with exchange market intervention for a long time if they continue merely to correct disorderly markets. Their role may be compared to that of the guards in the New York Federal Reserve Bank. Because the guards are to use their pistols only if there is disorder in the bank, many may never use their guns at all while on active duty. Both guards and official interventionists should resist the temptation to maintain order either by occasional shooting or by being regularly in the market.

Beyond this we have several important examples in recent financial history where *in orderly markets* expectations have carried exchange rates to levels which had no immediate relationship to basic economic facts. The development of the dollar at the end of 1973 and early 1974 was a case in point. At that time the market was expecting the bulk of the billions of oil dollars to come to the United States, although in fact this country eventually received only a small share of the OPEC surplus. Market expectations can be terribly wrong not only in the area of capital flows but also in the area of inflation differentials.

As I indicated earlier, I do not believe it is sufficient to approach these special situations (where markets are orderly) with the rule: Don't intervene because we don't know what rate is right. This approach is a dead end. The rule should rather be this: If there are many forces and factors responsible for moving an exchange rate, we ought to consider the use of many instruments (not merely official intervention) to influence the movement of the rate. In January 1974, the U.S. Treasury countered the exceptional strength of the dollar by abolishing capital controls, and this courageous and wise move had the desirable effects. In the United Kingdom the successful development of an incomes policy and the narrowing of the budget deficit will do far more for sterling than exchange market intervention. There are many situations where changes in monetary policy will have an effect on the rate that is quicker and more lasting than the effect of intervention. Even the United States should probably take a more positive view of occasionally using monetary policy in conducting its exchange policy. In some countries, such as Italy, exchange controls should not be ruled out as a means of curtailing capital flight. To sum up, my rule would be this: Provide the market with the maximum of relevant economic information, use exchange market intervention rather sparingly, and make more active use of the many other instruments that influence the exchange rate.

Marina v. N. Whitman

My comments here are in the nature of a series of questions that were raised in my mind as I listened to the discussion. But let me say first that I am struck by one point of unspoken agreement among the participants in this conference. However substantial their differences of opinion on some of the major issues, there is an analytical consensus, which I do not think existed two or three years ago, that the questions of rules for exchange market intervention and of international coordination of national economic policies are extremely closely related.

The reason is, quite simply, that there is more than one way to skin a cat. A country can maintain—or change—the relationship between its own currency and other currencies by direct intervention in the foreign exchange market. It can achieve the same result by taking other actions which appear, at first glance, to be far removed from the foreign exchange market, such as undertaking government or government-encouraged borrowing abroad rather than at home, or vice versa, or by changing the mix of monetary and fiscal policies. Therefore, one cannot really talk about rules for intervention or about behavior as regards exchange rates in isolation, without regard to a wide variety of financial and other policies that may be used to manipulate these rates.

Of course, all of this makes the problem of surveillance over exchange arrangements much broader and more difficult to manage. It is no wonder that the relevant section of Article IV of the proposed amended IMF Articles of Agreement is vague, inasmuch as no one has the foggiest notion of the way to go about such surveillance. This seems to be one of those situations in which our comprehension of the analytical complexities of the problem vastly outruns our knowledge of what to do about it. But, since understanding is at least the first step toward progress, the present state of affairs is not entirely discouraging. I think, though, that the implied controversy between Hirsch and Gutowski is dominated by uneasiness arising from a broad view of exchange-rate determination and by a strong desire to find some way of truncating the problem, of cutting off a piece of it and dealing with it separately, in order to make it more manageable.

Since, in considering guidelines for exchange rate policies, we find ourselves also raising questions about economic coordination, it may be useful to recognize at the outset that one can talk about such coordination at several different levels. The lowest level or least demanding form of coordination is simply the avoidance of explicit "beggar-my-neighbor" policies. I find both the stated intentions of nations and their recent record of behavior as regards such policies generally encouraging.

I would not have believed, when we headed into severe worldwide recession a year and a half ago, that we would collectively be able to avoid resorting to explicit "beggar-my-neighbor" policies to the extent that they have been avoided. There are a number of reasons for this, I am sure, but one very important one is that we were operating on a generalized system of floating exchange rates, however managed, rather than trying to maintain a system of pegged rates.

The next level of coordination can be described as taking into account the probable stabilization policy behavior of other countries— at least of major partner countries—in setting one's own. This type of policy coordination, which is obviously an iterative process, is important in order to avoid collective overkill on either the stimulative or the contractionary side. I would say the recent scorecard on this sort of behavior is mixed, at best. The recent recession may have been aggravated by a certain amount of contractionary overkill on the part of the industrialized countries as a group, but the fact that the beginning of this last recession coincided with a period of unprecedentedly high inflation makes it particularly hard to call the shots on this one. In any case, the level of coordination that involves keeping close track of what other countries are doing and/or are probably going to do, and taking these into account in one's own policy planning, is probably not as easy as it sounds.

Next comes a much more demanding level of coordination that involves making policy decisions, including decisions with respect to the timing of implementation, in common, with a real effort to avoid major inconsistencies. One could go beyond this to the level of genuine harmonization or joint policy making, but I think it is silly to spend much time discussing that level at the moment. We are a long way from a world central government, or from the kind of international institutions and procedures that would be required for that level of coordination.

Another important question that arises in considering the question of coordination is, which end of the problem does one try to approach first? That is, does one work first on the coordination of policy actions themselves or should the coordination of countries' macroeconomic policy targets (or at least the avoidance of major inconsistencies in those targets) come first? In a neat analytical universe, of course, one implies the other, and the problem is one of simultaneous determination of targets and policy instruments. But in the practical world of negotiation and procedure I suspect it may make some difference which end one starts from. A number of speakers here have emphasized the primary importance of making sure that the targets of the various nations are not blatantly inconsistent.

There was, it will be noted, a type of consistency mechanism operating under the Bretton Woods system. As far as balance-of-payments targets went, at least, the United States served as the "nth country"—a residual to provide consistency. Clearly, in the end that proved quite unsatisfactory, both for the United States and for everyone else. Today we must find some other way of insuring consistency of targets in the international system, and the necessity for doing this raises another question that has been implicit in much of the discussion. Should one take the position of Working Party III of the OECD, which attacks the problem from the side of balance-of-payments targets? Or is it better to focus primarily on the approach of the old Working Party I, which is today more or less carried on in Working Party IV, where countries discuss their broad macroeconomic targets, and the monetary and fiscal stances those targets imply, for the short and medium term? Again, in an analytical sense one implies the other, but in procedural terms the two approaches are quite different.

Incidentally, it is my impression that countries do not really have overall balance-of-payments goals at all, at least under the present system. What they do have is one of two things. They may have exchange-rate goals, which really are concerned with the relationship between exchange-rate changes and the internal price level, or they may have (and many countries long have had) targets for the current account or for the balance on goods and services. In the Bretton Woods days, current account targets masqueraded as overall balance-of-payments targets. Participants sat in Working Party III and talked about balance-of-payments targets when what they really had in mind were targets for the current account or for the balance on goods and services. With the advent of floating rates, the concept of overall balance-of-payments targets makes less sense than ever, and we might as well be explicit about the kinds of external targets countries actually have.

In any case, there clearly are inconsistencies, both in targets and in policy actions, and the whole question of the way one establishes a framework or procedures for resolving them is one we cannot answer at the moment. Moreover, managed floating has made the analytical issue somewhat more difficult in the sense that, in many cases, the conceptual framework we have in mind when we make comments on policy and policy coordination is still the framework in which most of us were trained, a framework more appropriate to the world of pegged rates than to the world in which we are operating today.

Managed floating has certainly made at least two important differences for guidelines for intervention and policy coordination. First, it has provided a degree of insulation for national policies, but that insulation has turned out to be a good deal more limited than many antici-pated. The insulation—or policy independence—afforded by floating rates has been limited partly by the high degree of international integra-tion of financial markets that exists today and partly by the fact that many of the world's economic problems over the past two years have been due in large measure to a series of common external shocks—especially the decisions of the OPEC cartel regarding petroleum supplies and prices. With hindsight, the rather limited insulation provided by floating rates is not surprising, but it is much less than had been generally anticipated. Certainly the issues raised by economic interdependence and the international transmission of economic disturbances are still very much with us.

The shift to managed floating has also posed some difficult technical problems regarding intervention and settlement. The whole question of the conditions under which countries are obliged—or permitted—to in-tervene in the exchange market becomes much more complicated than it was under the par value system. And a closely related question also arises: Under what conditions and at what prices will countries repur-chase the currencies acquired in the course of intervention? Under the pegged-rate system, the business of making swaps was fairly simple; at least countries usually knew at what price a transaction was going to be unwound. Under the present system, with exchange rates changing from day to day, it is by no means so obvious. All this relates back to the rules for intervention, because in the absence of some kind of agreement on the conditions under which countries do and do not intervene, *after* a country has piled up another currency through intervention, there may well be some nasty arguments as to whether those balances are going to be redeemed and at what exchange rate.

This is a technical problem, but I think it could be an important one for international economic relations and for the operation of the international monetary system. More generally, the whole issue we are discussing reminds me of when Washington's first subway was being built, not the big Metro system now under construction, but the little subway that runs under the Capitol, connecting with the Senate and the House office buildings. It seems that the subway tunnel was dug from both ends toward the middle. Everything went fine until the time came to meet in the middle and they discovered that the two sections were several feet apart.

I think we face a similar problem here. We are trying on the one hand to approach the question of consistency from the side of the exchange market and the formulation of rules regarding market inter-vention. On the other hand, we are trying to approach it from the side

213

of coordination of monetary and fiscal policy, of macroeconomic policies in the broad sense. Each of these sides has a close analytical connection with the other, but I keep wondering whether we are eventually going to meet in the middle or whether we will find that, at the supposed junction point, there are several feet of earth separating the figurative passages we have dug.

Another question that arises in connection with the coordination of macroeconomic policies is whether an increase in such coordination implies an increase in the synchronization of cyclical movements among nations and, if it does, whether this poses a problem of its own. We have always thought that one of the stabilizing factors in the world economy was that when some countries were up (in a boom phase) others were down (in contraction or recession), and that those that were up would help pull up the economies of those that were down, while those that were down would act as a restraining influence on those that were experiencing demand-induced inflationary pressures.

Clearly, this has not been the case recently, and one of the reasons that the most recent boom-recession cycle was so severe for everybody is that it was far more synchronized among many countries than were the previous postwar cycles. This is not the place to discuss all the factors that helped to produce this major cyclical swing in so many countries at more or less the same time, but the experience does highlight the dangers of increased cyclical synchronization. Increased synchronization might help to alleviate cyclical balance-of-payments problems but would also pose fundamental problems for global economic stability. We need to learn more about the relationship between policy coordination and cyclical synchronization, and to find ways of insuring that the one is not necessarily linked to the other.

One final comment is stimulated by the controversy between Sam Cross and Tom de Vries on the extent to which there should be rules or guidelines governing exchange rate movements, as opposed to allowing those movements to be determined exclusively by market forces. The fundamental point, it seems to me, is that if private markets were really universal—that is, if all international transactions and all domestic economic transactions were conducted among private nongovernmental entities—then the whole exchange rate question would appear in a very different light from the way it appears now. Analytically it is quite clear that, from the point of view of private transactions, the optimum currency area is the world. Thus, if the economic universe consisted only of private transactions, there would be a strong logical case for Mundell's view that the best of all possible systems is one of universal fixed exchange rates.

In the world we live in, however, that would be a terrible system. The citizens of every country include in their welfare functions not only private goods that can be bought and sold in the marketplace but also public or collective goods that cannot. Among these collective goods are stabilization and the achievement of redistributional and regulatory goals. Differences among countries in their consumption preferences for such collective goods—as regards the inflation-unemployment mix, for example—underlie the need for flexibility of exchange rates.

It seems to me that differences in countries' goals with respect to these collective goods will persist and should be allowed to persist. Why should countries not have differing views as to what constitutes the optimal market basket of these collective goods? But as long as such differences persist, exchange rates will have to be allowed to move to reflect these differences. For that reason, I see absolutely no inconsistency between a desire for greater coordination—or at least avoidance of gross inconsistencies—in general macroeconomic polices and a firm opposition to a return to pegged rates. It seems to me that these two positions are entirely consistent, merely reflecting an effort to narrow a very wide gap from both sides at once.

The existence of rate flexibility enables countries to pursue different mixes of public goods. At the same time, it is clear that flexible rates provide only partial insulation, that they certainly do not ensure total independence for national economic policies. Flexible rates do not make any possible set of national policies mutually consistent, and, as long as major inconsistencies can persist, this whole exercise in making more organized and systematic efforts to coordinate overall policies and policy targets is critically important. It is only by supporting both of these— the continuation of rate flexibility on the one hand and explicit efforts to eliminate gross policy inconsistencies on the other—that we can hope to narrow the present gap and establish a system that can function effectively over the long run.

Thomas D. Willett

I can be quite brief here because Marina Whitman has already said a good deal of what I had planned to say. Let me begin by saying that, in preparing for this session, I spent some time looking back over the past discussions on objective indicators, guidelines for floating, and similar matters, to see what were the main things I had learned from these exercises.

The main impression I came away with was that there just are not any easy or magic rules for assessing exchange rate behavior. We cannot look at exchange rates or reserve developments in isolation. What we should be groping toward when looking at standards for good behavior are analyses that enable us to make better qualitative judgments about what is actually going on and to what extent governments are following policies that may have substantial and perhaps inappropriate effects, direct or indirect, on exchange rates and the balance of payments.

For instance, no one will be able to give us (magically) a full set of necessary and sufficient conditions that everybody will agree upon for competitive depreciation or manipulation of the exchange rate. There are probably many policy actions, we would all agree, that would constitute manipulative practices, which should be discouraged or prohibited, and many others, such as limited exchange market intervention to help preserve orderly markets, that do not constitute manipulative practices. But there are policy actions that some of us might strongly believe were manipulative, while others would believe they were not, and still others would feel that a reasonable case could be made either way.

The point is to try to chip away over time at this gray area. In doing so, we must, I think, rely heavily on a case history approach, building up over time a set of common law interpretations or precedents. *A priori* theoretical analysis will, of course, be indispensable in arriving at such judgments, but I doubt that theorizing alone will take us very much farther on this issue. Eventually, we will run into the need for imparting to those theoretical concepts some empirical content, which can come only from the analysis of particular situations. Thus I would see the IMF's charge to develop specific principles for exchange rate surveillance as part of a continuing process of judgment and analysis, rather than requiring the speedy delineation of a long list of specific dos and don'ts.

In the process of developing such precedents or interpretations of principles of good behavior, I believe that it will be useful to keep in mind three basic categories or types of proposals. One category is what we might call positive guidelines or obligations, which essentially stipulate what all countries should do in the interest of the international community, as well as perhaps in their own interest. (An example of such a positive guideline would be the obligation to take actions to avoid disorderly exchange markets.) A second major category we might call negative guidelines—guidelines which seek to prohibit particular types of actions. Examples of these would be the avoidance of competitive depreciation or manipulation of the international monetary system. And a third category would encompass proposals that one would neither want to require for all countries in the system nor prohibit, but which may be suggested as good ways for individual countries to behave. In other

216

words, the international community could encourage a much broader range of policies than would formally come under the first two categories. This category would also include suggestions of ways in which two or more countries might want to coordinate their policies more closely within the broader framework of the IMF system. Certainly there are a variety of instances in which individual countries might want to pursue a higher degree of policy coordination than might be possible for the entire system of over 100 countries.

In closing, let me stress that the first two categories I listed— positive and negative guidelines—do not necessarily correspond with undertaking positive or negative actions. For instance, the obligation to promote orderly markets might require less official intervention in foreign exchange markets at times rather than more. In several instances under the current float, disorderly conditions in the exchange markets have emerged as the result of official attempts to maintain unrealistic values of managed exchange rates, rather than because of inadequacies in the functioning of the private market (which would necessitate official intervention on efficiency grounds).

One of the strongest lessons of the international monetary experiences of the last several decades is that today the greatest challenges to the smooth operation of the international adjustment process come from attempts to preserve a given level or range of the exchange rate for too long, rather than from overt attempts to manipulate exchange rates for competitive advantage such as the Bretton Woods exchange rate arrangements were designed to avoid.

REJOINDER

Sam Y. Cross

I have found this discussion extremely interesting and helpful, and I certainly would not try in this brief comment to respond to the many different views on matters which have been touched upon. But I will note that there is much I would agree with, much I would disagree with, and a few things that I found surprising. I heard one surprising comment from each of the de Vries present.

I was surprised by Tom de Vries's comment, which seemed to imply that the United States was interested in underlying stability in order to get back to the par value system. This is not the basis of our concern about the necessity of trying to restore greater stability to the underlying conditions in the world economy—something which is quite important, for its own sake, regardless of the exchange rate arrangements to be followed. And I was surprised by Rimmer de Vries's view that governments ought to be concerned about the exchange rate, inasmuch as it suggests that governments are *not* concerned about them. I do not think that point is really at issue. The only question is how best to manifest that interest and that concern—through a concentration on the proper management of the economy, or through a greater emphasis on the degree of intervention in exchange markets. No one would question that exchange rates are an obvious concern of governments.

I was also interested in Fred Hirsch's observation about the spate of books coming out on the reform exercise, including books by those who regard it as a triumph and books by those who regard it as a failure. I guess their assessment is determined by the objective the author had in advance. That is to say, those who were looking for a highly structured and rigid system may consider this reform not a triumph because it has not yielded that. It has yielded—in my view—the kind of flexible and evolutionary system which is appropriate to today's world.

On the question of (1) relying on guidelines or principles of the rather general inhibiting type, or (2) moving towards something closer to what Hirsch was proposing, I favor the first category. At this stage, we should be looking towards fairly broad and general principles for avoiding practices clearly seen to be internationally destructive. I doubt that the state of the art is such that—even if we wanted to—we could move to proposals of the kind he and Jack Polak were talking about, where countries establish balance-of-payments aims and then turn the exchange rate computer loose to determine the appropriate equilibrium rate.

Experience has not been encouraging in that respect—certainly to the extent I have followed efforts to agree on balance-of-payments aims (which usually turn out to be current account aims, as Marina Whitman pointed out). And I am dubious that it is possible to determine medium-term equilibrium rates. It does assume a certain knowledge about government policies over the medium term that would be difficult to obtain.

Polak referred to the "merm." It has many limitations as it applies to the problems of the weights, to the problem of the indexes, to assumed elasticities, and to the problems of ignoring capital flows; and it is based on ex post concepts. There are many limitations to this approach.

For all these reasons, I agree with George Willis that we all should approach this with a certain humility. My own humility is such that I believe we should find it more profitable to be looking down the path suggested by Tom Willett, using positive and negative injunctions. But we are not, in any way, able to move to the kind of system where we can reach agreement and have international bodies determine the proper current-account structure of balance of payments and the appropriate exchange rates to achieve them.

SUMMARY OF THE DISCUSSION

The chairman of the session, Gottfried Haberler, opened the discussion by asking the participants to limit the scope of their remarks to the specific problem of guidelines for national financial and exchange rate policies. He suggested that the participants assume there can be no significant harmonization, or coordination, or synchronization of domestic policies among countries. Given that assumption, Haberler called upon the prospective discussants to direct their remarks to what should be the guidelines for balance of payments or intervention policies and to the need for such guidelines. He noted that it may be not possible to separate the problems of international coordination of economic policies from those of guidelines for intervention, but he thought that the framework he was proposing would help to streamline the discussion.

John Karlik remarked that one among many ambiguities that remained following the Jamaica Agreement was conspicuously absent in the preceding commentaries. If one compares the Outline of Reform proposed by the Committee of Twenty in 1974 and what actually came out at Kingston in January 1976, the Jamaica Agreement appears to be an effective endorsement of an inconvertible dollar standard and a continuation of that standard for the foreseeable future. It is uncertain in how large a part of the world this standard will apply, given (for instance) the fate of the snake.

Karlik thought it important to recognize this interpretation for three reasons. First, some years from now, it may be realized that this was, indeed, endorsed, and the sooner it is realized the less will be the animosity towards the United States.

Second, certain responsibilities will be imposed on U.S. monetary authorities. If the international monetary system is run as much by the U.S. Treasury and the Federal Reserve as by the IMF for as long as it takes to renegotiate certain provisions of the Jamaica Agreement, then the question arises: To what extent should U.S. monetary authorities take cosmopolitan, international criteria into account in formulating U.S. economic policy? Third, it is important that the United States

221

recognize its opportunity as a leader in setting the environment, the context, and perhaps some of the characteristics, of the system that will be evolving in the next few years.

Karlik next moved to raise questions associated with other ambiguities he perceived in the Jamaica Agreement. He contended that what lies behind concerns about unfair competitive advantage and firm surveillance of exchange rate policies is really an interest in the distribution of adjustment burdens, particularly among OECD countries. He noted that this interest will increase as export competition among industrialized countries intensifies, particularly competition directed towards OPEC countries. Also, as developing countries proceed with their industrialization programs, one can expect increasing problems with imports of manufactured goods from those countries into OECD areas.

Industrial countries' concern about exchange rates is, and will remain, a reflection of their concern about the distribution of adjustment burdens, particularly as they relate to the maintenance of domestic full employment. As is well known, however, adjustment burdens can be shifted not only by exchange rate changes but also by means of demand-switching policies—export subsidies, import tariffs, various sorts of non-tariff restrictions, and so forth.

Karlik found it difficult to consider the problem of appropriate exchange rate levels without simultaneously taking into account the commitment of industrial countries to maintain full employment. Thus, in considering appropriate exchange rates and exercising surveillance over exchange rate practices, the International Monetary Fund should cast an eye on domestic employment policies as well. One rule that it would be possible to establish in this connection is that if a particular country had not made what was generally judged a reasonable effort to maintain or stimulate domestic employment, the exchange rate of its currency should not be allowed to drop.

Turning to Gutowski's comments, Karlik remarked that his suggestions were not as unrealistic as they seemed. They do not necessarily imply close international coordination of economic policies. Instead, they essentially call for a policy of publicly announced policy targets. To Gutowski's description of how such a policy has been implemented in West Germany, Karlik added that in recent years the Federal Reserve had begun announcing its targets for the growth in money supply. In addition, the Congress is attempting to implement a budget reform that would, to a large extent, outline what fiscal policy the United States is likely to follow in the medium future. If the path of the economic policies of the major countries for the next year or two can be known in the markets, then Gutowski's suggestion may not be so "heroic" as it first appeared.

In a brief remark, Gutowski agreed with Karlik's interpretation of his own suggestion and offered further clarification of its meaning. Gutowski recognized that his suggestion had given rise to some misunderstanding, especially between Hirsch and himself. He believed this misunderstanding could be attributed to the fact that he had taken the topic of international guidelines for national financial policies too literally. He emphasized that attaining the goal of stable medium-term expectations should result in relative stability of exchange rates among different currencies, but need not lead back to fixed par values. He acknowledged that the odds are against successful implementation of his proposal. The experience of the Common Market countries in this respect is not very encouraging. Nevertheless, the proposal has the undeniable advantage of allowing a policy to influence the market process without suppressing it.

George Willis believed that a large part of the deliberations on this subject could be reduced to the discussion of the proper role for the national authorities, for the IMF, and for the market. The role of national authorities cannot be limited to intervention in the foreign exchange market. Willis agreed with John Karlik and Marina Whitman that the questions of exchange rate determination, management, consistency, and so forth cannot be approached without specifically considering a whole array of national policies.

He acknowledged that the international community has not sorted out—and will probably take a long time to sort out—what is, or should be, the interplay among the national authorities, the IMF, and the market. Willis was struck by a certain amount of humility on the part of all speakers, whether they represented academia or private banks, or government agencies, or the International Monetary Fund. Nevertheless, he detected some undeniable progress in approaching and formulating problems associated with exchange rate policies. He found it encouraging that current discussions center on functional aspects of exchange rate behavior, on rules, procedures, and practices that would apply to all countries, no matter whether they peg or float their currencies. This shift in emphasis is quite important because, given that countries do have current account objectives, those objectives can be effectively pursued by freezing the exchange rate at some level or imposing a limit on how far it can rise. In other words, the notion has evidently gained recognition that the danger of suppressing adjustment by too much stability is at least as great as the danger of unnecessary adjustment entailed by too much instability.

Willis pointed out that as an exchange rate structure based on greater flexibility evolves, new forces determining exchange rate levels may emerge. For instance, he noted, as firms become increasingly sophisticated in avoiding foreign exchange exposure, capital movements out of strong into weak currencies are becoming more and more difficult. This, no doubt, adds another dimension to the problems the world may have to face. Still, taking the political drama out of discussions about exchange rate levels and concentrating instead on the degree of intervention or, more generally, on the distribution of responsibilities among the market, the IMF, and the national authorities, will make the very process of negotiation of exchange rates somewhat easier.

Saul Srole brought up the intimate connection between exchange rate policies and trade policies. He believed this issue had been neglected by most of the discussants, and pointed out that current trade negotiations within the GATT are not limited to further tariff cuts but include abolition of non-tariff barriers, among which subsidies figure prominently. It is thus recognized that trade restraints and subsidies have a harmful effect on world trade. He emphasized that for trade policy to be consistent with exchange rate policy, the latter should be directed at avoiding exchange rates that have the same effect as trade restraints or subsidies.

Robert Roosa remarked that present diversity of exchange rate regimes provides ample opportunities for experimental testing of alternative arrangements. In particular, areas with relatively fixed exchange rates in a world of generally flexible or floating rates, especially the European snake, should make it possible to test the advantages of both fixity and flexibility of exchange rates.

The snake can conceivably help to settle the question whether it is possible to rescue some of the useful features of a system of fixed parities. Of course, adherence to the snake presupposes a well-defined objective of exchange rate policy. That objective inevitably influences the framing of domestic economic policy, which must be consistent with domestic economic policies of other participants in the snake.

Roosa noted that achieving consistency in economic policies among countries through pursuit of exchange rate objectives is the reverse of what Gutowski suggested. Roosa acknowledged that economic policy is the basic determinant of the exchange rate. But he stressed that there can be important reverse directional influences, when the exchange rate objective provides guidance for overall economic policy and, perhaps, insures the necessary discipline. This is possibly the case of the smaller members of the snake who, through pegging to the deutsche mark, may be virtually compelled, if not to match, then at least to approximate the standards of performance maintained by the West German economy. A fruitful area for further study could be the extent to which exchange rate considerations within the snake influence and contribute to the consistency of its members' economic policies.

Next, Roosa raised the possibility of going back to an arrangement similar to the Tripartite Agreement of the 1930s to produce reasonable exchange rate relations among leading currencies that float vis-à-vis each other. He wondered whether the situation is ripe for explicitly trying to negotiate more stable paired relationships between the dollar and the mark or the dollar and the yen. He remarked that those bilateral exchange-rate rate relationships are of concern mainly (though, of course, not exclusively) to the pairs of countries involved. Those countries, and other leading industrial countries, should feel free of guilt in trying to resolve their own problems alone.

Roosa pointed to a difficulty inherent in the implementation of Gutowski's suggestion. The exchange rate of the mark is essential in formulating West German economic policy, hence in trying to reconcile national economic policies, and ultimately (one hopes) in producing reasonably stable exchange rate relationships. The alternative approach is to start with the assumption that it would be possible to get a rough idea of a range within which the dollar-mark exchange rate ought to be located and then to deduce what this exchange rate (or this range of exchange rates) may imply for the economic policy of both countries.

Roosa recognized that his suggestions may encounter some resistance on the part of those who want to rely exclusively on free market forces for the determination of exchange rates. However, his belief was that within the broad framework of flexible exchange rates there is room for improving the performance of the system through testing the effectiveness of alternative approaches characterized by partial or selective fixity of exchange rates.

Marina Whitman, clarifying one of her points made earlier, pointed out that the need for flexibility of exchange rates arises from the fact that free markets are by no means universal, that in every country there is a certain amount of government interference into and regulation of the economic life. The degree of interference and regulation varies from country to country because of different views on where to divide the roles of private agents and the government. For example, an American and a Briton are unlikely to agree on whether economic welfare is advanced by freedom of capital movements.

The diversity of views among countries explains the difficulty involved in establishing a set of rules to be incorporated in a monetary system. It is clear, though, that those differences in views must be taken into account.

Closing the discussion, Thomas Willett noted that the issue of guidelines for national financial policies is a part of a broader problem of the adjustment of payments imbalances. In turn, the latter problem is intimately connected with the question of international liquidity to which Part Five is devoted. He found it quite appropriate to continue discussing selected aspects of the adjustment process in the next session, especially as they relate to the problem of liquidity.

PART FIVE

INTERNATIONAL LIQUIDITY UNDER FLEXIBLE EXCHANGE RATES

INTERNATIONAL LIQUIDITY ISSUES UNDER FLEXIBLE EXCHANGE RATES

Robert L. Slighton

I have been asked to consider whether the difficulties with control of international liquidity that were so troublesome during the Bretton Woods regime will continue to be a major problem in the presently evolving period of greater exchange flexibility.

There is a persistent undercurrent of complaint that the Jamaica reform is incomplete, that the international monetary regime we have negotiated implies a bias toward an excessively elastic supply of international liquidity which will persist until the mechanism of liquidity creation is placed under international control. There is an equally persistent feeling among the major architects of the Jamaica reform that these criticisms are at best exaggerated and at worst misguided.

My objective is to confront the arguments embedded in some of these criticisms with the arguments of the policy maker in the hopes that we can gain better understanding of the reasons for these persistent differences in policy conclusions. These differences have multiple origins: different perceptions of the way the international economy actually works; differences in fundamental values; and, perhaps in the largest part, different perceptions of what is politically feasible—what reductions in national sovereignty are reasonably negotiable in the foreseeable future.

The subject of this session is extremely broad. It is international liquidity, not international reserves. It has been noted many times that international liquidity is in many ways an unhappy concept. It is a multidimensional concept whose operational specification requires careful consideration of at least three important analytical distinctions—the distinctions between official and private, gross and net, and actual and potential liquidity. International liquidity is not susceptible to description in terms of one variable; it is not readily susceptible to quantification in all its important dimensions.

In short, international liquidity is not a functional concept; for this reason most discussions with liquidity in their title have been transformed

229

into discussions of international reserve issues. Such transformations are luxuries in which we indulge too often.

On the domestic side, there is a reasonably convincing argument for substituting a concern for the various monetary aggregates for a more general concern for measures of liquidity, even though none of these monetary aggregates really measures the limits of spending power. The argument is the pragmatic sanction that the relationships between these monetary aggregates and the macroeconomic parameters by which we judge the performance of the economy are sufficiently stable to be useful.

On the international side, the pragmatic argument is considerably less compelling. The relationships between international reserves (however measured) and the international price level as well as the size and pattern of world trade are extremely loose. Reserves do matter, but so do other factors. Control of gross international reserves does not establish control over the volume and pattern of international transactions.

The argument for extending the scope of our discussion beyond the narrower concept of reserves and reserve policy is, I think, compelling, even though extension is necessarily bought at the cost of a certain loss of formal rigor. But how should broadening the scope of the discussion be accomplished? The solution I have adopted is to accept the priorities set by critics of the Jamaica reform.

I shall attempt to discuss three hypotheses critical of the greater exchange flexibility that have been frequently articulated both in the current literature on international monetary policy matters and in international policy negotiations: first, the present system is likely to result in an excessive growth of official reserves and hence exacerbate world inflationary tendencies; second, under the present system acquiring reserves through borrowing is so easy that countries with severe payments imbalances are under insufficient pressure to adjust; and third, the mobility of private international capital under the present system implies an unacceptable diminution of government control of national monetary policies and a further tendency toward international inflation.

These three criticisms have been introduced as hypotheses, but they are better phrased as questions. Although I promise only a response, not an answer, I hope that my response will stimulate a counterresponse from the participants in this discussion.

Are International Reserves Uncontrolled?

The most common criticism of the international monetary regime negotiated at Rambouillet and Jamaica is that it affirms a reserve-creation mechanism that has already been proved uncontrollable. There are two quite separate lines of argument for this conclusion. According to the first, the growth of international reserves in the period of floating rates has been far in excess of any reasonable formulation of incremental world needs. The second, more serious criticism is a commentary on the character of the reserve-creation mechanism itself. The usual formulation of this criticism is that international reserves are under no effective control because they are demand-determined.

If the first argument is to have any significance it must be phrased as a commentary on the recent workings of the adjustment process. It is quite true that international reserves have increased very rapidly during the period of floating, but the large size of this increase carries with it absolutely no presumption about its inappropriateness. The increase in international reserves since 1974 is the result of an apparently permanent change in the terms of trade between the OPEC countries and the rest of the world that was of such a dimension as to preclude rapid adjustment.

A decision to fund the deficit of the non-OPEC world by reserve transfers rather than reserve creation would most likely have resulted in some reduction of world inflationary pressures. It would also have resulted in widespread restrictions on international trade and investment as well as a major reduction in global output. The issue is not whether it is appropriate for world liquidity in the form of official gross reserves to increase under present circumstances but whether the various oil-importing countries are making an appropriate effort to adjust to the changed circumstances. I would like to postpone this question for a moment.

I would also like to note that the effect of the increase in official reserves in the period after 1973 on the world money supply is dramatically different from the monetary effects of the increase in reserves in the 1970–1973 period, which resulted from the external imbalance of the major reserve currency country. The earlier increase in reserves was distributed across many countries. The increase in reserves today is concentrated in a few countries whose absorptive capacity is relatively limited. In current circumstances, the distribution of incremental reserves is far more significant than the aggregate dimension of that increase.

The second, more serious line of argument claims that the system currently evolving is a demand-determined system in which each country will obtain the amount of reserves it prefers through borrowing or exchange rate manipulation and which is thus bound to reinforce world inflationary tendencies.

My initial reaction to this claim is that it is an exercise in hyperbole. In the first place, the system is not, strictly speaking, demand-determined.

A country wishing to acquire reserves through borrowing does not face an infinitely elastic supply schedule of loanable funds. Private credit is rationed both by price and by quota, and the system of international public lending is hardly structured to guarantee that all shortfalls resulting from limitations on supply of private credit will be covered from public sources. One may argue about the effectiveness of market discipline, but it is surely wrong to argue that there is no such discipline at all.

More important, in assuming extensive manipulation of exchange rates, this claim assumes that the signatories of the Jamaica Agreement will make no effort to honor their obligations under that agreement. I have two responses to this assumption. First, although it is certainly naive to assume that ratification of the Jamaica Agreement implies compliance with its provisions, the assumption that there will be a general, willful, quantitatively significant pattern of evasion of those obligations is unwarrantedly pessimistic. Second, if it is concluded that there is so little willingness to cooperate in the international monetary arena that there will be minimal adherence to the obligations of the Jamaica Agreement, how can it possibly be argued that an agreement embodying greater restrictions over reserve creation could be negotiated?

In the form I have given it, this criticism of the current liquidity-creation mechanism is just as unreasonable as a claim of optimality for the current regime on the grounds that in a floating world, the supply of international reserves will automatically adapt itself to the demand for reserves. The problem with the first argument is that it presumes that the acquisition of reserve assets has little to do with the demand for reserve assets as reserves. The problem with the second argument is that it presumes that reserve assets are never acquired to achieve an exchange rate objective. The obvious conclusion from both arguments is that international liquidity and exchange market intervention are intimately related, something we already knew. Effective control over international reserves presupposes effective control over intervention.

In this sense the critics are quite right. There is much unfinished business. National monetary authorities must be discouraged from accumulating large additions to their foreign exchange balances in the name of suppressing erratic fluctuations. However, proponents and critics disagree over the appropriate means to achieve that end. The architects of the Jamaica Agreement have proposed to monitor intervention activities through a network of continuous consultative arrangements that involve finance ministries, central banks, and the International Monetary Fund. The critics have predicted that these arrangements will have little success.

But what are the alternatives? One suggestion is the adoption of an asset settlement scheme with convertibility at market values. But the acceptability of such a proposal presupposes international acceptance of rules governing the choice of intervention currencies and concrete guidelines as to intervention limits. A more radical proposal would be to shift the focus of intervention decisions from national monetary authorities to a radically transformed International Monetary Fund. Yet it is reasonable to ask how such agreements might be thought negotiable if it is believed that the less restrictive consultative network envisaged in the Jamaica Agreement will be ineffective.

There is, I think, very good reason to believe that the critics are excessively pessimistic. The volume of official reserves that will be held in the current regime of generalized floating is likely to approximate the amount of reserve assets that monetary authorities desire to hold as reserves much more closely than under the Bretton Woods system. If this presumption proves false, we may take some solace in the fact that the behavioral relationship between expansion of official reserve holdings and increases in national spending is not of the same kind as the relationship between increases in national money supplies and increases in national spending. Reserve expansion may permit a relaxation of the constraints imposed by balance of payments on exchange rate targets and hence induce some governments to follow more expansionary demand-management policies. This chain of events is by no means automatic, however.

Unfortunately, some critics tend to blame the increased rate of world inflation in this decade on the expansion of international reserves. The reserve expansion of the 1970–1973 period was undoubtedly responsible in some part for the rapid growth in national money supplies over that period, but it is surely an exaggeration to place reserve growth as the key element in the causal mechanism of world inflation. Much of the argument for the inflationary importance of reserve growth derives from studies of the relationship between aggregate world totals for reserves and national monies. The relationships that have emerged from such studies can be highly misleading, however. The relationship between individual official reserves and national monetary aggregates varies considerably among countries. For that matter, because the subject is the causal mechanism of inflation, we would do well to be cautious in ascribing causal significance to these measured relationships even if they were more stable than they are. Monetary expansion may well reflect an accommodation to inflationary pressure as well as an initiating cause of inflation. Control of international reserves would help bring the rate of international inflation under better control, but it is neither a necessary nor a sufficient condition of achieving that objective.

Are Deficit Countries under Sufficient Pressure to Adjust?

A second persistent criticism of the current monetary regime is that countries with severe payments imbalances are under insufficient pressure to adjust. Obviously, this criticism is closely related to the complaint that official reserves are growing excessively. Both criticisms are variants of the basic theme that the supply of liquidity under the current international monetary regime is excessively elastic.

The line of criticism focused on control of the adjustment process has a greater scope, however, in that it often is stated in compound form. That is, it is claimed that countries in deficit are under insufficient pressure to adjust today but will be under excessive pressure to adjust tomorrow. This second line of criticism expands the argument that the rate of reserve creation will not be optimal under the present regime into the larger argument that neither the quantity nor the distribution of reserves will be optimal.

I have already touched on this line of argument. My response was the obvious point that the level of foreign borrowing, official or private, does not really tell us very much about whether a country is responding appropriately to a current imbalance in its external payments. There are no clear-cut criteria for judging the appropriate mix of finance and adjustment in responding to external imbalance. We can only talk about relevant considerations such as the range of effective adjustment instruments available to a country and the extent to which external imbalance is believed to be the result of transitory factors.

Judgmental conclusions about the adequacy of a country's adjustment measures necessarily leave a significant area for reasonable disagreement. In present circumstances, with the uncertainties associated with partitioning imbalances into cyclical and noncyclical components and estimating the long-term impact of the oil price increase, this area of indeterminacy of reasonable judgment is enormous. Nevertheless, the critics have a point. Some countries' adjustments to their external imbalances have been feeble if not perverse.

The quarrel between the critic and the policy architect is once again essentially a quarrel over prescription rather than diagnosis. The more radical critical prescriptions apparently call for formal international control over the allocation of international public and private credit among countries. Such control could be accomplished either by a licensing system or by the radical transformation of the IMF into an international central bank with an exclusive franchise for exchange market intervention and autonomy in the issue of international reserve assets. The policy architects have called for prompt implementation of those collaborative arrangements called for in Article IV of the recently amended IMF Articles of Agreement.

In the eyes of the critics this prescription is inadequate. It is akin to a call for moral suasion from a source without moral authority. It is a prescription to be administered by national authorities in light of their national interests. It is a sanction without teeth. From my point of view these charges are considerably overdrawn.

My first defense of the currently evolving arrangements is that they do not imply a diminution of the role of IMF in overseeing the adjustment process. The collaborative arrangements called for in the Jamaica Agreement most specifically assign the Fund the responsibility of exercising firm surveillance over its members' exchange rate policies. In short, the prescription of the policy architects is not a prescription to be administered by a few national authorities solely in light of their own national interests.

The most serious charge against the current system of oversight of the adjustment process is that it has no teeth. A country that is unwilling to bite the adjustment bullet has the option of funding its deficit from private sources outside the surveillance mechanism. If stated in such terms, it is easy enough to argue that this charge is exaggerated. It is certainly not true that the private external funding option is a widow's cruse.

Private financial markets most certainly impose their own form of liquidity discipline on borrowers. But simply to say this is not to say that the problem raised by the critics can be safely dismissed, because there is a fundamental difference between the kind of discipline that private markets can impose and the kind of discipline possible through public lending, particularly lending by international organizations. The difference is the effective capability or right of public lenders to impose policy constraints.

This conditionality constraint has seldom been imposed in recent years. In large part, this restraint reflects the large unused lines of international credit with which most countries entered the period of higher oil prices. In some part it reflects the erosion of the applicability of the conditionality principle within the IMF that has resulted from the expansion of the compensatory finance facility and the increase in the credit tranche.

We are rapidly approaching the time, however, when this credit slack will have been fully utilized by many countries. For these countries the conditionality constraint will soon become an effective constraint. It is the recognition of this process that prompts the criticism that the process of adjustment of liquidity flows under the current regime will prove inadequate—that we shall move abruptly from a situation of excessive liquidity (insufficient adjustment) to deficient liquidity (inefficient adjustment).

The problem raised by this criticism is not unimportant. But neither is it insurmountable within the context of the current regime. Its dimensions depend mainly on two factors: the resumption of substantial and relatively noninflationary growth in the industrial countries, and a cessation of the trend toward loosening the conditionality standards of the IMF.

There is no question but that private lenders will be unwilling to supply liquidity in the amounts and terms of the recent past to countries whose external debt service position has deteriorated markedly. This change is an integral and proper part of the adjustment process. To expect an abrupt discontinuity in the flow of private liquidity that would preclude orderly adjustment is another matter, however. This expectation is equivalent to the presumption that there will be no significant decline in the liquidity demands of deficit countries—a supposition that the reduction of the recession-induced shortfall in export earnings, particularly in less developed countries, will be a long drawn out process and that the principle of conditionality is not effectively involved in the supply of public liquidity.

The first supposition appears patently false. The second is somewhat more difficult to evaluate. What is certain is that an ever-increasing number of countries will have used up their credit slack and will have to resort to public borrowing, in most cases from the IMF. It is also certain that the conditionality principle gives an importance to IMF lending that transcends the volume of liquidity directly supplied, because the quantity of private international lending is intimately related to the strength of the insurance function provided by the conditionality constraint. A final certainty is that the U.S. government is pressing for a more rigorous application of IMF conditionality. What is uncertain is whether we shall be successful in this effort. If we are not, the adjustment process may not operate in an appropriately orderly fashion.

Is Private International Capital Unacceptably Mobile?

The third common criticism of the current international monetary system that I would like to discuss is the familiar charge that the mobility of private international liquidity implies an unacceptable diminution of national control of domestic monetary policy.

Given the presumption that monetary policy will have a stronger effect on the domestic economy in a floating regime than in one with fixed exchange rates, the persistence of this complaint might be thought surprising. We should know better. The complaint persists because monetary authorities do not wish to pay the price in the form of exchange rate movement required to pursue a particular interest rate objective successfully. The flow of interest-sensitive capital into many countries is large enough relative to national financial markets to limit sharply the monetary authority in pursuing exchange rate and interest rate objectives independently.

Where private international liquidity is highly mobile, the advent of floating enhances national freedom of choice over monetary policy, but it does not necessarily guarantee the degree of freedom that the monetary authority may desire. In these circumstances, the national authorities have the choice either of changing domestic policies in conformance with monetary developments in foreign markets or of resorting to capital controls. The degree of policy conformity or stringency of capital controls depends on the degree of substitutability of foreign and domestic assets. That is, it depends on the degree of exchange rate uncertainty.

The preferred initial tactic in attempting to recover freedom of choice of monetary policy is thus the negative factor of refusing to intervene to counter the exchange rate movements engendered by domestic monetary policies. As we have seen, such intervention is only a partial prescription for the problem, but it is difficult to go very far beyond it. It is difficult to assess the relative costs of exchange rate fluctuations and of capital restrictions with equal effect in deflecting capital flows.

With the current degree of mobility of private capital, the demand for some degree of national autonomy in conducting monetary policy is likely to result in more national restrictions on international capital movements. This is hardly to be applauded, but the potential cost need not be serious so long as the monetary authority accepts the need for a reasonable degree of uncertainty as to the exchange rate.

I cannot be so unperturbed, however, with respect to the suggestion that the Euro- or xenocurrency markets should be brought under international control. The view that these markets have been a major factor in the inflation of recent years is at best exaggerated and at worst incorrect. It derives from a confusion over the appropriate measure of the size of the market, an underestimate of the extent to which xenocurrency liabilities are a substitute for the liabilities of national institutions, and the mistaken presumption that a market which is not controlled directly is undisciplined.

The usual measure of the size of the Eurocurrency market is the Bank for International Settlements estimate of net liabilities of xenocurrency banks in eight European countries. For any given definition of money, however, that total is not equal to the difference between the world money stock and the sum of the national money stocks. That difference is not the net liabilities of the xenocurrency system but rather that part of net liabilities which are held by nonbanking institutions. Increases in world money aggregates resulting from bank-lending to xenocurrency institutions are reflected in increases in national monetary totals. To compute the world money supply as the sum of national money supplies and net Eurocurrency liabilities as ordinarily measured would thus represent considerable double counting. For example, at the end of 1974 the BIS estimate of the net size of the Eurocurrency market was $177 billion. Only $31 billion of that total, however, represented nonbank claims.

Further, although the size of Euromarket liabilities to nonbanks is the relevant accounting measure of the contribution of the Euromarket to world liquidity, it does not follow that this figure measures the difference between the current world monetary stock and what that stock would have been if the Euromarket had never been established. In large part, movement to the Euromarket represents credit substitution rather than credit creation. To the extent that nonbank deposits simply represent the substitution of Eurocurrency liabilities for domestic liabilities, even this modest statistic overstates the contribution of the Euromarket to world monetary expansion. The greatest contribution to inflation from the Euromarket's operation probably derives from shifts from liabilities of other central banks to Eurocurrency liabilities in central bank portfolios. From an accounting point of view, the increase in monetary aggregates resulting from this shift is reflected in national monetary statistics and cannot be evaluated by examining Euromarket data.

This review of the apparent effect of Euromarket operations on the total world money supply underscores what theoretical analysis of that market has told us all along. The specter of uncontrolled credit expansion made possible by a multiplier that is nearly infinite is quite illusory. A demand for international control of xenocurrency markets founded on the claim that they will contribute in a major way to world inflationary pressures if left "uncontrolled" is an ill-founded demand.

The second argument for international control of the xenocurrency markets is based on the claim that their operation diminishes national autonomy over monetary policy. This argument has meaning, however, only to the extent that the functioning of these institutions enhances the international mobility of capital. It seems to me that the causal relationship is almost entirely the other way. The growth of the Euromarket reflects the increased mobility of capital.

If increased national autonomy over monetary policy is deemed essential, it would thus seem less costly to work toward that end by establishing capital controls at the national level rather than imposing regulatory costs on Euromarket institutions.

COMMENTARIES

Franz Aschinger

The early 1970s saw the failure of a system of the deliberate creation of appropriate international reserves through the introduction of special drawing rights, and, in the years when the more disciplined growth of reserves was expected, there was an enormous explosion of international liquidity. The embarrassing effects of this have not yet been overcome.

There is no consensus as to the real nature of the problem of international liquidity and how it should be solved. The Jamaica Agreement makes rather scant reference to this question. Its official directives were confined to the guideline that the member countries of the IMF should pursue "a reserve policy aiming at the better control of international liquidity and the development of SDRs into a most important reserve asset."

To this end, the IMF has begun to diminish the role of gold as a reserve. Moreover, the executive directors of the IMF have been advised in the official communique of the conference in Kingston to continue "their consideration of the subject of a *substitution account* without delaying completion of comprehensive draft amendments."

It is doubtful, however, whether this direction will be pursued further. For one reason, it has become evident that an international consensus along such lines is very difficult to obtain. Second, questions have arisen about the problem of international liquidity since the late 1960s, namely, Hasn't it changed its fundamental character? and Doesn't this problem require a new approach?

A gold substitution account at the International Monetary Fund, through which national gold stocks could be exchanged into SDRs, would not be workable because no country would voluntarily substitute the gold stocks for SDRs, either at the old official gold price or at the market price.

The situation is similar for the complementary proposal of substitution accounts for reserve currency assets against SDRs. Exchanging dollars into SDRs would not be attractive for countries belonging to the

241

dollar area. Moreover, in the long run, the exchange and debt risks could be lower for the dollar than for the SDRs. Last but not least, a substitution account would not be workable in an unbalanced international payment situation in which foreign exchange reserves would sharply increase. Recognizing the infeasibility of the SDR monopoly through the creation of substitution accounts, the managing director of IMF recently advanced another proposal. It recommends controlling global international reserves, without drastic reduction in the role of reserve currencies, through the introduction of a compulsory minimum proportion of SDRs. According to this system, adjustments in the aggregate volume of SDRs and their reserve ratio should bring about international management of the global amount of liquidity.

It is doubtful, however, that the aggregate of international liquidity could be effectively manipulated by an indirect and marginal method, such as the minimum proportion of SDRs in countries' reserve portfolios. Furthermore, as long as the international payment situation is unbalanced and as long as the reserve currency assets continue to increase in large volumes, total world reserves cannot be effectively manipulated by any artificial method of control. The same problems apply to the proposal to integrate the different reserve assets in the multiple reserve system, through a so-called asset settlement account.

Apart from this, all these methods would, as their proponents recognize, scarcely be workable under flexible rates. Only when a well-balanced pattern of international payments is restored will it be possible to control the growth of aggregate reserves. To tackle the reserve problem effectively, there is no alternative but to aim at a better international payment situation through adequate domestic economic policies.

This is the fundamental thesis developed by Edwin Yeo, and I think also by Robert Slighton. Yet, they do not limit themselves to this statement. If I interpret them correctly, they also express the opinion not only that central administrative control of international liquidity is not feasible, but also that it is not necessary. Their main motivation for this thesis is that international liquidity has no major impact on inflation; that under flexible rates, there is no reliable standard for the appropriation of international reserves; and that international liquidity is today already disciplined through the market.

I share the opinion that central control of international liquidity is difficult and that international reserves cannot be kept within boundaries without an appropriate domestic economic policy. I cannot follow Yeo, however, when he questions even the necessity of controlling international liquidity.

First, in my opinion, there can be no doubt that the explosion of international liquidity from $74 billion to $184 billion between 1970 and 1973—more than has been accumulated in the world's previous financial history—has much to do with the worldwide hyperinflation of those years. Moreover, excessive international reserves induced many countries to neglect adjustment measures.

Besides, if international liquidity really had no implication for inflation, the dispute about the increase in the official price of gold would have been groundless. Furthermore, if this were the case, SDRs, which were established to serve as a yardstick for appropriate global reserves, would have lost their original sense.

Second, the structure of the international liquidity in the last few years has become more complicated and less controllable because official reserves have been complemented increasingly by enormous amounts of private reserves, especially from the Euromarket. Also, private reserves have, in large amounts, shifted into official reserves.

The Euromarkets, which have grown considerably in recent years and which contain a built-in credit-creation mechanism, in 1974 and 1975 provided the main financing for the enormous imbalance of world payments caused by the multiplication of the oil price. Every deficit country, provided it is still credit-worthy, can today boost international liquidity simply by borrowing in the Euromarkets. Official borrowing facilities have also increased to a degree that, together with the borrowing from private sources, has created a tendency for looser international discipline.

Third, after the skyrocketing of the oil price in 1974, reserve creation by borrowings, instead of financing out of existing reserves, was an adequate solution in light of the following recession. That is no proof, however, that liquidity creation is today generally disciplined by the market.

The international payment situation is still largely in imbalance, and the creation of international liquidity is potentially still influenced by many arbitrary factors. In addition, the fact that aggregate reserves for the first time in years returned to a growth rate of 3.2 percent—that is, to a percentage that was considered normal and appropriate in the late 1960s—can be no reason for neglecting the international liquidity problem.

Compared with the period of the par value system, the concepts of an appropriate growth rate and an appropriate aggregate stock of official liquidity have, of course, changed under flexible rates. It has become more difficult to define what is appropriate. But it would be exaggerated and wrong to say that the concept of appropriateness of aggregate reserves has lost its relevance. After all, without such a concept how would one still be able to decide on the allocations of SDRs?

To summarize, it is my view that the problem of international liquidity cannot be solved either by impractical centralized controls or by a new theory of benign neglect. As the growth, the volume, the composition, and the use of international liquidity all bear on stability and prosperity, surveillance of these aspects must remain an important task of the International Monetary Fund. But the Fund's ability is, in this respect, limited. Appropriate growth of reserves finally depends on the extent to which individual governments are prepared to adopt prompt balance of payments adjustment measures.

The problem of international liquidity, which has been neglected in the framework of international monetary reform, requires an intensive fresh approach. But one should avoid going from one extreme to the other.

Fritz Machlup

If Dr. Slighton conceived his task as being, so to speak, a defense attorney for the signers of the Jamaica Agreement against the charges of the prosecution, then I must say that he was hampered in this task by an unusual degree of fairness and honesty. As a matter of fact, if one reads his paper carefully, one realizes that he concedes practically every good point that has been made by the prosecution. He does not concede, of course, the stupid points made by the prosecution, which should not have been taken seriously anyway.

Had he confined himself to the sound arguments of the critics made by good economists, he would concede everything. One can see evidence for this: he starts out saying that there is a persistent undercurrent of complaint that the Jamaica reform is incomplete. And then he shows that it is incomplete. In other words, the good arguments of the prosecution were absolutely correct. Several sentences in his paper provide further evidence.

Slighton shows that it is necessary to bring the mechanism of liquidity creation under international control. And he admits that one has to try to find a way of doing it, although it is, of course, quite clear that reserve creation is neither a necessary nor a sufficient condition for world inflation. For example, if a German alchemist succeeded in creating a hundred billion dollars worth of gold out of garbage and gave it as a gift to the Deutsche Bundesbank, I am sure that nothing would happen. If, however, this alchemist were not German, but Brazilian or Greek or French or Belgian or Danish, we should expect something to happen. The point is that a reserve increase is certainly not an automatic mechanism. It is similar to an increase in money supply in a domestic monetary system: if lots of money is created and given to certain persons who sit on it, nothing happens. It all depends on who gets the additional money or reserves, and in what way he changes his policy.

However, we are quite convinced that it involves a question of adjustment. Many countries will, if they have ample reserves, postpone adjustment. And we also know that other countries will, by intervening in the market and buying foreign currencies, increase their money supplies.

We really need not quarrel on these issues. If we say that the new system does not have a good adjustment mechanism, we also know that it does not have a system of orderly creation of liquidity. The two things hang together.

I would like to discuss for a moment the point about the role of the market as a disciplinary force. Perhaps there is something missing in this argument and perhaps also in the argument which Aschinger made, though I am not sure.

We know that one can borrow reserves in the market. We know that, in the United States, one commercial bank can borrow reserves from another commercial bank. This action may do something to increase the velocity of circulation of reserves, but it is not really an engine of inflation. There is a specified asset that is called reserve under the control of the Federal Reserve Banks.

In the international private market, there is no similar ultimate reserve of a limited size. Thus there is the possibility that some of the lenders—perhaps even monetary authorities—consider their claims as reserves. In other words, it is not merely a question of velocity, like the exchange of reserves among banks that takes place in the federal funds market in the United States. Instead, there is a borrowing of reserves in a manner that does not keep the total stock of reserves unchanged.

At one point Slighton said that control of international liquidity would not be really negotiable. If a good system is not negotiable, it does not mean that what *is* negotiable should necessarily be called a good system. It simply means that the negotiators have failed in negotiating a good system and that, maybe, we should try again. We should certainly not give up and call the little that was done a reform or a new system. It is neither a reform nor a good system.

I believe we should stop talking about nonnegotiable or politically impossible proposals. I do not think that it is still a secret that in 1967 some of us, even in the sacred halls of the U.S. Treasury, were saying that the dollar was overvalued and ought to be devalued. We were told it was politically impossible to speak about it. There was also the question of flexible exchange rates, and, here as in other countries, it was politically impossible to speak about it in official conferences and announcements. Yet, after a while all these things became politically possible.

What is politically possible is a matter of education and a matter of making things understood. One should never give in to a defeatist excuse that some plan or proposal is nonnegotiable. I conclude that even the U.S. Treasury should discuss politically impossible recommendations from now on.

One of these supposedly nonnegotiable ideas is the control of international liquidity. Few experts doubt that such control is essential for a good international monetary system. Hence, if we want to get a good system, we have to provide an apparatus that controls the creation and destruction of liquidity.

We must, of course, distinguish between various ways of creating liquidity. There are, first of all, the increases in exchange reserves. It may be possible, perhaps even politically possible, to get rules about this increase in reserves via the rules about intervention in the foreign exchange markets. If we have good rules about intervention that prevent countries from purchasing foreign currencies under certain conditions, it may be possible to control this type of reserve creation. Thus, we would have rules on liquidity creation through rules on exchange rate flexibility and guidelines for intervention in the exchange markets. I do not say that this is the best way of doing it, but it is, perhaps, a way of starting it.

Next is the question of liquidity creation through gold reserves. No one can know what will happen in the future, especially with the Jamaica provisions regarding gold. Little, if anything, will happen in the next two years, but no one can say what a small club of central banks or other monetary authorities may decide to do after two years.

I would not be as defeatist as Aschinger is about the substitution account. One thought that crosses my mind looks politically quite impossible and may even be laughed out of court, or out of a round-table of academic economists. My thought relates to a substitution account with a gradual reduction in the exchange rate between gold and the SDR. If the managers of the substitution account were to purchase gold with SDRs at so and so much per ounce until a certain day; afterwards, at 5 percent less; and a little later, at another 5 percent less, some official holders of gold might find early substitution attractive.

246

This is similar to my old 1960 plan with the periodic decline in the gold price. In present circumstances anything can happen to the gold price, depending on official sales and official support purchases. If my plan were adopted, the substitution account would receive gold as some official holders—for example, the United States—could offer gold from time to time. With a gradual reduction in the exchange ratio, other official holders may prefer to dispose of some of their gold at, say, $120 per ounce at this time rather than hold it until the exchange ratio is down to $100 or $80. Holding gold would become excessively expensive if a gradual depreciation were added to the loss of interest.

I suppose this device could make a substitution account practical. After all, why should anyone believe there will be an increase in the market price of gold, a metal of which we have a stock of at least sixty years' production in the cellars of our central banks?

Picasso did not keep a stock of sixty years' production of his paintings in his house, but he kept a relatively large quantity. If only two years of Picasso's output were put on sale at once, his paintings would become of very little value. Their value depends on their being kept off the market. If too many paintings were offered for sale, they would fetch a rather low price, unless a consortium were formed to take them off the market and continue the policy of keeping them locked up and therefore scarce.

The scarcity of gold, likewise, depends on five or six governments' willingness to keep their gold locked up and off the market. Thus, there is no necessity for the price of gold to increase or to stay at its present level. Its price is independent of the industrial demand and of private hoarders' demand because so much of it is available in the cellars of the central banks. I conclude that gold, by wise management by the authorities and intelligent agreements among them, need not ever become a source of additional liquidity.

The third source of monetary reserves is SDR creation, and there should be no difficulty in arriving at workable provisions. If we have rules on reserves either directly or indirectly through rules or guidelines on exchange interventions, and if there is some beginning of the operation of a substitution account, then I believe there can be something like the Witteveen Plan. Under this plan, total monetary reserves are somehow locked in with a percentage requirement of SDR holdings. Something of this sort should be feasible and would allow a degree of control over reserves.

Nothing of what I have said is well thought out: I have spoken impromptu. But I think we must have the courage of saying foolish things because, eventually, out of foolish things, wise things may be distilled.

Walter Salant

To pick up one of the issues raised by Fritz Machlup, let me observe that the argument that the market can exert adequate control sounded like the position of the Banking School in argument with the Currency School prior to the passage of the Bank Act of 1844 in England. It also bore some resemblance, I thought, to the needs-of-trade argument embedded in the original Federal Reserve Act—not to say buried there, because it is not much noticed. In any case, I thought that Dennis Robertson disposed of that argument some forty or so years ago.

I want to make two points about the implications of a flexible-rate system for liquidity as well as a more general point growing out of this issue. We all remember that ten or more years ago it was widely believed that reserves would not be needed in a freely floating exchange rate world and that they would be needed in much smaller amounts in a world of managed flexibility than in a world of fixed rates. If I recall correctly, only Roy Harrod was skeptical about this proposition.

What seems to have given rise to the current debate is the vast increase in the supply of reserves, which has raised fears of further world inflation. There is no logical reason, however, why that increase should refute the previous reasoning that flexibility enables countries to control their own price levels.

If we ask why this vast increase in the supply of reserves has given rise to this fear, I think we have to conclude that there is an implicit assumption—and its implicit character is the thing to which I want to draw attention—that the demand for reserves has not increased or not increased as much as their supply.

As Robert Solomon pointed out earlier in this conference, nearly all the reported increase in official reserves is in the hands of the OPEC countries and really represents assets that would be better characterized as long-term investments rather than as reserves. Although I think this is true, I would prefer to emphasize that what we call them is not crucial to the question of whether the increase creates a danger of inflation.

The increase in these assets can be regarded as an increase in the supply of reserves, or as an increase in a substitute for reserves, but whichever definition is chosen the essential question is, How has the demand for those holdings changed in relation to their supply?

It seems doubtful that a great renewal of inflation need result from the growth of world holdings. The growth in world reserves can be seen as a big shift in the distribution of income and wealth in favor of people who have a high propensity to hoard money. In a domestic context, such a shift causes a big increase in the demand for money, and if it is not to have a deflationary effect, it should be matched by an increase in the supply. An increase in the supply, in that case, would not be inflationary; it would merely be antideflationary.

On this point, I agree with both Under Secretary Yeo and Robert Slighton that allowing this increase to occur was better than preventing it.

In regard to the change in the exchange rate system, the demand for reserves is obviously going to depend, among other things, on the degree of intervention. More precisely, it will depend on the relationship between the degree of fluctuation that would occur in the absence of intervention and the degree of fluctuation that the authorities are willing to tolerate. In other words, it depends in large part upon policy makers' behavior. This is, in effect, the same conclusion that Fritz Machlup reached when he said it depends on who gets it and what they do with it. It leads me to conclude that the question of how much reserves are needed cannot be answered without some assumptions as to the likely behavior of the monetary authorities.

My final point is a more general observation, one concerned not with reserves or liquidity alone, but with how we talk about many of these economic questions. The question of whether reserves are redundant is only one of many questions, it seems to me, that cannot be answered unless something is stipulated about the behavior of policy makers who are part of the economic system. Either their behavior must be stipulated exogenously, or it must be treated as endogenous—that is, as part of the model.

Assar Lindbeck has tried to do that in a long paper called, "Stabilization Policy in Open Economies with Endogenous Politicians." He summarized his findings in the Ely lecture he gave at the meeting of the American Economic Association in December 1975.

One illustration of a possible error in ignoring this consideration can be found in Josef Molsberger's paper presented at the first session of this conference. He said that West German controls to restrain capital inflows resulted from the commitment of West Germany to maintain the snake margins. Underlying that proposition is the assumption that without that commitment, West Germany would have accepted an appreciation of the mark—that is, an implicit assumption about the behavior of the West German monetary authorities.

If one assumed that they would not have accepted appreciation either, even if they had not been in the snake, then one could not be satisfied to blame the imposition of exchange controls on their having joined the snake. One would have had to ask, instead, why they joined the snake. The answer might be that they preferred it to the alternative of a possible need for currency appreciation. In that case, the exchange controls are not a reflection of their having joined the snake. That is a superficial manifestation of something more fundamental in their behavior.

The other illustration of the proposition that the behavior of the policy makers must be included in the model arises from an often debated question: whether a fixed or flexible rate system is more inflationary for the world as a whole.

I would say that one cannot answer this question without specifying the difference made by the system in domestic monetary policies. Without specifying that, it is an unanswerable question. There are more unknowns than equations. But the debate goes on, as if specifying the behavior of policy makers did not make much difference.

One can assume that the policies are the same under the flexible rate and the fixed rate systems, or that policies are related to variables affected differently by the systems, such as the exchange rate movements themselves, or reserve movements, or price-level movements, or employment. But one must specify something about the relationship of policy to the exchange rate system.

Until we begin to specify the behavior of policy makers, we are asking questions that cannot be answered. I suggest that we either make good the omission or stop asking unanswerable questions.

Wolfgang Schmitz

Speakers from countries that have large structural deficits in their balance of payments and that demand more SDRs in order to finance those deficits, rarely hold the view that global liquidity is generally lacking. I will start with the very simple statement that the task of any monetary system, whether national or international, is first to provide the community concerned with the necessary means of payments and second to control their amount.

The first task, I think, is performed rather satisfactorily by the mechanism creating convertible currencies and SDRs. No one complains about the system not producing enough means of payments. However, the ability of an economic system to create acceptable means of payments is by no means self-evident. The monetary community of the COMECON countries, for instance, has no means of international payments of its own. It uses the currencies of the free world to finance its foreign trade with non-Communist countries and even partly its own internal commercial transactions.

250

The second task, the control of liquidity, is not fulfilled, however, and no one is even claiming that there is a mechanism to that purpose at all. There was no mechanism under Bretton Woods, nor is there one currently under the present system of mixed managed floating. It would be a happy coincidence if a system without a mechanism for controlling liquidity would not create too little or too much money.

Nobody seriously complains anymore that we have not enough liquidity. That time has passed, at least for global liquidity. There are, however, quite a few who fear that there is too much liquidity.

It is rather hard to discuss the problem of international liquidity briefly. Among the matters that should be discussed systematically are the different sources of general liquidity, such as deficits in the balance of payments of key currency countries, diversification of reserves (including Petrodollar investments in pound sterling), currency markets outside the country of issue (for example, the Eurodollar market), drawings with the IMF, central bank credits to monetary authorities, revaluation of official gold holdings, substitution of the one-sixth of IMF gold that is to be sold in favor of developing countries, and additional allocations of SDRs. Moreover, the remedies should be elaborated in terms of their controls and the kind of conclusions necessary to activate central bank agreements, policies of key currency countries, rules to be followed by worldwide money and credit markets, provisions of the IMF agreements (including the power of the IMF not only to create and cancel SDRs but also to freeze larger amounts of international reserves), and other controls.

In the meantime I shall concentrate on the paper by Robert Slighton, the basis of today's discussion. I found this paper rather stimulating because of its excellent analysis of arguments. I share Machlup's view that Slighton primarily aims at defending the U.S. government's policy at the Jamaica conference, rather than approaching the individual arguments from a critical point of view. This purpose undoubtedly is legitimate but restricts the scope of the problem. The question as to what is politically realistic and feasible is to be answered in a different way for the short and for the long run. Because of lack of time to evaluate the positive aspects of this paper, for instance the concept of official and nonofficial reserves (the latter playing an increasing role), I shall confine myself at first to those statements I do *not* agree with.

For example, Slighton says: The relationships between international reserves (however measured) and the size and pattern of world trade and the international price level as well as the size and pattern of world trade are extremely loose. Reserves do matter, but so do other factors. Control of gross international reserves does not establish control over the volume and pattern of international transactions. This is true. This holds true, however, for any purely monetary approach also: money matters, but not alone.

Then Slighton says that the present system is likely to result in an excessive growth of official reserves. Rather, I would say not only is it *likely* to result, it did result. And it is likely to result in an even larger increase: the Jamaica decision allowing the revaluation of gold at near-market prices provides for still more temptations to increase liquidity. If countries can obtain credit facilities without being forced to use their own reserves, including gold, we shall have a more or less automatic increase of international reserves. This means that deficit countries are not forced to push forward their adjustment process as hard as they would otherwise.

Next, Slighton states that it is quite true that international reserves have increased very rapidly during the period of floating. The fact that this increase was and is large holds true; it is essential to note, however, that this increase was inappropriate and too large. Absolutely misleading is the hint that this increase happened during the period of floating: the inappropriate increase of reserves occurred also and even more remarkably during the fixed exchange rate period.

The supposition that this increase was inappropriate is confirmed by the relatively much slower expansion, or even reduction, of world trade. Also, the aggregate reserves of petroleum-importing countries did not change, despite the huge surplus of oil exporters. The oil-importing countries financed their balance of payments deficits with newly created reserves, rather than with their own reserves. This means that there is no sufficient pressure on governments and business and labor to make the adjustment process in accordance with the heavy changes in the terms of trade. Any price increase of gasoline—in Austria as well as in any other country—has been financed entirely by wage increases, because every increase in the gasoline price is entered into the price index, which often serves as the basis for wage contracts. The adjustment process would have been accelerated if these countries had been induced to make greater use of their own reserves and thus were left exposed to the pressure of diminishing reserves.

Slighton then goes on to say that a country wishing to acquire reserves through borrowing does not face an infinitely elastic supply schedule of loanable funds. The supply of loanable funds surely is not infinitely elastic but it is much too elastic. Quite a bit of time may pass by before a country with a triple A rating loses its creditworthiness. Despite the fact that this happened to Italy, ample reserves still seem to be available. For other countries still enjoying a high rate of creditworthiness, there will be no pressure on government expenditure as long as credit facilities of the Eurodollar market are readily available. The ample supply of reserves diminishes private market discipline whereas the credit multiplier remains fully potent. It was stated in one of the papers that it is just the loan-banking deposits that count in the Eurodollar market. This conclusion depends on one's point of view. Insofar as the adjustment process is concerned, the deposits of private commercial banks and the deposits of multinational companies as well as the deposits of central banks are subject to the multiplier in the Eurodollar market. These sources together provide an unlimited source of financing for balance of payments and budget deficits.

Slighton mentions further that the behavioral relationship between increases in national money supplies and increases in national spending is not the same as the relationship between expansion of official reserve holdings and increases in national spending. Although they may be not the same, they are rather similar. Reserve expansion may permit a relaxation of the constraint enforced by the balance of payments on exchange rate targets and, hence, allow governments to follow more expansionist demand-management policies. The chain of events is by no means automatic; it is, however, very likely to occur, as experience shows. And this is enough to make the oversupply of liquidity a matter of serious concern. Low liquidity forces everybody to fight inflation.

Slighton says that the reserve expansion of the 1970–1973 period was undoubtedly responsible in some part for the record growth in national money supplies over that period, but it surely is an exaggeration to consider reserve growth the key element in the cause or mechanism of inflation. It may not be *the* key element, but nevertheless it is a very important element. And if we were looking for elements, it would be difficult to find just one key, among the many elements in the inflationary process.

He further indicates that control of international reserves would help to bring the rate of international inflation under better control, but it is neither a necessary nor a sufficient condition of achieving that objective. It is certainly not sufficient, just as a restrictive monetary policy is not sufficient to fight inflation at home. The control of international reserves may not be absolutely necessary for a single country but is very, very helpful in easing worldwide inflationary pressure.

I would like to underline some statements in Slighton's paper with which I agree very much. He says the conditionality constraint has seldom been imposed in recent years by public lenders. This failure was a mistake. Any credit facility of any kind whatsoever—from one central bank to another, from an international institution to a country—

of necessity creates liquidity. If the pressure on the adjustment process is removed by newly created liquidity, it should at least be replaced by conditions that encourage the debtor countries to follow responsible economic policies. I will not touch upon the question of suitable conditions in individual cases. I only would like to underline the importance of making international credits conditional. In Austria, for example, we would not have our good central bank legislation if the League of Nations had not applied pressure in the 1920s in connection with an international loan. That pressure forced the Austrian government to adopt a law forbidding the central bank from financing the federal or regional government or even community administration in any way.

According to Slighton's paper, the U.S. government is pressing for a more rigorous application of IMF conditionality. What is uncertain is whether the U.S. government will be successful in this effort. I believe that any enlightened person really should assist these endeavors. Generally, any international financial assistance should be granted with economic conditions that help achieve monetary stability and balance of payments equilibrium. One principle, however, should be adhered to strictly: conditions should be equally binding on large countries as well as on small ones.

I should like to point out one more thing. After having drawn your attention to the fact that the control of liquidity is insufficient in the present system, I should like to refer to the paper of Edward Bernstein. His views about the relationship between international reserves and the floating rate system are contrary to Slighton's opinion. Bernstein said an amplitude of plus or minus 10 percent in floating rates between the dollar and the deutsche mark is too large to reflect underlying economic conditions alone. This raises the question: What causes markets to react in such a way?

I think the reason is that the international markets, the exchange rate markets included, are operating under inflation and changing exchange rate policies. Such markets, as we know, do not tend to an equilibrium. These fluctuations of plus and minus 10 percent are created by what Bernstein calls speculators. If we analyze the different types of speculation, we find investment in short-term money, leads and lags in payments, transactions of multinational companies, and speculation in the narrowest sense—borrowing in order to speculate.

All those engaged in activities of these types can function only if they can find enough liquidity to finance their transactions. I believe that the excess of liquidity is one reason why exchange rates fluctuate too much. Quick movements of huge amounts of short-term money indicate strongly that there is too much liquidity.

Egon Sohmen

The Unimportance of Being Earnest about International Liquidity

In contrast to some previous speakers, I would not lament the failure of the Jamaica Agreement to deal with the question of international liquidity and reserve creation. It seems to me that this issue has always been highly overrated. I think this verdict is justified both with respect to the level of total reserves and to their composition.

We recall the discussion of the early 1960s when it was widely believed that an expansion of world trade required a more or less parallel expansion of whatever was believed to fall under the heading of "international liquidity," and that failure to plan for such expansion by concerted international action might bring about a collapse of world trade and a general depression. This view, appropriately dubbed the international quantity theory, probably has few remaining followers today. Much of the underlying notion nevertheless continues to crop up inadvertently in current discussions and to find its way into agenda for monetary reform.

In our day, this notion finds expression, among other ways, in the claim that there has been an excess of reserve creation during the early 1970s in contrast to earlier days and that this excess is primarily responsible for the acceleration of inflationary trends over the past few years. This claim seems to appear particularly convincing to many observers when Eurodollar (or Eurocurrency) deposits are included in the figure for "world liquidity" because it is this financial market that has seen a particularly impressive expansion in recent times.

The defects of the international quantity theory and associated notions are many and space is too short even to summarize them here. Its basic fault seems to me to lie in the tendency to attribute to governments and central banks the same type of behavior with respect to monetary assets that we can expect with some confidence from private profit or utility maximizers. The economizing calculus followed by private decision makers will (at least for a sufficiently large number) lead to a fairly stable relation between the aggregate volume of transactions and the monetary assets held to handle them.

There is, it is true, a formal similarity in that official reserves are also held for the purpose of bridging deficits in the balance of all autonomous foreign exchange transactions. The forces that determine the various components of the totals on both sides of the foreign exchange market, however, are manifold and complex and are themselves influenced by various kinds of government interference as well as of

255

pressure groups. Therefore, any attempt at establishing a direct link between the volume of international transactions and the level of contingency holdings of monetary reserves is likely to be a caricature of reality.

The same objection applies if the imagined chain of causality is reversed. It is rather unlikely, at least for policy makers of the highly developed countries, that they base the degree of laxness or stringency of their monetary and fiscal policies primarily on the level of a country's official reserves. The only instance when this consideration approaches a reasonable degree of realism is when the reserves of a country approach the vanishing point and its government nevertheless refuses to abandon supporting its currency on the foreign exchange market.

This brings us to the main topic of this session, the role of reserves in a system of flexible exchange rates. Because official reserves are only required to support the exchange rate of a currency when it is under pressure, common sense reasoning suggests that the need for reserves disappears when a country is free to let exchange rates for its currency float in the free market. For the world as a whole, this belief obviously has to be modified to accommodate currency blocs in which certain countries agree to peg their exchange rates within specified limits with respect to each other.

Put into reverse, the same consideration suggests that neither the aggregate level of reserves nor their rate of change could possibly affect the rates of inflation in countries that let exchange rates for their currencies float freely. Concern over the rapid increase of world reserves as a cause of inflation could consequently make sense only before the general abandonment of exchange rate pegging in 1973.

The view has occasionally been expressed that transferring a substantial part of newly acquired dollar reserves from the oil-producing countries to European banks tended to accelerate inflation in the recipient countries. The exact opposite is true: when exchange rates are flexible, an inflow of money that is not absorbed by the central bank in the form of higher reserves has a *deflationary* effect. The only takers of the additional offer of foreign exchange, in that case, must be commercial traders, and the mirror image of the money inflow must consequently be an increase of imports relative to exports by exactly the same amount. This is a decidedly *de*flationary phenomenon. (This remark is, of course, not intended to inspire a deflationary scare, for it is one of the advantages of flexible rates that a country is not slavishly constrained in its monetary and fiscal policies by developments in its balance of payments.)

The Eurodollar Market

I have so far limited myself entirely to the role of *official reserves*. A word should perhaps be added on the Eurodollar market that caters both to the holders of official reserves and to private depositors. Most of what has been said so far about official reserves applies to official Eurodollar holdings as well. However, the contention that the Eurodollar market has operated as an inflation machine is also applied to its private deposit component.

Much of the apparent mystery that surrounds the Eurodollar market undoubtedly stems from the dollar denomination of its deposits and the tempting conclusion that these deposits are U.S. currency in the same sense as deposits in banks located in the United States. Because an overly rapid monetary expansion in the United States has undoubtedly contributed to inflation in the rest of the world on various occasions in the past, many people assume it causes any expansion of the Eurodollar market as well. I believe this mistaken identification of Eurodollars with genuine U.S. dollars is at the root of much confusion over this issue.

Let us take Eurodollar deposits in a London bank as an example. This bank has undertaken a commitment to honor specified liabilities toward its customers in U.S. dollars on maturity. This commitment should not lead us to believe that these deposits are part of the U.S. money market. The deposits in question are liabilities of a bank that is legally and economically part of the British economy. Its debits and credits are consequently first and foremost part of the British banking system and the London money market. Funds deposited with such a bank are used by it to make loans to customers. Funds deposited on Eurodollar accounts will, apart from a small contingency cash balance and with due consideration to risk factors, always go to the highest bidders, just as funds deposited in a regular account denominated in pounds sterling. The only difference of some significance is that British foreign exchange controls may prohibit certain types of foreign loans in one case and not in the other. In the absence of exchange controls, we should not expect British banks to differentiate between their customers in any other way.

Banks can, however, always be expected to watch their foreign exchange positions carefully, particularly when many currencies including the pound float freely. Prudence will call for an approximate matching of credits and debits denominated in each currency. To a large extent, this objective can be achieved by taking open forward positions of the appropriate amount and maturity structure while extending regular loans in domestic or any other currency.

257

This latter consideration suggests a description of Eurodollar deposits that may help to avoid some of the surrounding mystery. In all important respects, they are equivalent to regular deposits denominated in home currency, but endowed with an exchange rate guarantee in U.S. dollars. As noted above, British foreign exchange regulations may introduce another differentiation, but one unlikely to have any substantial bearing on whether the Eurodollar market can engender inflation anywhere outside Britain (or wherever Eurodollar banks may be located).

One peculiarity of the British banking system is that there are no legal reserve requirements, not even on the Eurodollar activities of British banks. This is undoubtedly one reason why this market has been centered in London. Banks that can profitably relend a higher share of the funds deposited with them obviously can offer more attractive conditions to their customers than banks in countries that impose strict reserve requirements.

Bank safety as well as the objective of more effective control of the money supply might well suggest the introduction of legal reserve requirements in the United Kingdom. Such requirements may also be suggested by considerations of competitive equality between British banks and those in other countries. Such a measure would undoubtedly lead to a drastic reduction of Eurodollar activities of British banks, but it is unlikely that the global size of the Eurodollar (or Eurocurrency) market would be much affected. If any government had the impression that such a reallocation of Eurodollar deposits leads to an undesirably large monetary expansion, it could always use the appropriate instruments of central banking to discourage such an extension.

This consideration holds just as well at the present time; however, it is first and foremost for the British monetary authorities. There is no basis for attributing to the Eurodollar market an inflationary impact that could not be fully neutralized by any national government—at least under a regime of freely floating exchange rates.

Use of Reserves to Reduce Excessive Exchange Rate Movements under Flexible Rates

There has long been some notable dissent from the opinion that the need for reserves is smaller the higher the degree of flexibility of exchange rates. Even if there is no legal requirement, every country will obviously want to prevent exaggerated gyrations of exchange rates for its currency.

Before the general move to basically flexible rates, we had to rely mostly on armchair theorizing to evaluate the question how wild or mild exchange rate movements might be in the absence of specified limits of variation. We now have some empirical evidence. Certain observers interpret this evidence as having convincingly refuted those who used to point to a number of autonomous stabilizing forces.

To begin with the easy cases, most of us certainly failed to anticipate a number of major destabilizing factors ten or fifteen years ago, such as the long poker game that eventually ended in a quadrupling of the oil price about a year after the general move to flexible rates in 1973, or more localized events such as the deepening agony of the Christian Democratic party that has deprived Italy of a forceful—and hence predictable—government for so many years.

Before I turn to other factors that contribute to exchange rate instability, let me stress that the imaginary economist who would have opposed official exchange market intervention under any and all circumstances is, as far as I can tell, a mere straw man. At a time when the vast majority of informed observers—and nearly all the uninformed ones—were convinced that perhaps not the world, but at least world trade might come to an end if central banks were no longer under strict orders to stabilize exchange rates, it was necessary to point to a number of market forces that would tend to prevent excessive fluctuations under normal circumstances. Because circumstances are, as we all know, rather abnormal more often than we care to see, official smoothing operations should certainly not be ruled out completely. Strong opposition to massive intervention against the overwhelming trend of the market is perfectly compatible with an endorsement of an intelligently managed stabilization system.

The Canadian practice during most of its flexible years (excepting the last two or three years before the end of the first decade of flexibility in 1962) can still serve as an example of sophisticated stabilization. I have always had difficulties in following those who used to defend unrealistic parities to the bitter end as long as the Bretton Woods system lasted, yet were quick to denounce even moderate smoothing interventions during times of flexibility as "dirty floating"—an expression that is obviously not intended to be a word of endearment. On the whole, it seems to me that central banks have operated in the foreign exchange market in a satisfactory way since the abandonment of the Bretton Woods rules. The only significant exceptions are again those cases in which an attempt was made to practice Bretton Woods *en miniature,* as in the abortive attempt of the European snake to swallow a politically restless France.

Acceptance of smoothing interventions that do not stubbornly oppose an obvious trend should not be misread to imply acceptance of the view that there is a predictable and calculable level of "optimal" reserves for every given volume of international trade. International liquidity, according to the usual definition, is needed only for stabilizing interventions in the *spot* markets for foreign exchange. Interventions in forward markets are an easy substitute, at least for all advanced countries with well-developed money markets. In addition, skillful handling of monetary policy can go a long way toward avoiding undesirable exchange rate fluctuation even without deliberate interventions, in spot or forward markets.

Possible Explanations for the Instability of the Deutsche Mark–Dollar Rate

While we should be open-minded on the issue of official exchange market intervention, we have every reason to welcome all autonomous market forces that tend to stabilize the movement of exchange rates over time. There is a long history of controversy over the question whether speculative foreign exchange transactions are likely to contribute toward stability or the opposite. It can be shown that speculation necessarily tends to be a stabilizing force the closer the following conditions are fulfilled:

- Foresight by market participants is perfect.
- Individual speculators have negligible market power.
- Entry into the "business" of speculation is free, a condition that assures a sufficiently elastic supply of funds for speculative activity.

What can be expected in the real world will obviously depend on the closeness with which these conditions are approximated. If governments frequently act in rather erratic and unpredictable fashions in an unstable political environment, it can hardly be expected that their actions can be predicted with reasonable accuracy by speculators or anybody else. Oil prices during the 1973–1974 period serve as a persuasive practical example.

Who can be expected to perform the speculative activities discussed in theoretical writings on the subject, and how important is speculative activity likely to be in practice? It can bear repetition that the group of people one could legitimately designate professional speculators is probably rather insignificant by comparison with the total volume of transactions. Most speculative engagements in foreign exchange presumably arise as a side effect of basically nonspeculative transactions, such as failure of exporting firms to hedge against their foreign exchange risks. Even when these implicit speculative commitments are added to those of "pure" speculators, it may well be that they still amount to a relatively small part of total foreign exchange transactions at most times. It is to be expected that speculative positions are unable to counteract the weight of major changes in a country's trade balance or large nonspeculative capital flows that may be prompted by basic policy adjustments.

Let me illustrate this proposition by the convenient practical example of the deutsche mark–dollar rate. Most observers seem to have been at a loss to explain the rather dramatic appreciation of the deutsche mark during the first months of 1975, starting from a level that was already considered to be remarkably high. A strong downturn indeed developed in the following months and the mark finally settled around what might be considered a reasonable equilibrium rate after August 1975.

Why were profit-maximizing (professional or implicit) speculators unable to foresee this development and cash in on it? Or is it even possible that speculative activity behaved in such a way as to *intensify* the cyclical swing?

To begin with the latter question first, it may be recalled that the failure of the Herstatt bank had occurred in 1974 as a result of large-scale speculative commitments in foreign exchange. I consider it a reasonable conjecture that its failure must have sharply reduced the desire of West German banks to speculate in foreign exchange and that it must have sharpened the watchful eye of governmental bank supervisors over such activities. Neither would it surprise me if this change had also reduced the willingness of banks to encourage speculative commitments by their customers. Whatever happened on the exchange market after the Herstatt failure is therefore likely to reflect a *reduction* of speculative activity rather than an increase.

The major reason for the substantial appreciation of the mark at the beginning of 1975 can, however, probably be sought in the choice of macroeconomic policy assignments by the West German government and the Bundesbank. This choice of assignments is stated succinctly in the annual report of the Bundesbank for 1974:

> In 1974, the monetary policy of the Bundesbank pursued the primary goal of bringing about a break in the inflationary trend by limiting monetary expansion. This was done in the frame-

work of a concerted strategy that assigned to the fiscal policy of the Federal government the objective of supporting the employment level by moderately expansionary action.

This policy mix implies that monetary policy was more restrictive and West German interest rates consequently higher than they would have been in the case of a more symmetrical division of labor between the two principal macroeconomic policy instruments. At the same time, the federal budget tended toward higher deficits than would otherwise have arisen. During most of 1974, West German interest rates nevertheless did not appear to be overly high by comparison with interest rates in other countries, as revealed by the fact that both long- and short-term capital moved outward at a rather impressive pace throughout most of the year. This made the deutsche mark relatively cheap and encouraged the huge West German export surplus of that year, by far the largest in history.

As the worldwide recession set in toward the end of 1974, interest rates started a general decline everywhere. At least when they are seen in conjunction with expectations about the future course of the deutsche mark, interest rates in West Germany appear to have been relatively high by international comparison. A rather pronounced change toward a net inflow of short-term capital developed during the first few months of 1975: after a short-term capital *out*flow of about DM 20 billion for 1974, the year 1975 brought a net *in*flow of short-term capital totaling about DM 5 billion. This is the simple explanation of the excessive appreciation of the deutsche mark during the first quarter of 1975, a development that could easily have been prevented by a more determined monetary expansion by the Bundesbank.

Its reluctance to loosen credit is understandable in that the rate of inflation was still at about 6 percent, an excessively high level by West German standards. It also reveals, however, that Bundesbank policy had not yet fully adjusted to the new environment of flexible rates. Under this monetary system, any change in the balance of capital flows across a country's borders transmits itself almost instantaneously into an equivalent change in the current account balance.

In the episode under review, this meant that the unusually high export surplus of 1974 (about DM 41 billion) was reduced to only DM 26 billion in 1975. The impact on domestic business activity was traumatic, but could have been predicted by carefully watching the development of capital movements and the induced course of exchange rates for the deutsche mark. The latter indicator is available from day to day and might have served as a warning sign that a more expansionary monetary policy was indicated. Even if it is argued that it is impossible to extend the domestic credit base with sufficient speed, it is always possible to bring about the desirable monetary expansion by purchases of foreign exchange. The Bundesbank indeed bought up dollars at that time, but apparently at somewhat too cautious a pace.

I do not want to give the impression of being overly critical of Bundesbank policy. By and large, especially in comparison with the activities of other central banks, West German monetary policy deserves rather high marks for flexibly steering the West German monetary system through rather difficult times.

Bundesbank policy also had to react to developments elsewhere in the economy that were not always progressing ideally. In particular, West German unions had deviated too much from their almost proverbial restraint in the two preceding years and made the task of the Bundesbank considerably more difficult than it has usually been.

To a large extent, we are still suffering from the heritage of the final years of the Bretton Woods system, during which West Germany as well as other countries were insufficiently able to isolate themselves from the worldwide wave of accelerating inflation. Like most other countries, West Germany has had to defuse gradually the inflationary expectations engendered at that time, and it has not been possible to accomplish this task without driving up unemployment to a level of 5 percent and beyond for an extended period.

Given the international pattern of interest rates that existed in 1974 and 1975, as well as the irresistible pull that resulted for short-term interest-arbitrage flows first in one and then in the other direction, it would be rather hopeless to expect that the cyclical time path of exchange rates that was induced by all this could be sufficiently dampened by private speculative engagements. The need for occasional support by central bank intervention on the foreign exchange markets is, as should be sufficiently clear from my discussion, indicated not only by the goal of preventing undesirable exchange rate instability, but even more by the more basic desire to keep business activity on a reasonably even keel.

Though it is obviously impossible to remove all sources of conflict for monetary policy simultaneously, it seems that the twin goals of external and internal balance can be approximated in a system of flexible rates by an alert and flexible monetary policy. To a large extent, differentiated operations directed at different ends of the time structure of interest rates may be used to reach these goals, but to go further into this topic is obviously beyond the scope of these remarks.

Robert Triffin

I had originally hoped to keep my remarks as uncontroversial—and as persuasive—as possible by confining them to the topic of international liquidity proper and skirting the quicksands of the broader debate on exchange rate flexibility. I am afraid, however, I will, as usual, be a nonconformist in this debate. My main point is that fundamental reforms in the present international reserve system are essential to the proper functioning of any exchange rate arrangements, whatever their degree of presumptive stability or flexibility.

The postwar reserves system was legally anchored on gold at a fixed price of $35 an ounce but in fact was increasingly anchored on the use of one or a very few major currencies for market interventions, settlements, and reserve accumulation by central banks. Eleven years of nearly continuous debates and negotiations in the IMF Executive Board, the Group of Ten, the Committee of Twenty, et cetera by 1974 had elicited at long last a nearly unanimous consensus on the following basic reforms needed to remedy the obvious shortcomings of the system:

(1) a process of erratic reserve creation, biased toward inflation, which had increased world reserves over three years (1970 to 1972) by more than in all previous years and centuries;

(2) the basic frustration of the balance of payments adjustment process, owing to a double asymmetry in the system: first, the ability of the reserve-center countries to finance large and continuing deficits with their own IOUs (as, for instance, 93 percent of the more than $50 billion overall deficits incurred by the United States from 1970 to 1972); and second, the parallel ability of surplus countries to avoid exchange rate readjustments through large and continuing purchases of foreign exchange with their own currency;

(3) the investment of the bulk of world reserves in a few of the richest and most capitalized countries, conferring upon them the awesome power and responsibility of "recycling" reserves toward the countries most in need of foreign capital;

(4) the stimulation of speculative capital flows between major money markets and into gold.

The general recognition of these basic defects of the system had prompted a large intellectual agreement—still spelled out in the *Outline of Reform* issued by the Committee of Twenty on June 14, 1974—on a number of essential reforms aiming, for example, at a better management of liquidity creation, more symmetrical adjustment and convertibility

264

processes, and cooperation in dealing with disequilibrating capital movements. None of these proposals was agreed on in Jamaica, and none survives in the draft amendments of the IMF Articles of Agreement.

Yet, the under secretary of the Treasury denounces any charge that the Jamaica reform is "incomplete" as reflecting "a failure to perceive the evolution which has taken place in the international monetary system" and "the profound change which has taken place in thinking about the world monetary system."[1]

I can hardly believe that four of the profound changes cited by Under Secretary Yeo are either real changes or have gone unperceived by the critics of the Jamaica Agreement:

(1) Changes in the Bretton Woods provisions on gold and exchange rates that "stem from a common idea: the view that . . . monetary stability can be achieved only by developing underlying conditions of stability in the major economies. . . . This is the reverse of the Bretton Woods focus."[2]

I for one, and I am sure many others, never had any doubt about this commonplace observation but felt that international agreement on some monetary rules might help preserve or restore "underlying conditions of stability" better than the free-for-all provisions of the Jamaica Agreement.

(2) The Bretton Woods par value provisions were based on an assumption that has "proved wrong"—that is, that "exchange stability could be achieved" by "using the threat of reserve losses or the eventual shame of a forced devaluation as the leverage to influence domestic policies."[3] This seems to me a failure by Under Secretary Yeo to perceive the fact that the Bretton Woods provision on changes in par values was precisely designed to meet the cases in which this leverage would not be sufficient, and was used far more frequently than he implies, even though belatedly at times.

Par values—or effective exchange rates, when no par value was adopted in 1946—were changed or suspended one or many times by all countries except the United States, from the 1946 declaration of initial par values until August 15, 1971. Though these changes were rather infrequent for the industrial countries—thus confirming, rather than infirming, the expected leverage of reserve losses on domestic policies— nearly half these major currencies devalued by 27 percent to 79 percent over this period. Par value changes were, of course, far larger and more

---

[1] Edwin H. Yeo III, "International Liquidity," *The Department of the Treasury News* (Remarks delivered before the Institutional Bond Club of New York at the City Midday Club, N. Y., N. Y., March 30, 1976), pp. 2, 3.

[2] Ibid., pp. 4, 5.

[3] Ibid., p. 3.

frequent for the many other nonindustrial countries, and particularly for the LDCs.

The formidable exception of the U.S. dollar—and its consequent appreciation in terms of other currencies—is precisely explained by the fact that the special status of the dollar in the international reserve system, ignored throughout by Under Secretary Yeo, enabled the United States to finance most of its deficits by piling up IOUs to foreign monetary authorities rather than through reserve losses. The U.S. deficits on official settlements from 1950 to August 15, 1971, totaled close to $50 billion, of which nearly three-fourths were financed by increased indebtedness to foreign monetary authorities and the IMF, and only one-fourth by losses of gross reserves.

(3) Most extraordinary, to my mind, is Under Secretary Yeo's claim that the pre-Jamaica proposals for reforms would have substituted "decisions of an international bureaucracy for market mechanisms" and that "international liquidity, in the present market-oriented world economy, is mainly disciplined by the market."[4] Were the $106 billion of foreign exchange reserves accumulated by central banks since mid-1971 (85 percent of total reserve increases) and $43.5 billion since the generalization of floating rates in March 1973 (91 percent of total reserve increases) created and disciplined by the "market" or by the "bureaucratic decisions" of the central banks that purchased them?

(4) We can all agree, however, with the concluding remark of Under Secretary Yeo: "*If* each nation will *individually* manage its affairs responsibly, and *if* we *all* remain firm in our commitment to international cooperation and trade matters, we can look forward to future progress without concern about excessive international liquidity."[5] Granted, but are those safe assumptions on which to build international monetary institutions, or assumptions repeatedly proved wrong in the past and likely to be proved wrong in the future, even more obviously than the assumptions underlying the Bretton Woods agreement?

Under any less optimistic—but, I am very much afraid, more realistic—assumptions, we may still have to concern ourselves tomorrow with the problems of international liquidity, swept under the rug in Jamaica. I am not sure indeed that such concern has been or can be effectively lessened by flexible rates, without serious costs to other legitimate policy objectives.

The main changes that have occurred so far in the evolution of international reserves are, first, that the industrial countries other than the United States have ceased to be the main reserve gainers (to the

---

[4] Ibid., pp. 6, 13.
[5] Ibid., p. 19 (italics added).

tune of nearly $70 billion from January 1, 1970, through March 1973), the OPEC countries accounting for practically all the $48 billion growth of world reserves from March 1973 through December 1975; and second, reserve losses (gross or net) are no longer practically confined to the United States, but are now widely distributed among many countries.

These two major changes, however, are far more likely to reflect the impact of the energy crisis on balances of payments than the impact of flexible rates. Indeed, of the six industrial countries whose reserve gains switched to reserve losses after March 1973, West Germany is the only one for which this switch could be credited to the appreciation of its currency. The dollar exchange rate of two of the other countries in this group (Canada and Denmark) did not change significantly, and that of the other three countries declined—rather than appreciated—very substantially: Japan by 12 percent, Italy by 15 percent, and the United Kingdom by 18 percent.

The other seven industrial countries all continued to gain reserves after March 1973 (up to approximately $9.5 billion in 1975 alone, as against $20.5 billion between January 1970 and March 1973), although their currencies all appreciated in terms of dollars, moderately or substantially: up to 10 percent for the Netherlands, 12 percent for Austria, and 24 percent for Switzerland.

I have no doubt that some of the exchange rate changes of this period were preferable to larger reserve gains or losses (particularly in Italy and the United Kingdom), but neither the overall changes in other major exchange rates nor especially their repeated wide swings could be interpreted as reflecting and correcting parallel changes in fundamental price and cost competitiveness. Unit labor costs rose far more abroad than in the United States over this period; these relative rises were accentuated—rather than corrected—by exchange rate changes (except again for Italy and the United Kingdom), and they certainly bore no relation to the huge, reversible swings in dollar exchange rates of the major countries.

I very much agree with Under Secretary Yeo that the main source of reserve increases since March 1973—that is, the $41 billion accumulation of foreign exchange by the oil-exporting countries—helped avoid a sudden elimination of oil-importing countries' deficits "through an infeasible reduction in imports of oil," and that "had there been a strict international control over liquidity creation—public and private—during that period, one wonders whether those charged with that control would

267

have had the courage and foresight to provide for expansion of official reserves in the magnitudes needed." [6]

Yet, this hardly means that the problems of liquidity creation, accumulation, and recycling can be safely entrusted to market forces in the future. The U.S. proposals for a "safety net," as well as many other proposals, testify that such an assumption is not relied on by our own officialdom.

Though the greater flexibility of exchange rates, particularly vis-à-vis the dollar, may relieve some pressures on international reserves, it may also aggravate them for three reasons.

First, flexibility seems to have elicited wider (in terms of participation *and* currencies) and more continuous interest in exchange rate speculation and capital movements—aggressive and defensive—than was the case previously.

Second, an increasing portion of official reserves and official as well as private lending and borrowing is now channeled through the Euromarket, where resulting claims, not very safely lodged, can be easily switched at any time from one currency to another, aggravating currency crises and instability. The volume of Eurobond issues and publicly announced Eurocurrency bank credits doubled from $13 billion in 1972 to $26 billion in 1973 and rose further in both 1974 and 1975 to about $30 billion a year.

The so-called recycling burdens and risks of these types of investment are certainly greater and less fairly distributed than would have been the case if surpluses had to be channeled primarily, as previously proposed, into SDRs or other reserve claims on the IMF.

Third, the exchange rates between the dollar and other currencies may move up or down substantially from day to day not because of the United States balance of payments, but rather because other countries settle their surpluses and deficits with one another primarily in dollars. These countries may take a different view of the comparative advantages, or disadvantages, of reserve gains or losses through market interventions as an alternative to letting the dollar depreciate or appreciate vis-à-vis their own currency.

This factor had probably as much or more to do with the huge swings in dollar rates experienced under flexible rates than with the fluctuations in the U.S. balance of payments or basic competitiveness in world trade.

I cannot but conclude that the problems raised by the present international reserve system and previously emphasized in the reform negotia-

---

[6] Ibid., p. 10.

tions have not all been solved by the Jamaica Agreement. Even the so-called demonetization of gold and the sale or restitution of IMF gold holdings leave unanswered the question of what will be done with the huge gold holdings inherited by national monetary authorities from the previous regime. If the charge that the Jamaica reform is incomplete reflects an insufficient perception of recent changes in the international monetary system, the claim that it is complete certainly reflects a lack of perception of the persistent problems of international liquidity that will continue to plague us tomorrow as they did yesterday.

SUMMARY OF THE DISCUSSION

Recognizing that the problem of international liquidity has many facets, all of which cannot be adequately discussed in one afternoon, the chairman of the session, Henry Wallich, asked the discussants to concentrate just on a few points. Without attempting to prejudice the discussion, he suggested emphasizing the following three issues, which emerged from the paper presented by Robert Slighton, the address by Under Secretary Yeo on "International Liquidity," [1] and the commentators' remarks: (1) the degree of need for control of international liquidity; (2) the means and their effectiveness of exerting such control; and (3) possible substitute measures to achieve what is thought to be accomplished by control of international liquidity if direct control is considered impossible or too difficult.

J. J. Polak started by saying that he basically agreed rather more with the propositions advanced in Slighton's paper than with the comments on that paper. He volunteered to provide two facts and one minor point of theory as a background for further discussion on "theoretical" (or as Sohmen said, "a priori") propositions concerning international liquidity.

The first fact, which Polak said one has to bear in mind all along, is that the so-called reserve explosion stopped in March 1973, as Robert Solomon had said earlier. The second fact is that since January 1974 the international community has repeatedly judged it necessary to introduce additional official liquidity because of the severe international economic disturbances.

The first source of additional liquidity was the introduction of the oil facility in the International Monetary Fund. The second was a significant liberalization of compensatory financing. The third source was the Jamaica decision to increase conditional liquidity from 100 percent of quota to 145 percent of quota. In addition to these three sources, one could mention the creation of the "safety net" and the regular increase in IMF quotas.

---

[1] Edwin H. Yeo III, "International Liquidity," *The Department of the Treasury News* (Remarks delivered before the Institutional Bond Club of New York at the City Midday Club, N. Y., N. Y., March 30, 1976).

Those two facts—the end of the reserves explosion in 1973 and the agreement on the need for additional liquidity—were thought by Polak to be relevant to any discussion of what ought to be done in the future about international liquidity.

The point of theory brought up by Polak was the less than ten-year-old proposition concerning conditionality of liquidity. According to that proposition, in a situation where liquidity is severely short, conditional and unconditional liquidity are far from perfect substitutes. In a situation where the international community has to deal with the provision of additional liquidity, it ought to judge where the objectives of economic expansion, abstinence from restrictions, containment of inflation, and the like are better served by the provision of conditional or unconditional liquidity, or perhaps by both, as well as the dosage required of each.

Although this proposition had gained wide acceptance, Polak noticed that it has been implicitly contradicted (without having been referred to explicitly) in the preceding discussion. The contradiction was manifested in the unrestrained support given to the provision of conditional liquidity and the criticism of any provision of unconditional liquidity. He concluded that the proposition he stated ought to be kept in mind when considering provision of liquidity.

Wilson Schmidt suggested that the problem of liquidity should be clearly distinguished from the question of whether some countries are under so great a strain that real resources at their disposal make the burden unbearable by international community standards. If the preoccupation is with the real resource position one should consider various schemes of increasing the development aid, not the liquidity at the disposal of such countries. Unfortunately, Schmidt pointed out, these two issues tend to be confused very frequently, even in the present discussion.

Fred Hirsch took up a point raised by Slighton and Under Secretary Yeo that indicates the attitude of the U.S. Treasury. The passage in Slighton's paper that he found objectionable reads:

> If it is concluded that there is so little willingness to cooperate in the international monetary arena that there will be minimal adherence to the obligations of the Jamaica Agreement, how can it possibly be argued that an agreement embodying greater restrictions over reserve creation could be negotiated?

Hirsch stated that the only way to argue this point is that the problem at hand is, fundamentally, a collective-good problem. In this particular instance, countries are asked to undertake certain cooperative action that involves some small private individual costs for each particular country.

The potential gain to the countries is the overall effect of the cooperation of everybody else. Their own participation in the cooperative effort is not going to give them the game.

According to Hirsch, the classical structure of the collective-good problem imposes a tighter system of restraints on individual freedom of action that could be expected to elicit more cooperation from any individual country.

Hirsch illustrated his point with an analogy. If within any cooperative arrangement members on the whole are expected to abide by the rules but also have a great deal of flexibility as to whether or not they will do so, as in the Jamaica Agreement, individual members of the cooperative may well be reluctant to abide by those rules. If, instead, there is a clear and unambiguous requirement that all members obey the rules, a member who would have resisted cooperating (when it was uncertain whether other partners would cooperate) might cooperate on this stricter and tighter basis. In conclusion, Hirsch charged that the agnostic approach exemplified in Under Secretary Yeo's statement and Slighton's paper misses the fundamental characteristic of international organization and cooperation.

Nicolas Krul began with a reminder that the very concept of international liquidity has remained ambiguous. Despite the efforts of Fritz Machlup and others over the last fifteen years to distinguish between loose definitions of liquidity and more restrictive concepts, little progress has been made. Experts still argue about volume, still search for adequate data on supply and demand flows, and still disagree about the desirability of controls as well as about the effective impact of the international market on domestic policy conditions or exchange rates.

Under such conditions, Krul posited, it is illusory and dangerous to theorize away the Euromarket—the existing pool of international, uncontrolled money, particularly in a monetary-financial environment marked by uncertainty and a weakened institutional framework—a far cry from the original tool intended to forge closer equitable international integration. Whatever the size of the pool of Eurocurrencies, it is without any doubt too big and too elastic in relation to the domestic money supply of the few European countries issuing preferred currencies. Similarly, the direct causal relationship between world inflation and the growth of international liquidity may be a matter of controversy.

Krul agreed with Schmidt's remark that the correlations between the rates of growth of international liquidity and the rates of inflation are far too close for comfort. He also expressed certainty as to the

273

direct causal relationship between the existence of the Euromarket and the persistence of disruptive capital flows. In support of his contention, Krul invoked a recent statement by Rinaldo Ossola to the effect that, were there no Euromarket, the destabilizing attitude of speculators and arbitragers could only be fed by the domestic monetary markets which are able to react and block financing; instead, the existence of the Euromarket gives these operations greater freedom of action since there is no authority to regulate it and because it seems to have a considerable capacity for expansion, although the limits of it have not yet been fully explored.

Krul also reminded the participants that the 1973 annual report of the Bundesbank spoke of the "turntable function" of the Euromarket and that it was no secret that the French opposition to Switzerland's entry into the snake had been directly related to the potential impact of the huge Swiss net Euro-assets on the intrasnake rates via the Swiss franc.

For commercial bankers the causal relationship is visible in the behavior of capital flows and interest rates. In February 1973, for instance, the deposit rate differential between the still pegged German mark and the already floating Swiss franc suddenly soared from the habitual 1 percent to around 7½ percent.

Krul concluded by saying that the pragmatic evidence of causal relationship between the operation of the Eurocurrency market and erratic capital flows made him persist in the belief that collective or coordinated national measures for Euromarket regulation remain desirable.

At this point Thomas Willett quipped that it was unusual to hear the U.S. Treasury's views on such issues as provision of liquidity being criticized as too liberal rather than too conservative. In a more serious vein, he pointed out that the U.S. Treasury had advocated all along *not* refraining from control of international liquidity; the Treasury has advocated what it considers the best ways to control liquidity.

In this regard, in Willett's view, the Jamaica Agreement made substantial progress toward better regulation of international liquidity, at least in the sense of allowing the governments to curtail the undesired expansions of international liquidity caused by obligations to maintain fixed exchange rates.

Willett indicated that the inordinately fast growth of international reserves in the early 1970s, deplored by Triffin, had been a consequence of fixed rates, still prevalent at that time, rather than of increased flexibility of exchange rates. In fact, since the advent of generalized floating in March 1973, the rate of growth of international reserves has slowed considerably.

In response to Machlup's criticism of the Jamaica Agreement, Willett readily conceded that it had not resulted in the adoption of any optimal or ideal method of control over international liquidity. He maintained, however, that the agreement had provided a basis for a clear-cut improvement in the effective control of international liquidity and, therefore, deserves fairly high marks on that score.

In a remark related only indirectly to the issue of international liquidity, Franz Scholl challenged Sohmen's interpretation of causes of changes in the dollar-mark exchange rate in 1974 and 1975. Though acknowledging that Sohmen's figures concerning the change in net capital flows from a DM 20 billion outflow in 1974 to a DM 5 billion inflow in 1975 were correct, Scholl pointed out that these figures pertain only to short-term capital movements.

What actually happened, in Scholl's opinion, was that sizable outflows of short-term capital in 1974 reflected large-scale financing of the West German export surplus in the form of credits granted by West German exporters. The value of such credits fell drastically in 1975, first because the Federal Republic experienced a substantial net long-term capital outflow, and second, because West Germany was the only industrial country enjoying an increase in real imports in 1975, with a concomitant increase in the demand for credit by domestic importers. Parenthetically, the decline in West German export credits became clearly visible in the third quarter of 1975, which gives it little relevance in explaining exchange rate changes at the beginning of the same year, that is, before this change.

Both in 1974 and 1975, Scholl continued, West German net (short- and long-term) capital outflows exceeded the surpluses on current account, and net foreign assets of the Bundesbank declined. It is debatable whether and to what extent the overall balance of payments positions were responsible for fluctuations in the exchange rate of the West German mark.

Scholl proceeded to offer an alternative explanation of the sharp appreciation of the West German mark at the beginning of 1975 that mystified a number of observers. The January 1975 figures indicated that the largest-ever monthly balance of trade surplus in December 1974 made the yearly surplus shoot up to 50 billion marks. At the same time, the Bundesbank, with full support of the government, announced its intention to pursue a restrictive monetary policy.

Scholl found it not surprising that, given the largest trade surplus on record, coupled with the announcement that it would not be diminished by inflating the domestic economy, the exchange markets reacted in the way they did and the exchange rate of the West German mark went up sharply. Later in the year an easier monetary policy was applied, liquidity increased, interest rates declined, and an outflow of capital occurred. As a result, the mark exchange rate went down—as everybody expected.

In an immediate response to Scholl, Egon Sohmen challenged this interpretation of the developments in the foreign exchange market in early 1975. Sohmen acknowledged that he had not mentioned long-term capital movements separately. He pointed out, however, that the dominating factor at that time had been short-term capital movements. Apart from the well-known difficulty in differentiating statistically between short- and long-term capital flows, what really is important is the overall balance of capital movements, which fell from an outflow of DM 25 billion in 1974 to an outflow of only DM 12 billion in 1975. This change was almost exactly equal to the change in the balance of goods and services. In other words, the Bundesbank's interventions in the foreign exchange market at that time were not very important.

Sohmen remarked that the swing in short-run capital movements at that time might not have been induced by trade flows. However, he thought it was quite easy to find out what had been the dominating factor by determining the effect on the exchange rate at the time. If, as the West German government claimed during 1975, the West German recession at that time had been prompted primarily by the recession in the rest of the world, one would have had to expect a depreciation of the mark. A decline in demand for West German exports in the rest of the world, as a result of stagnation there, would obviously have led to a weakening of the mark on the exchange markets.

Because exactly the opposite happened in early 1975, Sohmen tended to conclude that the dominating factor that led to the change in the current account balance was capital movements.

Sohmen stressed that his main point was not so much to criticize the Bundesbank or the West German government as to try to explain what had happened to the mark exchange rate, mainly because its behavior seemed to have caused some puzzlement. Although fluctuations in this rate need not necessarily be a cause for concern, it would have been possible to reduce those fluctuations by a slight change in the assignment of macroeconomic policy tools.

Robert Heller addressed a few points that had not been raised by other speakers. The first point was based on Slighton's argument that the effects of the recent expansion of official reserves on the world money supply are dramatically different from the monetary effects of the increase in reserves in the 1970–1973 period. Heller agreed that this may be true in the short run, but it would be mistaken to believe that the OPEC countries' reserves are permanently sterilized. Nearly all

OPEC countries spend their accumulated reserves as fast as they can. Once the current underutilization of productive capacity in the industrial countries is eliminated, OPEC spending may turn out to be a source of strong inflationary pressures. Certain real effects of large monetary accumulations will then become obvious.

Heller found it dismaying that the problem of more recent increase in international reserves was being slighted by attributing it to special factors. It reminded him of the arguments of the 1960s attempting to explain the U.S. balance of payments deficits. Instead of acknowledging an underlying deficit that needed correction, temporary and special reasons were formerly invoked to explain the balance of payments deficit in any particular year. Attributing recent increases in international reserves to balance of payments accounting procedures or minimizing their potential impact by emphasizing peculiarities in their distribution is not the right way to face the problem.

Second, Heller considered the concept of the appropriate stock of international liquidity under floating exchange rates. He noted that under fixed exchange rates, the appropriate volume of international reserves is largely related to the benefits that accrue to countries because they can avoid income adjustments. Under flexible exchange rates instead of income adjustments, countries with appropriate reserves can avoid exchange rate adjustments. Exchange rate adjustment implies a resource reallocation cost. Because these costs are very high in the short run, it was appropriate that the immediate impact of, for instance, the oil price increase was cushioned by a supply of additional international liquidity. Heller suggested that a fruitful way to look at the demand for international reserves, under both fixed and floating rates, would be to look at it in terms of a portfolio selection process, where countries hold a certain amount of liquid assets, and to set these liquid assets in some relation to foreign liabilities of domestic commercial banks, to foreign assets, and to the overall liability and asset position of the country vis-à-vis other countries.

Finally Heller brought up a point, raised in some recent discussions on the subject of international liquidity and related to the argument that the recent worldwide inflation has eroded many of the increases that have accrued in real international reserves. It follows from this argument that perhaps a further increase in international reserves is justified to restore the real international reserve balances that would be required. To illustrate that this view is grossly mistaken, Heller recalled the president of the Deutsche Reichsbank in the 1920s—in the middle of the German hyperinflation—when some people kept looking with concern at the declining real money stocks. The president of the Reichsbank announced that all economic problems in Germany would soon be overcome because the bank had just bought a new high-speed printing press that could restore the real balances to the levels which were needed.

In a brief intervention, Robert Triffin said that the observation about the explosion of liquidity having taken place mainly before 1973—that is, before the advent of floating—was essentially correct, a temporary sharp increase in 1974 notwithstanding. The correctness of this observation, however, does not undermine the claim that overexpansion of international liquidity is attributable to greater flexibility of exchange rates. That increased flexibility, Triffin stressed, goes back not to March 1973, but to May 1971, when a series of readjustments in exchange rates among several major currencies took place.

Gretchen Greene expressed her surprise at the presumption that in the past two years there has been an excess of international liquidity. From her vantage point at the foreign exchange desk at the Federal Reserve Bank of New York the concern appeared to be primarily over how to finance the very sudden and dramatic shift in global wealth distribution. It is true that there might have been excess liquidity in some national money markets, but this excess reflected maldistribution of liquidity among countries rather than excess global liquidity. This assessment was shared apparently by the IMF and other bodies that decided to provide various forms of additional liquidity to countries in need.

Next, Greene disagreed that the excess liquidity in the world markets had helped to finance speculation in foreign exchange markets. Though it is difficult to disprove that the increase in monetary aggregate contributed to stepped-up speculative activity since the beginning of the float, the much greater source of exchange rate movements due to speculation had been, in her opinion, a very sharp increase in velocity. From behind the foreign exchange desk at the Federal Reserve Bank of New York, the increase in velocity is easy to detect in the form of the same funds being passed from one trader to another, and thus contributing to exchange rate movements.

Greene said she was bothered more by the problem of diversification of reserves than by their aggregate size. First, she noted, a larger portion of official reserves is now being held in the Eurocurrency market, with a significant number of banks, and in many different forms in terms of denomination of assets and their maturities. Moreover, the dispersion of reserves among countries has also increased. Diversification of reserve holdings has already undermined, at least to some extent, an agreement among the ten industrial countries to employ reserves in national markets, rather than in the Eurocurrency markets. Proliferation of currencies taking on a reserve-currency status increases the potential for instability in the volume of international liquidity, and, of course, this potential grows even larger as the number of countries with diversified reserve holdings increases.

Wolfgang Schmitz remarked with approval that the majority of experts gave the impression that international liquidity matters. Unfortunately, there was not enough time in this discussion to look at the different sources of liquidity to distinquish which type of control is realistic and which is not. The sources of liquidity, Schmitz went on, range from the deficits of key-currency countries, the Eurodollar market multiplier and the diversification of reserves to additional international credit facilities.

The feasibility of measures to control given sources of liquidity differs greatly. For instance, only the creditor countries and the most important IMF members can determine whether additional credit facilities for countries with balance of payments difficulties will be made conditional upon a prior use of some of their own reserves, including gold.

Schmitz acknowledged that the supply of convertible currencies does not depend on the policies of the key-currency countries alone. However, he pointed out that a restrictive, or at least not expansionary, policy followed by them would be helpful in avoiding oversupply. Further, he suggested, the creation of additional reserves by means of reserve diversification can be avoided if the most important monetary authorities accept the rule that international official reserves can be invested only in the country of issue. An alternative might be a kind of restrictive open-market operation by the International Monetary Fund.

Schmitz warned that other ways and means, such as the control over the credit-creating power of the Eurocurrency markets, depend entirely upon a worldwide agreement. Otherwise the supranational money market would just shift to a different location. But even this solution, he noted, should not forever be regarded as unrealistic. It may come as a result of a learning process for all monetary authorities and national governments. The Bretton Woods agreement was also the result of a learning process lasting one or even two decades.

Franz Aschinger noted with satisfaction that the impression given by the papers of Under Secretary Yeo and Robert Slighton—namely, that the liquidity problem was, so to speak, solving itself—has been softened in the context of the current discussion. The discussion has revealed that the proponents of the new approach to the problem of international liquidity are not entirely neglecting the problem of controls.

Aschinger supported Machlup's appeal not to limit future negotiations to proposals that appear to be politically practicable. But he

279

warned against proposing destructive methods of controlling international liquidity, such as the proposal to implement a gold substitution account by gradually diminishing the price of gold. Forcing acceptance of a new reserve asset by artificially undermining the confidence in another reserve asset can never be a sound solution.

Aschinger concluded by voicing his reservations about attempts to phase out gold as a monetary reserve asset under present conditions. When Keynes said that gold is a barbaric relic, he may have been right in some respects, said Aschinger, but he disregarded one point: he did not know that we are still living in a barbaric age.

Robert Slighton, in a brief comment on the preceding discussion, sought to further dispel the notion that the U.S. Treasury sees no international liquidity problem. The problem of liquidity did not disappear with the advent of floating. If, however, intervention rules are adopted to prevent the accumulation of large balances of foreign exchange designed to do away with erratic fluctuations, the interesting dimensions of the liquidity problem will not be revealed by analysis of aggregate statistics on official reserves. Slighton acknowledged that nothing in the Jamaica Agreement charts the road to such a set of intervention rules. He concurred with Machlup's statement that attempting their specification is a first and critical avenue that must be pursued.

The most interesting aspect of the liquidity problem is the connection between liquidity distribution and adjustment policies. Although a claim that a country does not adjust appropriately is largely judgmental, there is ample evidence that many countries have not adjusted appropriately. The simplest reason for this, Slighton suggested, was that control over the allocation of international credit has shifted partially from the International Monetary Fund to private banks. He warned that unless there is a further expansion of public credit, a critical liquidity problem may emerge in the near future as some countries face severe adjustment problems. This, in turn, will intensify demands for additional allocations of aid-linked SDRs. In Slighton's view, this development would severely weaken the conditionality of the Fund's lending operations.

His last comment was made in reference to Machlup's call for considering even the so-called politically unfeasible solutions. Though Slighton agreed that discussions of international monetary problems should not be confined to what is politically feasible in the short run, political feasibility should be kept in mind. Certainly, the asset preferences of the OPEC countries constitute a constraint upon any reforms of the monetary system with respect to its capabilities of liquidity creation.

POSTSCRIPT
Issues in Exchange Rate Flexibility

Jacob S. Dreyer

Even those who greeted the advent of floating exchange rates with apprehension admit that the new regime enabled the industrial world to adjust to a series of economic shocks over the 1972–1975 period much more easily than would have been possible under a fixed rate regime. Yet, despite this evidence of unjustified fears in the last few years, some critics of the floating rate regime maintain that flexible rates did not perform as well as their early advocates had claimed they would. It seems worthwhile to summarize some of the charges aired during the conference, and to assess their validity. More generally, it is useful to catalog the issues discussed and to cull out the points of agreement and the reasons for disagreement.

Criticisms of floating exchange rates included the following charges: (1) they are ineffective in eliminating payments imbalances; (2) they facilitate the spread of inflationary pressures across national boundaries; (3) they result in allocative inefficiency; and (4) they inhibit international trade and investment.

In regard to the first two charges, it is clear that floating rates are not a panacea for balance of payments deficits or for the propagation of inflationary pressures. The charges would be more relevant, however, if it could be demonstrated that flexible rates are less able to cope with these ills than are alternative exchange rate regimes. So far, such evidence is lacking.

The third and the fourth charges stem from a perception by some observers that the fluctuations in some key exchange rates are excessive. The case in point is the dollar-mark exchange rate, which between the spring of 1973 and the fall of 1975 displayed significant and sometimes rapid changes.

The issue of volatility is important because it has often been alleged that excessive fluctuations of exchange rates have all sorts of pernicious consequences for the economy and should therefore be suppressed by public authorities.

The validity of this contention and the policy implications derived from it depend, however, on answers to several questions: (1) What is the criterion for declaring exchange rate fluctuations "excessive" and what causes them? (2) What is the precise nature of harmful effects, if any, of these fluctuations? More precisely, what are their welfare costs? (3) What is the probability that the policy of suppression of exchange rate fluctuations will be effective and what is the expected cost of implementing such policy?

The Issue of Exchange Rate Volatility. Concerning the first question, it was suggested that exchange rates should be considered excessively volatile if the changes in rates substantially and persistently exceed changes in the underlying economic determinants of those rates. This criterion, although valuable for its attempt to inject a measure of objectivity in assessing the behavior of flexible exchange rates, suffers from an obvious deficiency: it glosses over the role of expectations in the determination of exchange rates. But effects of such shifts on demand for and supply of currencies may be more powerful than the effects of trade balances, the flow of long-term investment, differential rates of savings among countries, and other variables thought to influence exchange rates. Moreover, the impact on exchange rates of shifts in asset preferences may be not only stronger than the influence of "economic variables" but also more rapid. Clearly, shifts in asset preferences, especially if they are abrupt, are less likely to occur if changes in key economic variables are more stable or predictable. But any such changes affect expectations and thus entail shifts in asset preferences that take place virtually simultaneously with changes in the economic variables generating them. As a result, if the role of expectations is not properly taken into account, the effect on exchange rates of changes in underlying economic factors may appear magnified.

Even if the role of shifts in asset preferences were recognized, the fluctuations in exchange rates could be judged excessive if exchange rates had a tendency to change under their own momentum. In fact, this claim is made by those who interpret persistent fluctuations of exchange rates around their long-term trends as evidence of "bandwagon" effects or as evidence of a "badly behaved" speculation in the foreign exchange market. A corollary to this claim is the assertion that foreign exchange markets are inefficient (in the technical sense of the term).

The Issue of Efficiency of Foreign Exchange Markets. The market can be said to be inefficient when systematic opportunities for above-normal profits remain unexploited. These opportunities arise when the market fails to incorporate economic information fully or rapidly enough. Market inefficiency occurs, for example, when the information contained in the past price series can be used to predict future prices. If a certain pattern of exchange rate fluctuation is apparent, an astute speculator could use it to earn supernormal profits. Specifically, if bandwagon effects were a systematic feature of exchange rate behavior, those able to detect this feature could always reap an advantage by going long in the currency when its rate begins to rise and going short in it when its rate begins to fall. Conversely, if such a bandwagon effect either is an isolated incident or occurs randomly, so that past experience is not helpful in either predicting or identifying this phenomenon, no supernormal profits can be earned by studying past price performance.

Intimately connected with the concept of market efficiency is the concept of speculation. In fact (barring extreme risk aversion on the part of speculators or unavailability of speculative funds) an efficient market implies that there is stabilizing speculation sufficient to prevent the actual price from remaining above or below the equilibrium price for any long period.

If changes in underlying economic aggregates are to be taken as a gauge for judging the appropriateness of exchange rate fluctuations, excessive fluctuations would imply the presence of destabilizing speculation or, at least, an insufficiency of stabilizing speculative activity.

There are no foolproof tests for market efficiency. Most tests applied to foreign exchange markets belong to the class of so-called weak-form tests. Some rely on a comparison between changes in exchange rates in different periods of time; a systematic correlation between such changes would create a presumption of market inefficiency. In another group of tests, a given trading rule is consistently applied ex post to see whether it would yield returns over and above profits that the buy-and-hold strategy would have yielded.

The results of many such tests reported at the conference, although far from being unchallengeable, tend to indicate that foreign exchange markets are essentially efficient. On the basis of this evidence, the often sharp fluctuations of exchange rates around the long-term trend would seem to reflect the instability of underlying economic conditions and policies, rather than defects inherent in the working of foreign exchange markets.

The Welfare Costs of Exchange Rate Fluctuations. The case for official intervention in the foreign exchange market rests on two claims. The first, that there is destabilizing or insufficiently stabilizing speculation, lacks strong empirical support, as just discussed. The second claim refers to the welfare losses caused by exchange rate fluctuations.

These losses may stem from two sources: unnecessary adjustment and uncertainty. It is reasoned that even if fluctuations in exchange rates were perfectly predictable, temporary changes in relative prices engendered by those fluctuations would shift resources alternately toward and away from export industries. Such an adjustment to price incentives would be generally wasteful. Moreover, fluctuations in exchange rates imply variability of income, especially if the foreign sector is relatively large. If stability of income is valued highly by the society, exchange rate fluctuations imply some reduction in the society's welfare.

Uncertainty is supposed to aggravate the problem. As the profits in domestic currency become to a large extent influenced by fluctuations in exchange rates, traders would shun foreign trade and investment activities or, at least, they would have to devote additional resources to hedging themselves against the consequences of such fluctuations. The total welfare of the society would thus be diminished either by the contraction of foreign trade and transnational investment or by the diversion of resources from productive uses to hedging.

The problem of such welfare losses could be analyzed in two steps: empirical validation of the theoretical reasoning sketched above, and an assessment of the advisability, feasibility, and cost of public policy measures to minimize the volatility of exchange rate movements. So far, claims of noticeable welfare losses arising from exchange rate fluctuations have not been substantiated empirically in a convincing manner. The evidence that flexible rates inhibit international trade and investment is conspicuously weak. Nor is there any serious empirical support for the view that exchange rate fluctuations result in needless shifting of productive resources among various sectors of the economy. The cost of foreign trading is no doubt higher under floating rates than it would have been under genuinely fixed parities, but this additional cost (mainly of hedging) constitutes a tiny fraction of the total cost of an exported or imported item. Not infrequently, hedging costs are incurred to conform with certain accounting rules rather than to satisfy a firm's economic objectives.

On a macroeconomic level, the deleterious consequences of exchange rate fluctuations most frequently highlighted in public discussions are the so-called ratchet effects and vicious and virtuous circles. At the heart of all arguments in support of this view are two propositions. One is that exchange rate changes are immediately and totally offset by changes in the prices of tradables that in turn lead to subsequent increases in prices of other goods and also wages. The other argument is that because of the general downward rigidity of prices, the effects of exchange rate changes on prices are asymmetrical. When the domestic currency depreciates, domestic prices rise so as to offset the depreciation, but when this currency appreciates, prices remain largely unchanged.

Few economists would deny that the relative rates of domestically generated inflation among countries are of primary importance in determining exchange rates among their currencies. And equally few economists would deny the existence of a feedback effect from exchange rate changes to relative price changes of the sort described above. Strong disagreement persists, however, as to the magnitude of this feedback effect. As with all cost-push inflation models, the results of empirical tests do not lend themselves to unambiguous interpretation. The least that can be asserted is that the proponents of the ratchet effect and vicious circles have failed so far to provide an unchallengeable proof of their validity.

The Issue of Exchange Rate Management. The desirability of an active policy for exchange rate management should be contemplated in the light of the preceding discussion. If, in fact, the harmful effects of exchange rate fluctuations are slight, the best policy would appear to be one of hands-off—especially if other economic policies could be used to smooth out fluctuations more efficiently or at a lower cost.

There seems little doubt that official intervention in the foreign exchange market is about the least efficient and most costly method of smoothing out changes in *equilibrium* exchange rates. The position that only appropriate macroeconomic management can secure long-run stability of the underlying equilibrium exchange rates barely needs to be defended. The relevant question concerns what provisions there should be, if any, to reduce fluctuations of exchange rates *around* their equilibrium values.

The very desirability of an active policy of exchange rate management ought to be evaluated in the light of whether or not the foreign exchange market is efficient, in the sense defined above. If it is efficient, no strong case can be made to justify official intervention. Since private parties operating in this market have access to the same information that officials have, there is no justification for the monetary authorities to try to influence changes in exchange rates. If, however, the monetary authorities are privy to privileged information about the current or future equilibrium rate—a matter of much dispute—this information can be made known on a regular basis to private parties, thus ensuring that at any time the efficient market will set a price which is appropriate.

285

Under certain assumptions, official intervention may be considered socially desirable. The first assumption is that officials do indeed have special knowledge or, if they do not, that the foreign exchange market is inefficient. A more general assumption is that exchange rates persistently fluctuate around their equilibrium levels so that their equilibrium and actual values coincide only occasionally. A final assumption is that when exchange rates are off their equilibrium levels, welfare losses exceed the cost of official intervention designed to bring actual rates in line with their equilibrium values, presumably known to the authorities.

If the validity of these assumptions could be confirmed, what would have to be the internationally agreed rules governing intervention in foreign exchange markets? The question is important since every exchange rate is of concern to at least two national governments. If their exchange rate objectives are contradictory or not fully compatible, it is possible that their intervention policies would clash and perhaps take the extreme form of "beggar thy neighbor." Even if not so blatantly protectionist, such policies are likely to generate difficulties in distributing the burdens of international adjustments and thus breed political animosity.

The coordination of exchange rate policies is made more difficult by the fact that in many cases the level and the rate of change of a particular exchange rate is of concern to more than the two governments directly involved. The International Monetary Fund (IMF), representing in a sense the world community, has an understandable interest in exchange rate policies. A set of very important amendments to Article IV of the Articles of Agreement of the IMF contains, among others, an admonition not to manipulate the exchange rate system, either to avoid adjustment or to gain unfair competitive advantage. The IMF is charged with the task of exercising "firm surveillance" over the exchange rate policies of its members. Development of specific principles for the guidance of members with respect to those policies is presently under discussion at the IMF.

In designing a set of detailed and operational rules for exchange rate management policies, the difficulty lies in the need to leave room for flexibility in the choice of economic policies in general and exchange rate arrangements in particular by individual IMF members. In other words, resolution of the surveillance problem implies reconciliation between the desire for national sovereignty and the need for international cooperation.

The Problem of Liquidity. One more criticism frequently levied against the system of flexible exchange rates is that it leads to an uncontrollable expansion of world liquidity. This criticism is based on an "empirical" observation and a theoretical argument.

The "empirical" observation refers to the very rapid expansion of the volume of international reserves during the early 1970s. Although the fact of that expansion is uncontestable, it is most debatable whether floating exchange rates were the cause. Since the advent of generalized floating coincided roughly with the jump in oil prices, it is not at all clear which event is responsible for the expansion of world reserves. Since 1973, reserve increases were concentrated largely in a small number of surplus OPEC countries, reflecting the oil-importing countries' collective preference for financing their balance of trade deficit through reserve creation rather than reserve transfers. Insofar as these reserves are being recycled, their accumulation by OPEC countries can be regarded as their capital exports approximately equal to their trade surplus.

The theoretical argument linking flexible exchange rates and liquidity expansion refers to the system as being demand-determined. What is meant is that a country can obtain as much reserves as it wishes either through borrowing or manipulation of exchange rates.

Even if one were to disregard the fact that the supply of both private and official credit is not infinitely elastic, it is difficult to see why a system of flexible exchange rates should make official borrowing any easier than it would have been had exchange rates been fixed.

The frequently expressed fear that governments would deliberately engage in extensive exchange rate manipulation in order to acquire more reserves is not unjustified. Incidences of such official manipulations have occurred in the last several years and are likely to be repeated in the future. If countries are unwilling to comply with international agreements prohibiting deliberate manipulation of exchange rates when they are floating, it seems unreasonable to expect that they would comply with agreements prohibiting competitive changes in parities (or, alternatively, competitive maintenance of parities) under a system of fixed exchange rates.

On the other end of the spectrum are those who adopt a purist position that international liquidity is irrelevant to flexible rates. This claim would be valid in a world with a fixed supply of reserves and governments' indifference to the levels of exchange rates of their currencies. In today's world neither is true, and changes in the global volume of liquidity as well as its distribution among countries are of legitimate interest to policy makers.

It is widely accepted that, in general, a solution to a balance of payments problem would be a mixture of adjustment and financing. Insofar as adjustment takes place through changes in exchange rates, the issues reserve and exchange rate policies are inseparable. On a policy-making level, no guidelines for exchange rate management would be adequate in the absence of rules governing reserve policy. Critics of the present international monetary system contend that its legal basis—the amended Articles of Agreement of the IMF—does not contain adequate provision for the orderly creation of liquidity. It should be pointed out, however, that the current rules under which new reserves are injected into the system are no more lax than they were before 1973. If anything, the rules governing official borrowing have become more structured in recent years, although there have never been any rules to govern the supply of reserve currencies. It may be argued, even though many would not subscribe to this view, that world conditions in the last decade or so have made an effective mechanism of liquidity creation more imperative than ever. In other words, a set of much more specific rules is needed under which the size of reserve increments and their allocation among countries would be agreed upon internationally. But again, as in the case of international surveillance of exchange rate management practices, the need for international cooperation must be reconciled with the wish to preserve national sovereignty.